Gems & Minerals

Gems & Minerals

Earth Treasures from the Royal Ontario Museum

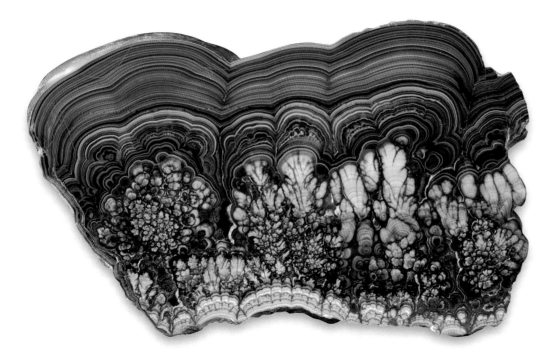

Dr. Kimberly Tait

 Royal Ontario Museum

FIREFLY BOOKS

A FIREFLY BOOK

Published by Firefly Books Ltd. 2011
Copyright © 2011 Firefly Books Ltd.
Text copyright © 2011 Kimberly Tait
Photographs copyright © 2011 Royal Ontario Museum, Toronto, Ontario, Canada.

First printing

Publisher Cataloging-in-Publication Data (U.S.)

Tait, Kimberly.
    Gems and minerals : earth treasures from the Royal Ontario Museum /
Kimberly Tait.
[   ] p. : col. photos. ;   cm.
Includes index.
Summary: Stunning and rare gems and minerals from the collection of
the Royal Ontario Museum.

ISBN-13: 978-1-55407-880-6
ISBN-10: 1-55407-880-6

1. Precious stones – Identification. 2. Gems – Identification. 3. Minerals –
Identification. I. Royal Ontario Museum. II. Title.
553.8 dc22   QE392.T358 2011

Published in the United States by
Firefly Books (U.S.) Inc.
P.O. Box 1338, Ellicott Station
Buffalo, New York 14205

Library and Archives Canada Cataloguing in Publication

Tait, Kimberly T.
    Gems and minerals : earth treasures from the Royal Ontario Museum /
Kimberly Tait.

Includes index.

ISBN-13: 978-1-55407-880-6
ISBN-10: 1-55407-880-6

1. Royal Ontario Museum—Catalogs. 2. Minerals—Catalogs and collections.
3. Gems—Catalogs and collections. I. Title.

QE386.C32T67 2011   549'.074713541   C2011-902340-7

Published in Canada by
Firefly Books Ltd.
66 Leek Crescent
Richmond Hill, Ontario L4B 1H1

Design and Layout: Joseph Gisini / PageWave Graphics Inc.
Editing and Index: Gillian Watts
Photography: Brian Boyle, MPA, FPPO, and Miguel Hortiguela, LPPO
Illustrations: Crowle Art Group

Printed in China

The publisher gratefully acknowledges the financial support for our publishing program by the Government of Canada through the Canada Book Fund as administered by the Department of Canadian Heritage.

Many of the minerals, gems and meteorites in this book are on display in the Teck Suite of Galleries: Earth's Treasures, at the Royal Ontario Museum, Toronto, Ontario, Canada.

Note: For illustrative purposes, some images in this book are shown larger than the object's actual size. Readers are encouraged to refer to the caption of each image for the object's actual dimensions. Dimensions in the captions refer to the entire gem or mineral; however, in some cases only a portion is shown.

Page 1: Cluster ring (see page 69)
Page 2: Cerussite "Light of the Desert" (see page 117)
Page 3: Malachite (see page 120)
Page 6: Mimetite (see page 139)
Page 248: Quartz (amethyst variety), Erongo Mountains, Namibia • 5 x 6 x 3 cm
Page 251: Calcite, Irai, Rio Grande do Sul, Brazil • 12.5 x 10 x 10.5 cm
Page 252: Gypsum rosette, Red River floodway, Winnipeg, Manitoba, Canada • 10.5 x 10.5 x 6.5 cm
Page 256: Labradorite (see page 171)

I would like to dedicate this book to my family.

To my daughter Emily: you have transformed my
life and encouraged me in so many ways —
you are my greatest achievement.

To Cecilia, for being a wonderful big sister and
a blessed addition to my life.

And to my husband, Sal, without whom this book
would not have been possible: thank you for
your dedication to us and our family.

Contents

Minerals: Products of a Changing Planet

The internal heat of Earth drives geological forces that are continually changing our planet. These changes are made dramatically apparent to us as spectacular mountain ranges, erupting volcanoes, earthquakes and even hot springs and caverns. But most geological activity occurs deep down beneath our feet, unseen by us, as Earth's crust is subjected to varying pressures and temperatures. Immense quantities of rock and their constituent minerals are altered and destroyed in these changing conditions. In the process, new minerals and rocks are formed.

RIGHT: Malachite with chrysocolla, Majdanpek, Serbia •
11 x 8 x 7 cm

LEFT: Fluorite, Taihang Shan Mountains, Hebei, China •
19 x 13 x 1 cm

The Wonder of Crystals

Huge quantities of minerals created over the course of Earth's history formed as the small, nondescript interlocking crystals that make up rocks. Under very special conditions, however, perfect crystals may grow to incredible size and beauty.

Most of the rocks in Earth's crust are composed of just a few minerals; quartz and the feldspar group are the most abundant species. These are the major constituent minerals in common rocks such as granite. The mineral grains in these rocks are actually crystals, but they typically have indistinct forms. However, given just the right geological conditions, these same minerals can grow into beautiful naturally formed crystals — true jewels of nature.

Crystals are solids with regular three-dimensional repetitive arrangements of atoms, and these atomic arrangements are called **crystal structures**. Natural crystals formed by geological processes are called **minerals**, but laboratory-grown (synthetic) crystals, although identical to their natural counterparts, are not considered to be minerals.

Biominerals

Crystals formed by biological rather than geological processes — called biominerals — are not considered to be true minerals. Pearls, shell, amber, coral and other materials created by living organisms do not qualify as minerals, even though they do contain fibrous crystals of aragonite secreted by the organisms. But there are exceptions to this rule. Some sulfur crystals grow as a result of bacterial action, yet these crystals are considered to be a mineral because they grow in rock.

Microcline, Crystal Peak, Colorado, USA • 12 x 9 x 5 cm

Vanadinite, San Carlos district, Chihuahua, Mexico • 8 x 4 x 2 cm

Mineral Species

Minerals encompass a great variety of chemical compositions and crystal structures. Each unique combination of elements and crystal structure is called a **mineral species** and has a specific name. More than 4,500 mineral species are known, but only about a hundred of them are common "rock-forming" minerals.

Exceptional Crystals from Special Environments

Some crystals are striking in appearance and spectacular in size. These rare specimens formed under extraordinary geological conditions: a combination of space for growth, sufficient time and an adequate supply of chemical nutrients. Well-formed crystals can develop only if they are able to grow freely, unimpeded by nearby crystals, in places such as open fractures and cavities in rocks. Large, perfect crystals also need long periods under suitable geological conditions to grow. As extended periods of stability are uncommon in our dynamic planet, this is another reason why these crystals are so rare. And large crystals require a steady supply of their chemical ingredients to grow. In many cases, these elements are dissolved in solutions that flow around the growing crystals, "feeding" them.

Given enough space, the right materials and sufficient time to develop, crystals can reach gigantic proportions. However, this convergence of conditions is so uncommon that giant crystals are rarely produced in nature. And once they have formed, these rare giants must face the destructive forces of the geologically active Earth that created them. There are few survivors, and fewer still are discovered and collected undamaged.

Many mineral crystals grow from molten rock (**magma**) deep inside Earth. The large, well-shaped crystals found in many volcanic rocks — such as feldspar and leucite — crystallized in a magma chamber deep underground; they were brought to the surface by the magma when the volcano erupted. Others, such as topaz crystals, can grow directly from hot gases, which carry the mineral's ingredients in vaporized form.

How Crystals Grow

Chemical Alteration of Minerals

As geological conditions change, minerals may be exposed to materials with which they chemically react, causing their elements to recrystallize as entirely different but stable minerals. Galena (lead sulfide) oxidizes to form anglesite (lead sulfate). Azurite (blue copper carbonate) can react to form malachite (green copper carbonate). If malachite produced this way keeps the original crystal shape of the azurite, it is called a **pseudomorph**, meaning "false form."

The resistance of minerals to change varies considerably. Some, like tourmaline, remain unchanged for hundreds of millions of years. Others, such as chalcanthite, may crumble when they are removed from the ground and exposed to light and air. Crystals may be partially dissolved or etched by corrosive solutions, as occurs with beryl, or they may be fractured by rock movements during or after crystal growth, as exemplified by tourmaline in schist, quartz or phlogopite.

Space for Growth

Cavities in rocks provide space in which minerals can grow unimpeded into well-formed crystals. The result may be just a few crystals, as with celestine and fluorite, or the cavity may become lined with inwardly growing crystals, as in septarian nodules — named for their angular cavities — with calcite (see photo opposite). Crystal linings that survive being freed from the rock by weathering — or by humans — are called **geodes**, which are very popular among mineral collectors and often used as decorative items.

Basalt is the most abundant volcanic rock on Earth's surface. Spherical or tube-shaped cavities are commonly found in this rock, created when hot gases were trapped in the basalt lava as it solidified. In some basalts of India and Brazil, these cavities are large enough for a person to stand in. Watery solutions rich in dissolved mineral components flow through the rock into these cavities, lining them with crystals. In the larger open spaces, the crystals can reach an impressive size. Among the many minerals found within these cavities are some of the world's finest crystals of amethyst, agate and a large family of silicate minerals known collectively as zeolites.

Growth Through Time

It is common for more than one mineral species to be present on a specimen. The minerals may have grown at about the same time, as happens with pyrite and quartz, or they may have grown one after the other, as in fluorite growth on celestine. Delicate crystals can be overgrown by another mineral that then serves to protect and preserve them. Rutile inclusions in quartz are a good example.

Growth in Veins

Veins are fractures in rock where crystals have grown. They grow from the fracture surfaces inward and may fill up the space. Veins commonly form in a variety of geologically active environments. In the upper crust, minerals may crystallize in wide fractures, resulting in well-formed collectible crystals such as gypsum (page 252) and epidote (page 221). Solid crystal-filled veins form when molten magma crystallizes in a fracture, producing such forms as aegirine pegmatite. As well, hot hydrothermal fluids often carry and deposit valuable minerals in veins.

The Stories Minerals Tell

Changes in the supply of ingredients or in the conditions under which they grew can often be seen in the crystals themselves. Zones of inclusions or colors in quartz (page 248) and tourmaline crystals (page 210), and the layered or banded growths in rhodochrosite (page 112) and agate (page 167), document these changes. Such features provide clues to the history of a specimen's geological environment.

Calcite (septarian nodule), San Juan County, Utah, USA • 18 x 24 x 8 cm

What Is a Rock?

Rocks consist of crystals of one or more mineral species that grew together or were cemented together naturally. The crystals in rocks are usually small, with interlocking and irregular shapes. There are three major classes of rocks — igneous, sedimentary and metamorphic — and each of these classes is then subdivided into groups and types based on their different compositions and textures.

Igneous Rocks

Igneous rocks form when liquid rock (magma) cools and solidifies. The faster the magma cools, the smaller the crystals in the rock. Geologists can figure out how quickly an igneous rock formed by looking at the size of its crystals. If the magma has escaped from below Earth's surface, it is known as **lava**. Lava on the surface cools much faster than magma beneath the surface, so **volcanic igneous rocks,** formed from lava, have much smaller crystals than **plutonic igneous rocks**, which form when magma cools and solidifies deep below Earth's surface.

Sedimentary Rocks

Sedimentary rocks can form from eroded bits of other rocks and minerals. These fragments of rock and mineral are deposited in layers at the bottom of rivers, lakes and oceans. Over time, the particles are cemented together to form new rocks. These are known as **clastic sedimentary rocks**. Sedimentary rocks can also form from the bodies of once-living creatures. For example, many creatures that live in the sea make shells from calcium carbonate. When they die, their shells sink to the floor of the ocean, where the calcium carbonate can eventually form limestone. Sedimentary rocks made in this way are known as **organic sedimentary rocks**.

Finally, sedimentary rocks can also form chemically. If water in an ocean evaporates, the chemicals in the remaining water become more concentrated. Eventually the chemicals become so concentrated that they form crystals and fall to the bottom of the ocean. When these crystals are pressed together to form rocks, they are known as **chemical sedimentary rocks**. Plants or animals trapped in this sediment sometimes form fossils.

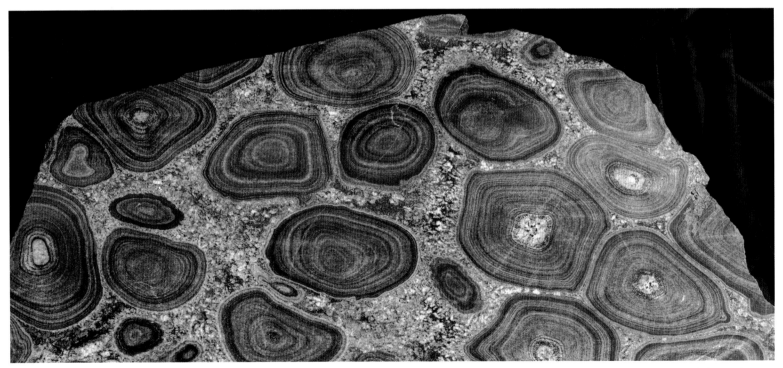

Orbicular granite, Finland • 99 x 74 x 31 cm. This uncommon type of intrusive rock has a unique appearance due to its orbicules — concentrically layered spheroidal structures. The orbicules are thought to have formed by nucleation around a grain of rock in a cooling magma chamber.

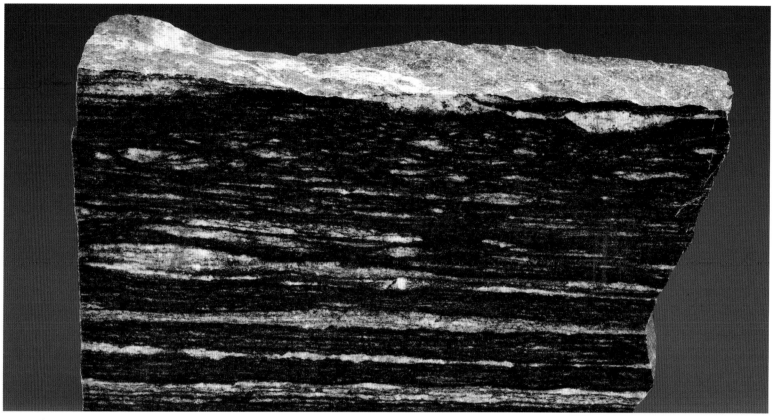

Acasta (Hadean tonalite) gneiss, Slave craton, Northwest Territories, Canada • 9 x 9 x 6 cm. Located on an island about 300 km (185 miles) north of Yellowknife, the Acasta River deposit is believed to be 3.5 to 4 billion years old — one of the oldest known rocks on Earth.

Metamorphic Rocks

Metamorphic rocks form deep within Earth, often beneath mountain belts. When igneous or sedimentary rocks are heated or subjected to immense pressure, their appearance and mineral content can change (*metamorphic* means "changed form"). For instance, the small calcite crystals in the sedimentary rock limestone change into larger crystals in the metamorphic rock marble. In metamorphosed sandstone, recrystallization of the original quartz sand grains results in very compact quartzite.

Earth's Recycling Program

Rocks can be recycled — but not in the same way that we recycle paper or cans. Over time, processes on and in Earth change rocks from one form — igneous, sedimentary or metamorphic — to another, and sometimes back again. It can take thousands, if not millions or sometimes billions of years for rocks to change in this way.

Magma is molten rock, and igneous rocks form when magma solidifies. If magma is brought to the surface by a volcanic eruption, it may solidify into an **extrusive igneous rock** such as basalt. Magma may also solidify very slowly beneath Earth's surface, creating an **intrusive igneous rock** such as granite. These rocks become exposed to wind, water and ice — the extrusive rocks first, of course, but eventually the intrusive ones also. As the igneous rocks undergo weathering and erosion, the bits of broken-off rock are transported by rivers and streams into the ocean, where they are eventually deposited on the seafloor as sediment. These loose bits of rock become **lithified**, or packed together, and become sedimentary rock.

As the rock is buried by additional layers of sediment and sedimentary rock, the heat and pressure increase. If the temperature and pressure become high enough — usually several kilometers below Earth's surface — the sedimentary rocks recrystallize. A new type of material forms: metamorphic rock. If the temperature gets even higher, the rock will melt and become magma again, and the cycle starts over.

Gemstones

Sapphires, rubies, diamonds . . . words we associate with kings and queens, the rich and famous, glitz and glamor. Humans have been fascinated by these sparkly stones throughout all time. If the conditions are just right, Earth can produce large, transparent crystals that can be cut into gemstones. Actually most minerals can be cut up to be used for jewelry, but the most desired are minerals that are hard, resist wear and breakage, and have the richest of colors. Or, in the case of diamonds, the most colorless and clear can be as valuable as the richly colored stones.

Gem cutters bring out the inner beauty of gems by creating small polished surfaces on the stone called **facets**, which play a trick with light. Facets allow light to enter the gem; once inside, the light bounces off its other angled faces. This causes it to disperse, or split apart, into the colors of the rainbow before it

leaves the gem, similar to what happens when you pass light through a prism. This is the sparkling color you see when you look at a gemstone.

Sometimes gems have different names depending on their color, though they are all varieties of just one mineral. For example, sapphires and rubies are actually the same mineral, corundum. The difference between the two is at the atomic level, something that can't be seen with the eye but which makes the colors different. Rubies are always red; sapphires can be any other color than red, but blue is the most commonly known.

In the gem-cutting process, sometimes more than half the mineral can be lost, so gemstones are cut into different shapes to maximize their size. The bigger and more perfect the stone is, and the rarer it is on Earth, the more valuable it becomes.

ABOVE: Imperial topaz, Ouro Preto, Minas Gerais, Brazil • 3.3 x 2.7 x 1.8 cm, 159.10 ct

RIGHT: Round brilliant-cut white diamonds, South Africa and Canada • 2.00 ct and 3.06 ct

Meteorites

Earth is not alone in space; it exists within a system of planets and moons that orbit a star — our Sun. This solar system, including Earth, formed more than 4.5 billion years ago. And there are other objects in our solar system: asteroids. They formed at the same time as the planets and range in size from a few tens of meters in diameter to as much as several hundred kilometers. Most of them orbit the Sun in a region called the asteroid belt, which is between the orbits of Mars and Jupiter.

Asteroids are our main source of meteorites. When asteroids slam into each other in the asteroid belt, pieces of one or both can break off and be launched into space in their own orbits. These bits of asteroid are called **meteoroids**. Some meteoroids end up on a collision course with Earth. They are moving tremendously fast — as much as 17 kilometers per *second* — so when they hit Earth's atmosphere they become white-hot, the way a space shuttle does during re-entry. During this white-hot phase they are called **meteors**. Eventually the atmosphere slows the meteor down and it falls to the ground, at which point it becomes a **meteorite**.

Meteorites are very important to our understanding of how the solar system formed and what it formed from. Earth is a geologically active planet, and plate tectonics (also known as continental drift) means that its crust is being continually recycled. Although Earth is more than 4.5 billion years old, we have no samples of our planet's very first rocks because they have all been recycled. However, it seems that most asteroids undergo little or no recycling activity. The rocks they are made of have changed very little, if at all, since the beginnings of the solar system. So meteorites show us what the very first rocks to form in our system were like.

There are three basic types of meteorites: stony, stony iron and iron-nickel. Stony meteorites, as you might guess, are made up of minerals similar to those we find on the surface of Earth. These meteorites come from the crust of an asteroid and are by far the most common type found. Stony iron meteorites are rare and very unusual looking. They are made of the greenish mineral olivine surrounded by shiny iron-nickel metal. These meteorites come from deep inside an asteroid, similar to the area deep inside Earth near the border between the core and the mantle. The third type is iron-nickel meteorites, which are made almost entirely of iron and nickel and so are extremely heavy and very magnetic. They come from the core of an asteroid.

Polished slice from the Springwater meteorite, a pallasite from Springwater, Saskatchewan, Canada • 20 x 14 x 1.4 cm, 1.85 kg

Not all meteorites come from asteroids. Some rare types actually come from our moon and from Mars. Both are much smaller than Earth, which means they have less gravity — which explains the images of lunar astronauts bouncing high off the ground. The Moon and Mars also get hit by meteoroids. If they are hit by a large enough piece of asteroid, the impact can actually launch rocks off the surface and send them into space, because there is so little gravity holding them down. Just like meteoroids from asteroids, these rocks may end up on a collision course with Earth, and if we are lucky they will be found so we can study them.

Meteoroids enter Earth's atmosphere at terrific speeds — the equivalent of traveling from Toronto to New York in about 30 seconds. Most meteoroids are small enough that the atmosphere slows them down to only a couple of hundred kilometers per hour. This means that they will partially bury themselves in the ground when they hit but they won't do a lot of damage (unless they hit a car, which has happened a number of times). However, if they are too big for the atmosphere to slow them down, they can do tremendous damage and create a large crater. The Pingualuit crater, a striking circular basin 3.4 kilometers (2 miles) wide, is one example in northern Quebec. It was the Royal Ontario Museum's Victor Meen who explored that crater for the first time, back in the 1940s and 1950s, with the National Geographic Society.

The Physical Properties of Minerals

There are currently more than 4,500 known minerals, and about 30 to 50 new ones are being discovered every year. How can we tell them apart? The first step a mineralogist takes is to look at the mineral's physical properties in order to identify it. Many minerals have very characteristic physical properties that no other minerals have, or at least the physical properties can help narrow down the possibilities. If a mineral cannot be identified by its physical properties alone, the experts use more sophisticated methods. This type of work is done in settings such as the mineralogy laboratory at the Royal Ontario Museum. ROM mineralogists have identified and described many new minerals; in fact, there are minerals named after almost every mineralogy curator who has worked at the museum — a fine way to recognize their hard work!

Hardness

It is sometimes possible to identify minerals by how hard they are. The Mohs hardness scale allows you to determine the hardness of a mineral by finding out what it will (and won't) scratch. The hardness of a fingernail is 2 and a steel nail is 5. For example, talc, which is 1 on the scale, is extremely soft and can be scratched by a fingernail — which is why it is used in baby powder. Diamond, at 10 on the scale, is the hardest natural substance on Earth and cannot be scratched by anything except another diamond. Diamonds are used for cutting other minerals.

Hardness 2
Gypsum

Gypsum (selenite variety), Galetta, Ontario, Canada • 12 x 13 x 5 cm

Hardness 3
Calcite

Calcite, Oklahoma, USA • 10 x 11 x 8 cm

Hardness 1
Talc

Talc, Mpumalanga, South Africa • 19 x 5 x 3 cm

Hardness 4
Fluorite

Fluorite, Madoc, Ontario, Canada • 5.5 x 7 x 6 cm

Hardness 5
Fluorapatite

Fluorapatite, Ontario, Canada • 13 x 13 x 21 cm

Hardness 6
Microcline

Microcline, Madagascar • 12 x 23 x 3 cm

Hardness 7
Quartz

Quartz, Mount Ida, Arkansas, USA • 14 x 15 x 10 cm

Hardness 8
Topaz

Topaz, Téofilo Otoni, Minas Gerais, Brazil • 14.5 x 14 x 13.5 cm

Hardness 9
Corundum

Corundum, Mozambique • 17 x 11 x 10 cm

Hardness 10
Diamond

Diamond, Kimberley, South Africa • 0.5 x 0.5 x 0.5 cm

Color

Minerals have been used as pigments since the dawn of history, either in powdered form, as paint and cosmetics, or as sources of color for ceramic glazes. Hematite and other iron oxides create reds and browns, while cinnabar and minium give us bright red and malachite is a source of green.

Color is one of the first things we observe about a mineral. Some minerals are found in only one color, while others, such as fluorite, may have a wide range of colors and hues. In some cases the color is due to the chemical composition of the mineral itself, but it can also be influenced by the presence of another mineral. As a result, color is one of the least definitive properties of minerals used for identification.

Minerals with a characteristic color are called **idiochromatic** minerals. Their color is caused by one or more of their major elements. For example, rhodochrosite ($MnCO_3$), regardless of where it is found in the world, is characteristically pink or red because of its manganese content. The characteristic green of malachite and blue of azurite are both due to copper, an element that can produce different colors in minerals with different crystal structures.

If all the spectral colors in white light are strongly absorbed by a mineral, then very little light leaves it. We see it as being very dark or black (for example, graphite). Alternatively, if very little of the color in white light is absorbed, the light leaving the mineral is largely unaffected and we see it as colorless or white (for example, gypsum).

Many minerals would be colorless if they were pure. But they almost always contain impurities or tiny defects in their crystal structures, both of which can interact with light to produce color. The result is that many minerals, including many gems, are found in a wide variety of colors. Minerals that appear in a range of colors are called **allochromatic**. For example, the many colors of smithsonite ($ZnCO_3$) are due not to zinc but to impurities. Blue and green specimens contain traces of copper, pink examples contain cobalt, and yellow ones contain cadmium.

Metallic and non-metallic minerals interact with light in different ways. Metallic minerals absorb nearly all of the light close to their surface and then immediately re-emit it. This is what causes the bright metallic luster and opaqueness of metals. Gold and copper absorb and re-emit orange to red colors of the spectrum slightly better than blue and green, giving them their warm yellow and reddish hues. Many minerals have an appearance somewhere between those of metals and the glassy minerals such as quartz. This is because these minerals are semiconductors —

when exposed to light some of their electrons behave as though they were in a metal. Sulfur owes its bright yellow color to this effect, as do the rare colored crystals of diamond.

The color in many minerals may derive not from the mineral itself but from small crystals of another mineral that were trapped in the larger one as it grew. Quartz is commonly colored red or brown by inclusions of iron-bearing minerals. The quartz gem chrysoprase is colored by inclusions of green nickel minerals.

Some minerals grow to form microscopic structures such as spheres and layers. These structures produce plays of color when light strikes them. Opals contain tightly packed spheres, there are layers of platy aragonite crystals in fossil ammonites, and the feldspar gem varieties labradorite and peristerite have layers with different optical properties. The play of colors on hematite comes from very thin surface layers similar to an oil film on water. Somewhat different are the pastel colors produced by the thicker layers in calcite, which cause light rays to scatter in several directions and interfere with each other.

RIGHT: Funerary jar and stand (China, Song Dynasty, 960–1279 CE), earthenware, painted with mineral pigments.

LEFT: Malachite, Bwana M'Kubwa Mine, Ndola, Copperbelt, Zambia • 22 x 26 x 16 cm

Crystal Habit

Habit is a general term describing the outward appearance of a mineral: as a single crystal or as an aggregate of crystals. A number of terms are used to describe these habits. As a crystal grows, some faces will develop faster than others, resulting in faces of varying sizes. Some crystals will be long and needle-like, while others will be short and stubby.

Massive Minerals with a massive habit have their crystals growing in a mass so that they cannot be seen individually.

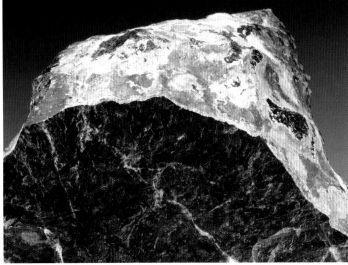

Massive sodalite, Namibia • 20 x 18 x 14 cm

Bladed The crystals look like a knife blade, tending to be long in one direction, and are thicker than acicular minerals.

Bladed stibnite, Ichinokawa Mine, Saijo, Shikoku, Japan • 10 x 1 x 1 cm

Acicular These minerals have slender, needle-like crystals and are typically very fragile.

Gypsum (selenite variety), Portman, Murcia, Spain • 14 x 11 x 5 cm

Dendritic These minerals grow by branching out like frost on a windowpane.

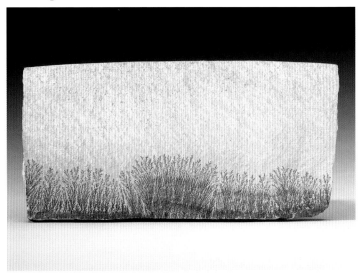

Dendritic manganese oxide on limestone, Solnhofen, Bavaria, Germany • 11.5 x 24 x 0.5 cm

Botryoidal This habit creates minerals that look like bunches of grapes or bubbles; they are rounded rather than having a more typical crystal shape.

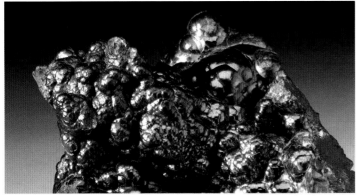

Botryoidal hematite with iridescent limonite coating, Parcocha Mine, Bilbao, Spain • 19 x 19 x 16 cm

Drusy These minerals have a fine coating of small crystals, like sprinkles on a donut or a fresh fall of snow on a winter day.

Drusy linarite, Bingham, New Mexico, USA • 9 x 7.5 x 2 cm

Radiating The crystals are arranged so that they spread out from a central point like the spokes of a wheel.

Rutile, Novo Horizonte, Bahia, Brazil • 5 x 3 x 0.6 cm

Stalactitic These minerals grow in a tall, tapered column that is slowly formed by dripping mineral-laden solutions.

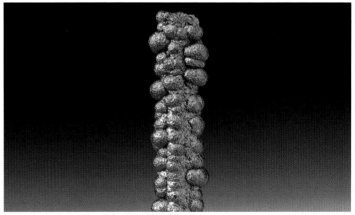

Goethite, Tintic, Utah, USA • 16.5 x 3.5 x 2.5 cm

Arborescent The minerals grow like tree branches in one or more directions.

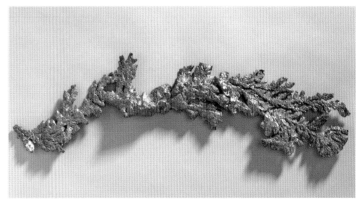

Arborescent copper, Michigan, USA • 35 x 8 x 1 cm

Platy In this habit the minerals form in very thin sheets.

Platy muscovite, José Pinto Mine, Jaguaraçu, Minas Gerais, Brazil • 12 x 19 x 6 cm

Capillary Also known as filiform, this habit gives minerals hair-like or thread-like crystals that are thin and flexible.

Aegirine, Mt. Malosa, Zomba, Malawi • 10 x 10 x 7 cm

Reticulated These minerals form crystalline fibers or columns that cross to create net-like formations.

Cerussite, Broken Hill, New South Wales, Australia • 7 x 6 x 6 cm

Reniform In this habit, minerals form rounded masses that resemble kidneys.

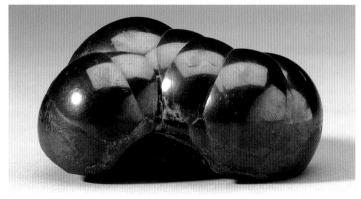

Hematite, Frizington, Cumbria, England • 6 x 9 x 5 cm

Tabular This habit creates crystals that have a flattened appearance like a book page or stone tablet; they are thicker than platy crystals.

Calcite, San Sebastian Mine, Charcas, San Luis Potosí, Mexico • 10 x 8 x 6.5 cm

Plumose Such minerals have tiny crystals arranged in branching patterns that resemble the structure of a feather.

Epidote, Brazil • 7 x 7.5 x 4 cm

Prismatic The crystals are elongated and prism-shaped, somewhat resembling a pencil.

Quartz (smoky variety), St. Gotthard, Ticino, Switzerland • 4 x 8 x 5 cm

Transparency

Transparency — also technically known as **diaphaneity** — describes how well light passes through a mineral sample. There are three degrees of transparency: transparent, translucent and opaque. You can see objects through a **transparent** mineral such as gypsum or diamond. You can see light but no objects through a **translucent** mineral such as actinolite. And you can't see anything at all through an **opaque** mineral such as graphite.

Transparent

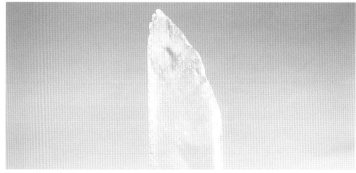

Gypsum, Bancroft, Ontario, Canada • 18 x 80 x 9 cm

Translucent

Massive jade (actinolite), New Zealand • 29 x 18 x 0.5 cm

Opaque

Graphite, Black Donald Mine, Renfrew County, Ontario, Canada • 14 x 11 x 10 cm

Density

Density is the mass per unit volume of a mineral, usually expressed in grams per cubic centimeter (g/cm^3). Like other properties of minerals, it is dependent on chemistry and crystal structure. While both diamond and graphite are made of carbon (C), diamond feels heavier than graphite because its carbon atoms are more densely packed. Thus there are more carbon atoms in a cubic centimeter of diamond than in the same volume of graphite. So although both minerals are made of the same element, diamond (at $3.52 \ g/cm^3$) has a density about 1.5 times higher than graphite ($2.15 \ g/cm^3$).

These carbonate minerals all have the same crystal structure; only the cation (positively charged atom) is different. Density increases with an increase in the atomic weight of the cation.

Mineral	Formula	Density	Atomic Weights	
aragonite	$CaCO_3$	$2.930 \ g/cm^3$	Ca	40.08
strontianite	$SrCO_3$	$3.785 \ g/cm^3$	Sr	87.63
witherite	$BaCO_3$	$4.308 \ g/cm^3$	Ba	137.36
cerussite	$PbCO_3$	$6.582 \ g/cm^3$	Pb	207.21

Aragonite, Tintic, Utah, USA • 11.5 x 12 x 8.5 cm   Strontianite, Oberdorf, Styria, Austria • 19 x 15 x 6 cm

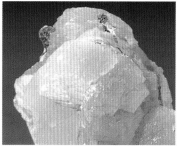 

Witherite, Rosiclare, Illinois, USA • 7 x 11 x 7 cm   Cerussite, Tsumeb, Namibia • 12.5 x 10 x 7.5 cm

Specific Gravity

Specific gravity is closely related to density but easier to measure. It indicates the mineral's relative density with respect to water, and is defined as the weight of the mineral divided by the weight of an equal volume of water at a temperature of 4°C.

Tenacity

Tenacity describes the strength or toughness of a mineral and how it resists the shock of being struck, crushed, bent or cut. Tenacity is an important property to know when mining or refining minerals. It also has important industrial applications. **Malleable** gold can be pounded into ultra-thin sheets known as gold leaf. **Flexible** minerals bend but do not break, while **elastic** minerals bend and then spring back to their original shape. **Brittle** minerals shatter when struck, and **sectile** minerals can be cut with a knife.

Flexible and Elastic

Phlogopite, Bedford, Ontario, Canada •
8 x 12 x 0.1 cm

Brittle

Fluorapatite, Wakefield, Quebec, Canada •
11 x 16 x 13 cm

Malleable and Sectile

Copper, Central Mine, Michigan, USA •
7 x 17 x 4 cm

Flexible and Inelastic

Stibnite, Ichinokawa Mine, Ehime, Shikoku, Japan •
20 x 2 x 1.5 cm

Cleavage

Minerals with **perfect cleavage** break along planes of weakness parallel to the layers of atoms in their crystal structures. More than one plane of cleavage is possible in some crystals; salt (halite) has three perfect cleavage directions, each parallel to one side of a cube. Cleavage is described by the number of directions and their directions with respect to the crystal structure. The angles between the cleavages and the degree of perfection of the cleavage are also important.

One Perfect Cleavage

Annite, Silver Crater Mine, Bancroft, Ontario, Canada • 14 x 6 x 6 cm

Two Cleavage Planes

Ferro-edenite, Bancroft, Ontario, Canada • 13 x 6.5 x 4 cm

Four Cleavage Planes

Fluorite, Benzon Mine, Cave-in-Rock, Illinois, USA • 18 x 12 x 5 cm

Fracture

Fracture refers to breakage of a mineral that does not take place along a cleavage plane or a parting. Therefore it is irregular in appearance, but it is sometimes distinctive enough to be used as an identification tool. Most of the terms used to describe fracture are self-explanatory, but a few need explanations. **Conchoidal** means shell-shaped fractures like those often seen on the edges of glass. **Hackly** refers to a break with a rough, ragged appearance.

Hackly

Silver, Gowganda, Ontario, Canada • 9 x 16 x 7 cm

Conchoidal

Quartz (citrine variety), Sete Lagoas, Minas Gerais, Brazil • 11.5 x 10.5 x 8 cm

Splintery

Wollastonite, California, USA • 22 x 13 x 6.5 cm

Streak

Some minerals will leave a different color when you scrape them across an unglazed ceramic plate, what mineralogists call a **streak plate**. The plate grinds away a tiny bit of powder whose color can help to identify the mineral. For example, even though calcite can occur in a variety of different colors, its streak is always white.

Calcite, San Sebastian Mine, Charcas, San Luis Potosí, Mexico • 10 x 8 x 6.5 cm

Magnetism

Some minerals react to a magnetic field. Some are attracted to a magnet, some are weakly attracted and some can even be repelled. There are also several minerals that are attracted to magnetic fields only when heated. Probably the most common magnetic mineral is magnetite, an iron oxide that owes its name to its characteristic physical property of being attracted to a magnet. Most minerals are not attracted to a magnet at all, but if a mineral is attracted, this is a key physical property by which to identify it.

Fluorescence

Fluorescence is visible light emitted by some minerals when exposed to invisible ultraviolet (UV) radiation. There are two effective ultraviolet sources, long-wave and short-wave. A variety of minerals will glow under only one source, while others will glow under both. The fluorescent color of a mineral is usually different from its color in daylight. Not every mineral is fluorescent; impurities known as **activators** must be present in the chemical makeup of the mineral. For example, manganese in very small quantities will cause calcite to glow red under UV. Other activators can cause minerals to glow in any color of the rainbow.

Crystallography

Space Groups

When you look at a well-formed crystal, the first thing that you notice is that the faces are symmetrically repeated. It is this symmetry that allows us to divide crystals into 32 possible classes, which can then be classified into one of seven crystal systems. This outward expression of faces is a result of the crystal's structure — the regular placement of the atoms that comprise the crystal. In crystallography, most types of symmetry can be described in terms of the apparent movement of an atom, such as some type of rotation, or **translation**. If you look at an equilateral triangle through 360 degrees, what you'll find is that a point occurs every 120 degrees. If you imagine identical atoms at each of these points in the triangle, as you rotate the triangle through 360 degrees, it repeats itself three times, or has three-fold rotation. The same is true for a square: each of the corners is equivalent, meaning that in 360 degrees it is identical four times, or has four-fold rotation.

At the atomic level, atoms or similar groups of atoms are repeated in three-dimensional space to result in what can be described as a space lattice. Fourteen possible space lattices can be described in crystals. Now think of our square in three dimensions, as a cube with six equivalent sides. More specifically, a cube (or hexahedron) has eight points, six faces, and twelve edges that are perpendicular to each other, forming 90-degree angles. This is the most symmetric crystal form and is the basis of the cubic crystal class, which includes minerals such as diamond, pyrite, fluorite and garnet.

There are three main variations of this cube, called simple cubic, body-centered cubic (bcc), and face-centered cubic (fcc, also known as cubic close-packed, or ccp), and then variations of these. The other numbers and letters in the space-group formula refer to other rotations and translations. Applying these symmetry elements, or **operators**, to the crystal structure, a total of 230 unique space groups can be described. For further information on the topic of crystallography, several references are provided in the back of this book.

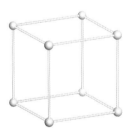

The *simple cubic* system (P) has atoms in each corner of the cube (*P* means "primitive" in a space group). Pyrite crystallizes in the space group *Pa*3, and its crystal form is that of a cube.

Another option is to have an atom in the center of the cube as well as at the corners. So *body-centered* means that there is one atom in the "body" of this cube. An *I* in the space-group formula means that it is body-centered. An example of this is garnet, which crystallizes in the space group *Ia*3*d*.

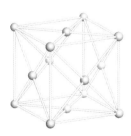

A third arrangement has atoms in each of the faces of the cube, which is referred to as *face-centered cubic*, represented by *F* in the space-group formula. An example of this is galena, which crystallizes in the space group *Fm*3*m*.

Crystal Systems

As you flip through the pages of this book, one of the first things you will notice is the seemingly endless variety of crystal shapes. It is true that there are many variations, but all of them can be related and assigned to one of six crystal systems. Since the outer shape, or habit, of a crystal depends on a regular build-up of unit cells — the mineral's building blocks at the atomic level — it is not surprising that each system has basic unit cells with characteristic angles and proportions. These systems are

- cubic
- tetragonal
- hexagonal and trigonal (usually referred to as a single system)
- orthorhombic
- monoclinic
- triclinic

Each system is defined by the relative lengths and orientation of its three crystallographic axes (typically written *a*, *b* and *c* if they are different lengths). These axes can be thought of as imaginary lines that describe the unit cell of the mineral.

The **cubic** system (also called isometric) is one of the six crystal systems. The cubic unit cell has the same dimension in every direction, including its edges, and the angles between the edges are all 90°. It is possible to generate the other six unit cells of the crystal systems by distorting this basic cube. Minerals that crystallize in the cubic system include gold, halite, copper, platinum, diamond, pyrite and galena.

If one edge dimension of the basic cubic cell is changed so that it either increases or decreases in size, a **tetragonal** unit cell is formed. The angles between the edges are still 90° but the cell is longer along one dimension. Some of the minerals that crystallize in the tetragonal system are cassiterite, zircon, chalcopyrite, wulfenite and rutile.

Pressing on the sides of the cubic cell and distorting it to form angles of 60° and 120°, then placing three of the resulting cells together, results in a six-sided **hexagonal** cell. The **trigonal** system, in which three like faces are repeated, is considered by some to be a subdivision of the hexagonal cell; others consider it to be a separate system altogether, resulting in seven systems. Minerals that crystallize in the hexagonal system include beryl and apatite, and in the trigonal system are quartz, tourmaline-group minerals and calcite.

Stretching the cubic cell in two directions at right angles to each other results in an **orthorhombic** cell. No pair of opposite sides is square and each pair of opposite sides differs in size, but all the angles remain at 90°. Minerals that crystallize in the orthorhombic system include olivine, topaz, barite (baryte) and marcasite.

Pushing on an edge of an orthorhombic cell so that it distorts in one direction results in a **monoclinic** cell, in which the faces of one pair of sides no longer have 90° angles. Minerals that crystallize in the monoclinic system are azurite, malachite, realgar and gypsum.

Starting with the orthorhombic cell and distorting it in three directions results in a **triclinic** cell. None of the faces has corner angles of 90°. Minerals that crystallize in the triclinic system are microcline, albite, kyanite and talc.

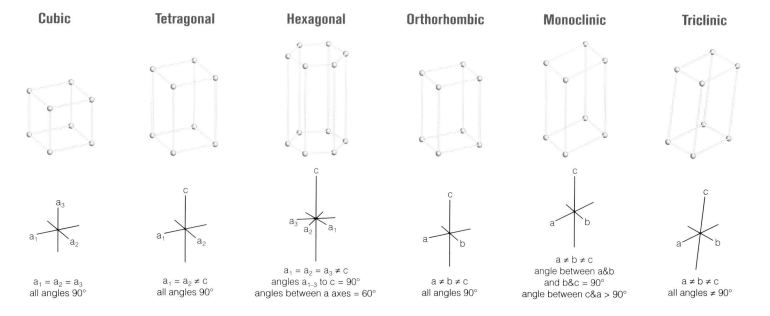

Cubic	Tetragonal	Hexagonal	Orthorhombic	Monoclinic	Triclinic
$a_1 = a_2 = a_3$ all angles 90°	$a_1 = a_2 \neq c$ all angles 90°	$a_1 = a_2 = a_3 \neq c$ angles a_{1-3} to c = 90° angles between a axes = 60°	$a \neq b \neq c$ all angles 90°	$a \neq b \neq c$ angle between a&b and b&c = 90° angle between c&a > 90°	$a \neq b \neq c$ all angles ≠ 90°

CHAPTER 1
Native Elements

Minerals that are made up of just one essential element are called native elements. They include the metallic elements, such as gold, silver, platinum and copper; semi-metals, such as arsenic; and non-metallic minerals, including diamond, graphite and sulfur. These substances have a wide variety of physical characteristics. Many uncommon minerals occur in this group because the conditions that cause an element to form in an uncombined state are in most cases very rare. For example, lead is an abundant element, but it hardly ever occurs in its native form. Copper, on the other hand, commonly occurs naturally in its free metallic state, sometimes in massive aggregates of up to several tons.

ABOVE: Medallion, William Smith and Charles Eaton (England, c. 1834–70), lead and copper alloy, 6 x 4.5 cm. "Billy" Smith and "Charley" Eaton were a couple of illiterate treasure hunters who made a modest living salvaging small articles from the Thames in the mid-1850s. In about 1857 they decided they could make more money by casting "medieval" objects in a lead and copper alloy, using hand-cut plaster molds. This medallion of a knight is a good example of this category of fake, now commonly referred to as "Billy and Charleys." The British Museum and the Royal Ontario Museum both own examples.

RIGHT: Sulfur, Sicily, Italy • 9 x 10 x 11 cm

LEFT: Gold, Bralorne (Pioneer) Mine, Bridge River area, British Columbia, Canada • 7 x 6 x 1 cm

Gold

Formula Au

Crystal System cubic

Space Group *Fm3m*

Hardness 2.5–3.0

Specific Gravity 15.2–19.3

Cleavage none

Fracture hackly

Tenacity very malleable and ductile

Gold nugget, near Greenville, California, USA • 16 x 10 x 7 cm

Habit Golden yellow color, inclining to silver yellow with increasing mixture of silver, or orange red from substitution with copper. Octahedral, dodecahedral and cubic crystals, typically crude or rounded; can also be reticulated, dendritic, arborescent, platy, filiform or spongy; massive; in rounded nuggets; or as scales and flakes. Metallic luster; opaque, except in the thinnest foils. Yellow streak.

Environment Forms in hydrothermal quartz veins associated with pyrite, arsenopyrite and other sulfide minerals, and in placers resulting from weathering of these deposits.

Notable Localities Found in almost every country worldwide; some famous localities are as follows. Canada: Klondike, Yukon; several in Ontario, such as Porcupine and Hemlo districts; Noranda district, Quebec. USA: Mother Lode belt and others in California; Silverton and Telluride, Colorado; Homestake Mine, South Dakota. Latin America: Serra Pelada, Pará, Brazil. Europe: Hope's Nose, England; Transylvania, Romania. Africa: Ashanti, Ghana; Witwatersrand, South Africa. Asia: eastern slope of the Ural Mountains, Russia; Mysore, India. Australia: Kalgoorlie, Coolgardie and Norseman, West Australia.

Name The etymology of the name has been lost, but it is believed to derive from the Sanksrit *jyal* and the German *geld*.

Gold's chemical symbol (Au) is from the Latin *aurum*, meaning "shining dawn."

The great ancient civilizations — Egyptian and Greek, Chinese and African, Aztec and Mayan — coveted gold for its beauty. Glowing like the sun, gold was also considered a sacred metal, worthy of offering to the gods. Unlike more practical metals such as copper and iron, its value is primarily symbolic: gold's worth is determined by the value we place on it. Eighty-five percent of the metal is used for jewelry, objects of art and other applications that have a purely aesthetic or luxurious purpose.

Gold's physical qualities led to its becoming a symbol of wealth and power, especially its color, luster and resistance to corrosion. Gold's malleability and ductility meant that it could be hammered into shapes and drawn into thin wires.

Gold occurs in two types of deposits: lode and placer. In lode deposits, pure gold is consolidated into rock and is commonly so fine-grained that it is invisible to the naked eye.

Placer deposits form when these gold-bearing rocks become weathered and eroded. The gold is washed out and carried away by streams and rivers. When the current slows, the relatively heavy particles of gold sink and accumulate, forming deposits. Canada's most famous placer deposits were discovered in the late nineteenth century in the Yukon Territory, sparking the Klondike Gold Rush (1897–98). Prospectors retrieved placer gold by panning and, later, by dredging.

ABOVE: Histamenon (Byzantine, 1028–1034), gold, diam. 2.5 cm, wt. 4.4 g. From the reign of Emperor Romanus III Argyrus, this coin, also known as a solidus, depicts Christ enthroned on the front (shown) and Romanus and the Virgin Mary on the back.

RIGHT: Crystallized gold emerging from quartz, Eagle's Nest Mine, Placer County, California, USA • 8.5 x 6.5 x 2.5 cm

Gold

LEFT: Plaque of a lion's head (Persia, Achaemenid dynasty, c. 400 BCE), gold with repoussé decoration, 4.9 x 0.2 x 5.7 cm. The robes of ancient royalty were often embellished with beads or embroidery, but an especially rich impression was achieved by using gold ornaments such as this one. Repoussé designs were created by hammering sheets of gold over a carved base to produce an image in relief. The resulting ornament would then be sewn onto the garment. The lion's strength was an attribute that particularly appealed to royalty.

BELOW: Cigarette case (Russian, c. 1912), 18-karat gold carved with acanthus leaves, 7 x 5 x 1 cm. In the late 19th century cigarette cases became a decorative personal accessory, along with lighters and compacts. By the early 1900s elaborate cigarette cases were being made in Russia, France and England. Russian cases of that period exhibited floral and geometric enamel designs, such as those made famous by Peter Carl Fabergé. After the First World War, when cigarette smoking was considered chic, Paris became the center for cigarette-case design.

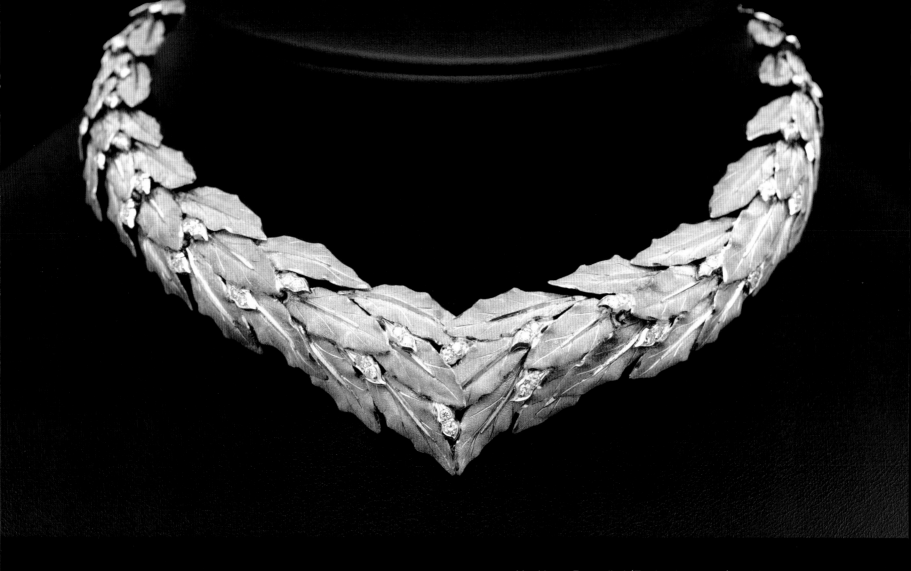

Necklace, Buccellati (England, c. 1970), gold with diamonds, 20 x 15 x 0.5 cm. Diamonds and gold are frequently used together in the world of expensive jewelry. Among the most desirable luxury goods in the world are pieces made by Van Cleef & Arpels and Buccellati, firms patronized by royalty, film stars and wealthy socialites.

Silver

Formula Ag

Crystal System cubic

Space Group *Fm3m*

Hardness 2.5–3.0

Specific Gravity 10.5

Cleavage none

Fracture hackly

Tenacity malleable and ductile

Habit Characteristically silvery white; tarnishes to gray or black. Cubic, octahedral or dodecahedral crystals, but reticulated, arborescent and wiry forms common. Metallic luster; opaque. Silver white streak.

Environment Widely distributed in small amounts. Larger deposits are probably the result of deposition of silver from hydrothermal solutions. Also formed through secondary processes of oxidation in deposits containing minerals rich in silver.

Notable Localities Canada: Cobalt mining district and Thunder Bay District, Ontario. USA: several localities in California and Colorado; Tombstone, Globe and Bisbee, Arizona. Latin America: Batopilas, Chihuahua, Mexico; Uchucchacua Mine, Peru; Potosí, Oruro and other localities, Bolivia. Europe: Kongsberg, Norway; Sainte-Marie-aux-Mines, Alsace, France; Schemnitz, Czech Republic. Africa: Tsumeb, Namibia. Australia: Broken Hill and Cobar, New South Wales.

Name From the Latin *argentum*, which is derived from a Sanskrit word meaning "white and shining." The chemical symbol (Ag) is also from *argentum*.

Much of the world's silver production is a by-product of refining lead, copper and zinc, but deposits of silver are also known.

Ring (Byzantine, 500–600 CE), silver, diam. 2.6 cm.

Wire silver, Silver Islet Mine, Thunder Bay District, Ontario, Canada • 11.5 x 14 x 11 cm

Silver has been used for thousands of years, for ornaments and utensils, for trade and as the basis for many monetary systems. Artifacts made from silver can be traced back as far as 4000 BCE. Silver is one of the easiest metals to work into shapes; it is second only to gold in terms of malleability and ductility.

Silver's natural brilliant white color has made it prized throughout the ages for jewelry and tableware. When polished, it has the highest reflectivity of all metals — nearly 100% — making it suitable for a number of applications in mirrors and coatings. What's more, silver has the highest thermal and electrical conductivity — measures of how well a material accommodates the movement of heat and electrical charges — of all metals.

ABOVE: Teapot, James Fry (Dublin, Ireland, 1834), silver, 20 x 25 cm.

LEFT: Silver, Keeley-Frontier Mine, South Lorrain, Ontario, Canada • 2.5 x 3 x 1.5 cm

Copper

Formula Cu

Crystal System cubic

Space Group *Fm3m*

Hardness 2.5–3.0

Specific Gravity 8.9

Cleavage none

Fracture hackly

Tenacity very malleable and ductile

Habit Light rose; tarnishes to copper red or red brown. Cubic and dodecahedral crystals common; often flattened or elongated in twisted, wire-like shapes; also filiform, arborescent, massive and as a coarse powder. Metallic luster; opaque. Reddish copper streak.

Environment Native copper is almost always a secondary mineral formed by the reduction of copper-bearing solutions by iron minerals.

Notable Localities Canada: Kamloops, British Columbia; Cap d'Or, Nova Scotia. USA: Santa Rita, Ajo and Bisbee, Arizona; Keweenaw Peninsula, Michigan. Latin America: Cananea, Sonora, Mexico; Corocoro, Bolivia. Europe: Cornwall, England; Rheinland-Pfalz, Germany. Asia: Yekaterinburg (Sverdlovsk), Ural Mountains, Russia. Australia: Broken Hill, New South Wales.

Name From the Latin *aes cyprium*, meaning "metal of Cyprus," where the metal was produced in early times. The chemical symbol is from the shortened Latin form, *cuprium*.

In Michigan copper is found as a primary ore; million of tons have been mined there.

Copper, New Cornelia (Ajo) Mine, Ajo district, Arizona, USA • 6 x 5 x 1 cm

ABOVE: Copper, White Pine Mine, Ontonagon, Michigan, USA • 12 x 23 x 6 cm

LEFT: *Hu* (China, Eastern Zhou dynasty, 500–450 BCE), bronze, copper and turquoise, ht. 34.8 cm, diam. 24.9 cm. This wine vessel, thought to be from Luoyang, in Henan province, was used for ritual purposes.

Sulfur

Formula S

Crystal System cubic

Space Group *Fddd*

Hardness 1.5–2.5

Specific Gravity 2.0–2.1

Cleavage {001}, {110} and {111} imperfect

Fracture uneven to conchoidal

Tenacity rather brittle to somewhat sectile

Habit Pale yellow to yellow brown. Dipyramidal crystals typical, but at least 56 crystal forms known; can also be massive, reniform or stalactitic. Resinous to greasy luster; translucent to transparent. Yellow streak.

Environment Well-formed sulfur is usually created as a sublimate from volcanic gases (H_2S) that encrusts volcanic vents and fumaroles. Massive sulfur can be found in thick beds in sedimentary rocks.

Notable Localities USA: Sulfur Mountain, Yellowstone Park, Wyoming; salt deposits in Louisiana and Texas. Latin America: Baja California, Mexico. Europe: Mt. Vesuvius; Solfatara di Pozzuoli, near Naples; Perticara, near Rimini; Carrara, Tuscany; Cianciana, Sicily — all in Italy; Conil, Spain. Asia: volcanic regions in Japan.

Name Derived from the Sanskrit word *sulvere* or Latin *sulfurium.*

Sulfur is used in detergents and pesticides and is a component of gunpowder. A bright golden yellow sulfur compound, orpiment, was used by artists all over the ancient world. It was replaced in the 18th century by an artificial (and highly poisonous) version.

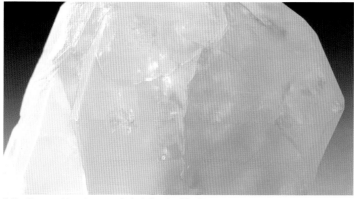

Sulfur, Cianciana Mine, Agrigento, Sicily, Italy • 8 x 7.5 x 5 cm

Arsenic, Sankt Andreasberg, Lower Saxony, Germany • 5 x 7 x 1 cm

Arsenic

Formula As

Crystal System hexagonal

Space Group $R\bar{3}/m$

Hardness 3.5

Specific Gravity 5.7

Cleavage perfect on {0001}; fair on {10$\bar{1}$4}

Fracture uneven

Tenacity brittle

Habit Tin white; tarnishes to dark gray. Crystals rare; usually massive, reniform or stalactitic, often with concentric layers. Metallic luster; opaque. Black streak.

Environment Typically found in hydrothermal veins, generally associated with antimony, silver, cobalt and nickel-bearing minerals.

Notable Localities Canada: Port Alberni, Vancouver Island, and Watson Creek, Fraser River, British Columbia. USA: Washington Camp, Arizona. Latin America: Pasta Bueno, Peru; Copaiapo, Chile. Europe: Sainte-Marie-aux-Mines, Alsace, France; Wolfsburg and Sankt Andreasberg, Lower Saxony, Germany. Asia: Akatani Mine, Japan.

Name From the Greek word *arsenikos*, meaning "potent" or "masculine," which was used to describe orpiment, an arsenic sulfide. The word was adopted into Latin as *arsenicum.*

Tellurium, Rainy River District, Ontario, Canada • 10 x 12 x 3 cm

Tellurium

Formula Te
Crystal System hexagonal
Space Group $P3_121$ or $P3_221$
Hardness 2.0–2.5
Specific Gravity 6.1–6.3

Cleavage perfect on $\{10\bar{1}0\}$; imperfect on $\{0001\}$
Fracture none
Tenacity brittle

Habit Typically tin white color. Massive to fine granular forms; rarely prismatic and acicular crystals. Gray streak.

Environment Found as a hydrothermal vein mineral associated with gold and silver tellurides, and in volcanic fumaroles.

Notable Localities Canada: Rainy River District and Frood Mine, Sudbury, Ontario. USA: Delamar, Nevada. Europe: Facebaj, Transylvania, Romania. Asia: Kochbulak, Uzbekistan; Kawazu Mine, Simoda, Japan. Australia: Kalgoorlie, West Australia.

Name From the Latin *tellus*, meaning "earth."

Lead

Formula Pb
Crystal System cubic
Space Group *Fm3m*
Hardness 1.5
Specific Gravity 11.34

Cleavage none
Fracture hackly
Tenacity very malleable, moderately sectile

Habit Gray white; tarnishes to dull dark gray. Commonly found in round masses and plates; rare as octahedral, cubic or dodecahedral crystals. Lead gray streak.

Environment Rare in nature; hydrothermal in origin, and found in placers.

Notable Localities Canada: Yukon Territory. USA: Franklin, New Jersey. Latin America: El Dorado, Gran Sabana, Venezuela. Europe: Ilimaussaq, Greenland; Långban, Filipstad, Värmland, Sweden.

Name From the Latin *plumbum*, which is why the chemical symbol is Pb.

Combined with other elements, lead forms a variety of interesting and beautiful minerals, all of which tend to be heavy because of their lead content. The most significant is galena (PbS), a lead sulfide.

Lead, Långban, Värmland, Sweden • 5.5 x 5.5 x 3.5 cm

Placer platinum, Tulameen River, British Columbia, Canada • Various sizes

Platinum

Formula Pt

Crystal System cubic

Space Group *Fm3m*

Hardness 4.0–4.5

Specific Gravity 19.0–21.0

Cleavage none

Fracture hackly

Tenacity ductile and malleable

Habit Whitish steel gray to dark gray. Rare in nature, typically occurring in flakes or grains; very rare in nuggets and even rarer as cubic crystals. Metallic luster; opaque. Grayish white streak.

Environment Found in or associated with mafic and ultramafic igneous rocks; also found in quartz veins associated with hematite, chlorite and pyrolusite.

Notable Localities Canada: Sudbury basin, Ontario; Rivière-du-Loup, Quebec. USA: Stillwater complex, Montana. Latin America: near Papayan, Cauca, Colombia. Africa: Bushveld complex, South Africa. Asia: Nelkan, Khabarovsk Oblast, Russia.

Name From the Spanish *platina*, a diminutive of *plata*, "silver," as it was once believed to be an impure ore of silver.

Graphite

Formula C

Crystal System hexagonal

Space Group $P6_3/mmc$

Hardness 1.0

Specific Gravity 2.1–2.2

Cleavage {0001} perfect

Fracture uneven

Tenacity flexible but not elastic, sectile

Habit Typically black or silvery gray. Commonly massive, columnar, granular or earthy masses; rarely crystals with well-defined hexagonal habit and spheroidal aggregates. Dull earthy or metallic luster; opaque, but transparent in extremely thin flakes. Black to steel gray streak.

Environment Formed by metamorphism of sedimentary carbonaceous material, such as limestones rich in organic material; also found as the primary mineral in some igneous rocks.

Notable Localities Canada: National Mine, Hastings County, Ontario; Buckingham, Quebec. USA: Ticonderoga, New York; Franklin and Sterling Hill, New Jersey. Latin America: Morodillas Mine, Sonora, Mexico. Europe: Egalugssuit and Disko Island, Greenland; Barrowdale, Cumbria, England; Passau, Bavaria, Germany; Piedmont, Italy.

Name From the Greek *graphein*, "to write," an allusion to its ancient use as a drawing pencil. Its chemical symbol (C) indicates that it is composed of carbon.

Graphite, mixed with clay, is still used to make pencils. Before the 18th century, graphite was called "plumbago" or "black lead," which is the source of the term "lead pencil."

Graphite, Kahatagaha, Kurunegala, North Western Province, Sri Lanka • 13.5 x 8.5 x 7 cm

Diamond

Formula C

Crystal System cubic

Space Group *Fd3m*

Hardness 10.0

Specific Gravity 3.5–3.53

Cleavage {111} perfect

Fracture conchoidal

Tenacity brittle

ABOVE: Diamond in matrix, Mir Pipe, Mirny, Sakha Republic, Russia • 3 x 2 x 2 cm

BELOW: Pendant (Spain, 17th century), gold, diamonds and enamel, 6 x 5 x 0.4 cm.

Habit Colorless and ranging from yellow to brown or black; rarely pink, green, blue, orange or red. Crystals octahedral, dodecahedral, cubic or even more complex; massive and fine-grained (carbonado) forms rare. Adamantine to greasy luster; transparent to translucent. No streak.

Environment A product of deep-seated crystallization of ultrabasic igneous magmas, in kimberlite pipes or lamproites; crystals also found in alluvial deposits, a result of erosion of such kimberlite pipes.

Notable Localities Canada: Ekati and Diavik mines, Lac de Gras region, Northwest Territories; Nunavut; Ontario. USA: Murfreesboro, Arkansas. Africa: several pipes around Kimberley, South Africa; Jwaneng and Orapa pipes, Botswana. Asia: Yakutia, Russia; Golconda region and near Nágpur and Bundelkhand, India. Australia: Argyle pipe, Kimberley, Western Australia.

Name Most likely from the Greek *adamas*, "invincible," for its extreme hardness. Its chemical symbol (C) indicates that it is composed of carbon.

Princess- and brilliant-cut diamonds, Ekati Mine, Lac de Gras, Northwest Territories, Canada • 7.9 x 7.7 x 5.6 mm, 3.00 ct; 9.6 x 9.6 x 5.6 mm, 3.10 ct

Diamond's rarity, brilliance, hardness and sparkling luster have made it one of the most sought-after gemstones since it was first found in India more than 2,000 years ago, in riverbed deposits of sand and gravel. It wasn't until 1871 that the geological source of diamonds, a rare volcanic rock, was discovered near Kimberley in South Africa.

"En tremblant" brooch, Bulgari (Italy, c. 1960), platinum with colored diamonds, 7 x 6 x 5 cm, 29.80 ct. Realistic floral motifs had been a common theme in French jewelry since the 18th century. In the late 1950s the Italian jeweler Bulgari purchased a large collection of colored diamonds and, influenced by earlier French designs, created a series of *en tremblant*, or "trembling," brooches. The gems are set in spring mounts so that they shiver and sparkle with the wearer's movements. The economic boom after the Second World War saw an increased interest in high-end jewelry distinguished by designs lavishly set with diamonds. Bulgari's en tremblant brooches were bestsellers during the 1950s and '60s.

CHAPTER 2
Sulfides & Sulfosalts

The sulfide minerals are made up of one or more metallic elements combined with the non-metallic element sulfur (S). They tend to have a simple structure and a highly symmetrical crystal form. Sulfides also possess many of the properties of metals, such as metallic luster and conductivity, and tend to be opaque. This group is an economically important class of minerals; most of the major ores of important metals such as copper, lead and silver are sulfides.

Sulfosalts are closely related to sulfides. In addition to sulfur and related elements combined with metallic elements, they also require one or more semi-metals — such as antimony, arsenic or bismuth — to form their structure. This is an extensive group of minerals, with over a hundred known examples, and is characterized by some of the most complicated atomic and crystal structures of any group. These minerals are generally soft, have a metallic luster and high specific gravity, and are fairly uncommon. Sulfosalts tend to form at low temperatures and are among the last minerals to crystallize, many of them in ore deposits.

ABOVE: Gem sphalerite is uncommon, as the mineral is typically opaque. However, a few localities such as Spain and Mont-Saint-Hilaire, Quebec, produce handsome transparent specimens.
TOP: Cut sphalerite gemstone, Las Manforas (Aliva) Mine, Camaleño, Cantabria, Spain • 19.3 x 13.9 mm, 37.80 ct BOTTOM: Cut sphalerite gemstone, Mont-Saint-Hilaire, Quebec, Canada • 20.30 ct

RIGHT: Orpiment, Picher Mine, Tri-State Mining District, Oklahoma, USA • 8 x 5 x 2.5 cm

LEFT: Orpiment, Quiruvilca Mine, Santiago de Chuco, La Libertad, Peru • 7 x 5 x 5 cm

Acanthite, Sandon, Slocan Mining Division, British Columbia, Canada • 7.5 x 1.5 x 7.5 cm

Acanthite

Formula Ag_2S

Crystal System monoclinic

Space Group $P2_1/n$

Hardness 2.0–2.5

Specific Gravity 7.2–7.4

Cleavage indistinct

Fracture subconchoidal

Tenacity very sectile

Habit Iron black. Pseudo-cubic or pseudo-octahedral crystals; can also be massive. Metallic luster; opaque. Black streak.

Environment Occurs worldwide in silver ores.

Notable Localities Canada: El Bonanza Mine, Port Radium district, Northwest Territories; Cobalt, Ontario. Latin America: Atacama, Chile. Europe: Liskeard, Cornwall, England; Kongsberg, Norway. Australia: Broken Hill, New South Wales.

Name From the Greek word for "thorn," referring to the shape of the crystals.

Chalcocite

Formula Cu_2S

Crystal System monoclinic

Space Group $P2_1/c$ or Pc

Hardness 2.5–3.0

Specific Gravity 5.5–5.8

Cleavage {110} indistinct

Fracture conchoidal

Tenacity brittle

Habit Black to lead gray. Crystals rare; usually massive and compact, with a drusy coating. Metallic luster; opaque. Black streak.

Environment Belongs to a group of sulfide minerals formed at relatively low temperatures, often as alteration products of other copper minerals. Concentrated in secondary alteration zones; can contain considerably higher content of copper than the primary ore. These alteration zones are often hydrothermal veins containing minerals such as quartz, calcite, covellite, chalcopyrite, galena, bornite and sphalerite as well as chalcocite.

Notable Localities USA: Bingham Canyon, Utah; Bisbee and Miami, Arizona; Flambeau Mine, Ladysmith, Wisconsin. Europe: St. Just and Redruth, Cornwall, England; Dognacska (Dognecea), Romania. Asia: Bogoslovsk, Ural Mountains, Russia. Africa: Tsumeb, Namibia.

Name From the Greek word for "copper."

Chalcocite is a common and widely distributed ore mineral of copper.

Chalcocite, Flambeau Mine, Ladysmith, Wisconsin, USA • 12 x 11 x 7 cm

Sphalerite, Elmwood Mine, Carthage, Tennessee, USA • 19 x 19 x 14 cm

Sphalerite

Formula (Zn,Fe)S

Crystal System cubic

Space Group $F\bar{4}3m$

Hardness 3.5–4.0

Specific Gravity 3.9–4.1

Cleavage {011} perfect

Fracture conchoidal

Tenacity brittle

Habit Yellow, brown, black or, less commonly, red or green; when iron-free, white to colorless. Crystals tetrahedral or dodecahedral, typically complex and distorted, with curved and conical faces common; also fibrous, botryoidal, stalactitic, cleavable, coarse to fine granular or massive. Resinous to adamantine luster; transparent to translucent, but opaque when iron-rich. Yellow to light brown streak.

Environment Occurs in hydrothermal ore deposits.

Notable Localities Canada: Watson Lake, Yukon; Kimberley, British Columbia; gem crystals at Mont-Saint-Hilaire, Quebec. USA: important deposits in Missouri, Wisconsin, Illinois, Kansas and Oklahoma. Latin America: Santa Eulalia and Naica, Chihuahua, and Cananea, Sonora, Mexico. Europe: Cumberland, England; Freiberg, Saxony, and Neudorf, Harz Mountains, Germany. Asia: Dal'negorsk, Primorskiy Krai, Russia.

Name From the Greek *sphaleros*, meaning "treacherous."

Sphalerite was given its name because the mineral occurs in several forms that can be mistaken for galena but don't yield lead. It is the most common zinc mineral and the principal ore of zinc.

Bornite

Formula Cu_5FeS_4

Crystal System orthorhombic

Space Group *Pbca*

Hardness 3.0

Specific Gravity 5.1

Cleavage poor

Fracture uneven to conchoidal

Tenacity brittle

Habit Copper red or brown to bronze on fresh surfaces; tarnishes to iridescent purple and black. Crystals rare; when found they are pseudo-cubic, dodecahedral or rarely octahedral. Metallic luster; opaque. Gray black streak.

Environment A common and widespread mineral in copper deposits, principally in hydrothermal veins along with minerals such as quartz, chalcopyrite, pyrite and marcasite. Also occurs in dikes, contact metamorphic deposits, pegmatites and basic intrusives. An important ore of copper.

Notable Localities Canada: Marble Bay Mine, Texada Island, British Columbia. USA: Kennecott, Alaska; Bisbee, Globe, Ajo and Magma, Arizona. Europe: Cornwall, England. Asia: Norilsk, Russia; Zhezkazgan, Kazakhstan. Australia: Mt. Lyell, Tasmania.

Name Named for Ignaz von Born (1742–91), an Austrian mineralogist.

Bornite is informally called "peacock ore" or "purple copper ore" because of its iridescent purple tarnish.

Bornite, Zhezkazgan, Karaganda Oblast, Kazakhstan • 7.5 x 6 x 2.5 cm

Pyrrhotite

Formula Fe_7S_8
Crystal System monoclinic
Space Group $A2/a$
Hardness 3.5–4.5
Specific Gravity 4.6–4.7

Cleavage none
Fracture subconchoidal to uneven
Tenacity brittle

Habit Bronze or bronze yellow to brown; tarnishes on exposure to air. Generally massive or granular but can form pseudo-hexagonal crystals. Metallic luster; opaque. Gray black streak.

Environment Occurs mainly in silica-poor igneous rocks, as an accessory mineral in metamorphic rocks and in sedimentary rocks. Commonly associated with pentlandite, pyrite and quartz.

Notable Localities Canada: Bluebell Mine, Riondel, British Columbia. Latin America: Potosí and San Antonio mines, Santa Eulalia, Chihuahua, Mexico; Morro Velho gold mine, Nova Lima, Minas Gerais, Brazil. Asia: Dal'negorsk, Primorskiy Krai, Russia.

Name From the Greek for "redness," in reference to its color.

Pyrrhotite is the second most common magnetic mineral.

Pyrrhotite, Morro Velho Mine, Nova Lima, Minas Gerais, Brazil • 18 x 8.5 x 4 cm

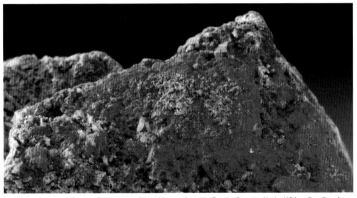

Cinnabar, Marion Mine, Camp Floyd Mining District, Tooele County, Utah, USA • 5 x 5 x 4 cm

Cinnabar

Formula HgS
Crystal System hexagonal
Space Group $P3_12_1$
Hardness 2.0–2.5
Specific Gravity 8.1–8.2

Cleavage {0101} perfect
Fracture subconchoidal to uneven
Tenacity slightly sectile

Habit Scarlet red; darkens on exposure to light. Rhombohedral, thick tabular, stout to slender prismatic crystals; also occurs as incrustations, granular or massive. Adamantine luster, inclining to metallic when dark, and dull in friable material; transparent in thin pieces but otherwise opaque. Red streak.

Environment Formed from low-temperature hydrothermal solutions (hot springs) in veins, and in sedimentary, igneous and metamorphic host rocks associated with pyrite, marcasite and stibnite.

Notable Localities USA: New Almaden and New Idria, California. Latin America: Charcas, San Luis Potosí, Mexico. Europe: Almadén, Ciudad Real, and Mieres, Asturias, Spain; Mt. Amiata, Italy; Nikitovka deposit, Gorlovka, Ukraine. Asia: Hydercahn, Kazakhstan; Tsar Tien Mine, Hunan, China.

Name From the medieval Latin *cinnabaris*, which probably derived from the Persian *zinjifrah* and Arabic *zinjafr*, meaning "dragon's blood," in allusion to the mineral's red color.

The most abundant mercury mineral, cinnabar has been mined for at least 2,000 years at Almadén in Spain. It was used as a pigment by ancient peoples and is still used to color Chinese lacquerware.

Cobaltite

Formula CoAsS

Crystal System orthorhombic

Space Group $Pca2_1$

Hardness 5.5

Specific Gravity 6.3

Cleavage perfect on {001}

Fracture conchoidal or uneven

Tenacity brittle

Habit Silver white to steel gray. Cubic and pseudo-cubic crystals with striated faces; also massive or granular. Metallic luster; opaque. Dark gray streak.

Environment Occurs in high-temperature hydrothermal deposits and in veins in contact metamorphic environments.

Notable Localities Canada: Cobalt and Sudbury districts, Ontario. Europe: Wheal Cock and Botallack mines, St. Just, Cornwall, England; Tunaberg, Södermanland, and Riddarhyttan and Håkansboda, Västmanland, Sweden. Africa: Bou Azzer, Morocco. Australia: Broken Hill and Torrington, New South Wales; Bimbowrie Station, South Australia; Mount Cobalt Mine and Cloncurry, Queensland.

Name From the element cobalt in its composition.

Cobaltite, Håkansboda, Lindesberg, Västmanland, Sweden • 4 x 3 x 3 cm

Molybdenite, Allies Mine, Deepwater, New South Wales, Australia • 8 x 6 x 3 cm

Molybdenite

Formula MoS_2

Crystal System hexagonal

Space Group $P6_3/mmc$

Hardness 1.0–1.5

Specific Gravity 4.6–4.7

Cleavage {0001} perfect

Fracture flaky

Tenacity sectile; lamellae flexible, not elastic

Habit Lead gray with a bluish tint. Hexagonal barrel-shaped or thin tabular crystals; commonly foliated, massive or in scales. Metallic luster; crystals nearly opaque. Silver blue streak.

Environment Occurs as an accessory mineral in some granites and pegmatites or high-temperature hydrothermal veins, and also in disseminated deposits of the porphyry type.

Notable Localities Canada: Con Mine, Yellowknife, Northwest Territories; Timiskaming District, Ontario; Mont-Saint-Hilaire and Moly Hill Mine, La Motte, Quebec. USA: Climax Lake, Colorado; Frankford Quarry, Philadelphia, Pennsylvania. Europe: Carrock Fell and Caldbeck Fell, Cumberland, England; Altenberg, Saxony, Germany. Australia: Kingsgate and Deepwater, New South Wales.

Name Derived from the Greek *molybdos*, meaning "lead."

Molybdenite was originally thought to be lead. It is the most common molybdenum mineral.

Galena

Formula PbS

Crystal System cubic

Space Group *Fm3m*

Hardness 2.5

Specific Gravity 7.6

Cleavage {100} perfect

Fracture subconchoidal

Tenacity brittle

Galena on matrix, Peterszeche Mine, Burbach, North Rhine–Westphalia, Germany • 7 x 5 x 5.5 cm

Lead is a soft gray metal that is incredibly dense. The medieval science of alchemy believed that lead could be turned into gold. While the alchemists never achieved their goal, lead was widely used throughout history. It was first used because it is easy to shape. In ancient China and Greece, craftsmen made lead into coins and ornaments. The Romans fashioned lead pipes to transport water for their cities. In fact, the Latin word for lead is *plumbum*, the root of our modern English words "plumber" and "plumbing."

The most common ore mineral of lead is galena, a lead sulfide. Galena is often found with sphalerite, a sulfide of zinc. The two are so commonly found together that they are referred to as lead–zinc deposits.

Habit Lead gray. Most commonly cubic, more rarely cubo-octahedral or octahedral, may be tabular and can form reticulated masses and skeletal crystals; also as cleavable masses, coarse to very fine granular, fibrous or plumose. Metallic luster; opaque. Lead gray streak.

Environment Forms in many different types of environments, including hydrothermal veins under a wide range of temperatures and contact metamorphic deposits. Limestones and dolostones are common host rocks.

Notable Localities Canada: Pine Point, Northwest Territories; Little Cornwallis Island, Nunavut; Bluebell Mine, Riondel, British Columbia; Kidd Creek, Ontario. USA: Tri-State Mining District (Missouri/Kansas/Oklahoma). Latin America: Naica and Santa Eulalia, Chihuahua, Mexico. Europe: Alston Moor, Cumbria, and Weardale, Durham, England; Příbram, Czech Republic; Trepča, Serbia. Africa: Tsumeb, Namibia. Australia: Broken Hill, New South Wales.

Name From *galena*, the Latin word for lead ore or dross from melted lead.

ABOVE: Galena, Blue Goose Mine, Tri-State Mining District, Missouri, USA • 3 x 4 x 3 cm

RIGHT: Galena, Naica, Chihuahua, Mexico • 6 x 7 x 5 cm

Arsenopyrite, Panasqueira, Castelo Branco district, Portugal • 11.5 x 9.5 x 4.5 cm

Arsenopyrite

Formula FeAsS

Crystal System monoclinic

Space Group $P2_1/c$

Hardness 5.5–6.0

Specific Gravity 6.0–6.2

Cleavage {001} distinct

Fracture uneven

Tenacity brittle

Habit Silver white to steel gray; tarnishes to brownish or pink. Flat tabular, blocky or prismatic, striated crystals; also compact, granular or columnar. Metallic luster; opaque. Dark gray to black streak.

Environment Occurs mostly in high-temperature hydrothermal veins, pegmatites and contact metamorphic deposits. Associated with significant amounts of gold.

Notable Localities Canada: Bluebell Mine, Riondel, British Columbia; Cobalt district, Ontario. USA: Franklin, New Jersey. Latin America: Santa Eulalia and Santa Barbara, Chihuahua, Mexico; Llallagua, Bolivia. Europe: Cornwall, England; Freiberg, Saxony, Germany. Australia: Torrington and Broken Hill, New South Wales.

Name From the older term for the mineral, "arsenical pyrites."

Arsenopyrite is the most common arsenic mineral.

Cubanite

Formula $CuFe_2S_3$

Crystal System orthorhombic

Space Group *Pcmn*

Hardness 3.5

Specific Gravity 4.1

Cleavage none

Fracture conchoidal

Tenacity none

Habit Brassy to bronze yellow. Thick tabular and elongated prismatic crystals; usually massive. Metallic luster; opaque. Black streak.

Environment Forms in hydrothermal deposits at fairly high temperatures. Commonly associated with chalcopyrite, pyrite, pyrrhotite, pentlandite and sphalerite.

Notable Localities Canada: Grey Rock Mine, Bridge River district, British Columbia; Strathcona Mine, Sudbury, Ontario; Chibougamau, Quebec. USA: Mackinaw Mine, Washington; Christmas Mine, Arizona. Latin America: Barracanao, Cuba; Minas Gerais, Brazil.

Name From its occurrence in Cuba.

Cubanite, Chibougamau, Quebec, Canada • 6 x 4 x 3 cm

Pentlandite, Sudbury, Ontario, Canada • 12 x 8 x 12 cm

Pentlandite

Formula $(Fe,Ni)_9S_8$

Crystal System cubic

Space group $Fm3m$

Hardness 3.5–4.0

Specific Gravity 4.9–5.2

Cleavage none

Fracture conchoidal

Tenacity brittle

Habit Pale bronze yellow. Massive or granular. Metallic luster; opaque. Light brown streak.

Environment Occurs in silica-poor intrusive rocks; also found in mantle xenoliths and undersea "black smoker" deposits. Typically associated with pyrrhotite.

Notable Localities Canada: Thompson, Manitoba; Sudbury, Ontario; Voisey's Bay, Labrador. Europe: Craignure, near Inverary, Strathclyde, Scotland; Outokumpu, Finland; Espedalen, near Lillehammer, Norway. Africa: Merensky Reef, Bushveld complex, Mpumalanga, South Africa.

Name Named for Joseph B. Pentland (1797–1873), the Irish scientist who first noted the mineral.

Realgar

Formula AsS

Crystal System monoclinic

Space Group $P2_1/n$

Hardness 1.5–2.0

Specific Gravity 3.5–3.6

Cleavage {010} good; {$\bar{1}$01}, {100} and {120} indistinct

Fracture conchoidal

Tenacity sectile; also slightly brittle

Habit Generally red to yellow orange. Short, prismatic crystals uncommon; also occurs as incrustations. Resinous to greasy luster; transparent when fresh, but crystals tend to fade when exposed to light. Orange to orange brown streak.

Environment Occurs as a minor phase in hydrothermal sulfide veins with orpiment and other arsenic minerals. Also forms as a sublimate around volcanoes and in hot springs and geyser deposits.

Notable Localities USA: Snohomish County, Washington; Norris Geyser Basin, Yellowstone National Park, Wyoming. Latin America: Noche Buena, Zacatecas, Mexico. Europe: Schneeberg, Saxony, Germany; Lengenbach Quarry, Binn Valley, Switzerland; Cavnic and Sacaramb, Romania. Asia: Shimen, Hunan, China.

Name From the Arabic *rahu al ghar*, meaning "powder of the mine."

Realgar has been used to make carvings and as a red pigment.

Realgar, Jiepaiyu Mine, Shimen, Hunan, China • 8 x 6 x 3 cm

Millerite

Formula NiS

Crystal System hexagonal

Space Group *R3m*

Hardness 3.0–3.5

Specific Gravity 5.3–5.5

Cleavage perfect on {1011} and {0112}

Fracture uneven

Tenacity brittle

Habit Brass yellow; tarnishes to iridescent. Needle-like crystals in radiating masses; massive also common. Metallic luster; opaque. Dark green to almost black streak.

Environment Low-temperature mineral often found in cavities in limestone and dolomite or as an alteration product of other nickel minerals.

Notable Localities Canada: Thompson, Manitoba; Temagami, Ontario; Malartic, Quebec. USA: Sterling Hill Mine, New Jersey. Latin America: Ojuela Mine, Mapimí, Durango, Mexico. Europe: Müsen and Wissen, Germany. Africa: Trojan nickel mine, Bindura, Zimbabwe; Mabilikwe Hill, Limpopo, South Africa. Australia: Kambalda and Black Swan Mine, Western Australia.

Name Named for William H. Miller (1801–80), the English mineralogist who first described the mineral.

ABOVE: Millerite, T-3 Mine, Thompson, Manitoba, Canada • 8 x 7.5 x 3 cm

LEFT: Millerite, Kerr-Addison (Kerr) Mine, Timiskaming District, Ontario, Canada • 7 x 7 x 5.5 cm

Millerite, Ojuela Mine, Mapimí, Durango, Mexico • 2 x 10 x 2 cm

Chalcopyrite

Formula $CuFeS_2$

Crystal System tetragonal

Space Group $I\bar{4}2d$

Hardness 3.5–4.0

Specific Gravity 4.1–4.3

Cleavage poor on {011} and {111}

Fracture uneven

Tenacity brittle

Habit Brass yellow; frequently tarnishes to iridescent. Compact crystals; often massive. Metallic luster; opaque. Dark green streak.

Environment Found in a wide variety of conditions, as a primary mineral in hydrothermal veins deposited at medium and high temperatures and in disseminations and massive replacements.

Notable Localities Canada: Sudbury and Kidd Creek, Ontario; Noranda Mine, Rouyn district, Quebec. USA: Tri-State Mining District; Bisbee, Tombstone and Globe-Miami, Arizona. Latin America: Cananea, Sonora, Mexico. Europe: Cornwall, England; Outokumpu, Finland; Rio Tinto, Spain; Siegen and Neunkirchen, Westphalia, Germany. Asia: Japan.

Name From the Greek *chalkos*, copper, and from "pyrite," for its copper content and its resemblance to pyrite.

Chalcopyrite is the primary mineral in several porphyry-copper deposits and a widespread copper ore.

Chalcopyrite, Arakawa Mine, Akita, Honshu, Japan • 18 x 15 x 7 cm

Covellite, Butte, Montana, USA • 1.3 x 3.5 x 1.5 cm

Covellite

Formula CuS

Crystal System hexagonal

Space Group $P6_3/mmc$

Hardness 1.5–2.0

Specific Gravity 4.6–4.7

Cleavage perfect on {0001}

Fracture none

Tenacity flexible in thin leaves

Habit Indigo blue to black; sometimes highly iridescent to brass yellow and deep red. Generally massive and foliated; can form hexagonal plates that when thin enough are flexible. Submetallic luster, ranging to resinous; opaque. Gray to black streak.

Environment Associated with other copper minerals in the zone of secondary enrichment; rarely occurs as a primary mineral.

Notable Localities Canada: Copper Mountain Mine, British Columbia. USA: Arizona; Butte, Montana; Franklin, New Jersey. Latin America: Sierra de Famatina, La Rioja, Argentina. Europe: Mt. Vesuvius, Campania, and Alghero, Sardinia, Italy. Asia: Kedabek, Caucasus Mountains, Azerbaijan. Australia: Moonta, South Australia.

Name Named for Niccolo Covelli (1790–1829), the Italian mineralogist who first described the mineral.

The first named specimens of covellite were taken from the slopes of Mount Vesuvius, the famous Italian volcano.

Greenockite

Formula CdS

Crystal System hexagonal

Space Group $P6_3mc$

Hardness 3.0–3.5

Specific Gravity 4.8–4.9

Cleavage {11$\bar{2}$2} distinct; {0001} imperfect

Fracture conchoidal

Tenacity brittle

Habit Shades of yellow and orange, rarely deep red. Single-ended pyramidal crystals, prismatic or tabular; also as earthy coatings. Resinous to adamantine luster; nearly opaque to translucent. Red, orange or light brown streak.

Environment An alteration product of cadmium-bearing minerals that forms earthy coatings on sphalerite and other zinc minerals. Rarely forms crystals in cavities in mafic igneous rocks and in high-temperature hydrothermal vein deposits.

Notable Localities USA: Mono County, California; Friedensville, Pennsylvania; Franklin and Sterling Hill, New Jersey; Arlington Quarry, Leesburg, Virginia. Latin America: Asunta Mine, Potosí, Bolivia. Europe: Bishopton, Renfrewshire, Scotland; Příbram, Czech Republic. Africa: Tsumeb, Namibia.

Name Named for Charles Murray Cathcart, Lord Greenock (1783–1859), who discovered the mineral in Scotland.

Greenockite, Golden Gate Mine, Mono County, California, USA • 9.5 x 13 x 5 cm

Stibnite, Xikuangshan Mine, Lengshuijiang, Hunan, China • 17 x 14 x 7 cm

Stibnite

Formula Sb_2S_3

Crystal System orthorhombic

Space Group $Pbmn$

Hardness 2.0

Specific Gravity 4.6

Cleavage perfect on {010}; imperfect on {100} and {110}

Fracture subconchoidal

Tenacity highly flexible but not elastic; slightly sectile

Habit Lead gray; tarnishes to blackish or iridescent. Complex aggregates of acicular crystals; also in radiating or columnar masses, often striated or grooved parallel to *c*. Metallic luster, splendent on cleavage surfaces; opaque. Dark gray streak.

Environment Occurs most commonly in hydrothermal vein and replacement deposits.

Notable Localities Canada: Prince William Mine, New Brunswick. USA: San Benito County and Ambrose Mine, California; White Caps and Murray mines, Independence Mountains, Nevada. Latin America: San José and Oruro, Bolivia. Asia: Nerchinsk, Siberia, Russia; Xikuangshan Mine, Hunan, China; Ichinokawa Mine, Saijo, Shikoku, Japan.

Name From the Latin *stibium*, the old name for the element antimony (which is why the chemical symbol for antimony is Sb).

Dyscrasite after silver, Uranium Mine No. 19, Příbram, Czech Republic • 20 x 10 x 18 cm

Dyscrasite

Formula $Ag_{3.2}Sb_{0.8}$

Crystal System orthorhombic

Space Group $Pm2m$

Hardness 3.5

Specific Gravity 9.76

Cleavage {001} and {011} distinct; {110} imperfect

Fracture uneven

Tenacity sectile but brittle

Habit Silvery; tarnishes to lead gray. Prismatic to platy striated crystals; usually massive, foliated or granular. Metallic luster; opaque. Silver streak.

Environment Occurs in hydrothermal veins with other silver minerals as both a primary and secondary mineral.

Notable Localities Canada: Tanco pegmatite, Bernic Lake, Manitoba; Cobalt district, Ontario. USA: Highbridge Mine, Belmont district, Nye County, Nevada. Europe: Ilímaussaq intrusion, southern Greenland; Hiendelaencina, Guadalajara, Spain; Wolfach, Baden, Germany; Příbram, Czech Republic. Australia: Consols Mine, Broken Hill, New South Wales.

Name From the Greek words meaning "a bad alloy."

Nickeline

Formula NiAs

Crystal System hexagonal

Space Group $P6_3/mmc$

Hardness 5.0–5.5

Specific Gravity 7.8

Cleavage none

Fracture conchoidal to uneven

Tenacity brittle

Habit Pale copper red; tarnishes to gray or black. Crystals rare; usually massive. Metallic luster; opaque. Dark brown to black streak.

Environment Occurs in ore deposits with other nickel and arsenic minerals and in veins containing silver and copper.

Notable Localities Canada: Great Bear Lake, Northwest Territories; Silver Islet, Thunder Bay, and Cobalt-Gowganda, Timiskaming District, Ontario. USA: Copper King and Gem mines, Colorado. Latin America: Cochabamba, Bolivia. Europe: Sangerhausen, Saxony, Germany; Schladming, Styria, Austria. Asia: Ban Phuc nickel-copper deposit, Vietnam.

Name From the nickel component in its formula.

Nickeline was called *kupfernickel* in German, meaning "devil's copper," because the mineral was first believed to contain copper but then yielded none.

Nickeline, Helbra, Mansfield Basin, Saxony-Anhalt, Germany • 4 x 4 x 2 cm

Orpiment, Men-kyule River, Sakha Republic, Siberia, Russia • 17 x 11 x 1 cm

Orpiment

Formula As_2S_3	**Specific Gravity** 3.5
Crystal System monoclinic	**Cleavage** {010} perfect
Space Group $P2_1/n$	**Fracture** uneven
Hardness 1.5–2.0	**Tenacity** sectile

Habit Lemon yellow to golden or brownish yellow. Distinct crystals uncommon, short and prismatic when occurring; usually foliated columnar or fibrous aggregate, and may be reniform or botryoidal. Resinous to pearly luster; transparent. Yellow streak.

Environment A low-temperature hydrothermal mineral found in veins and hot springs deposits; also occurs as an alteration product of other arsenic-bearing minerals.

Notable Localities USA: Mercur, Utah; Getchell and White Caps mines, Nevada. Europe: Tajov, Slovakia; Baia Sprie, Romania. Asia: Zarshuran Mine, Iran; Guizhou, Hunan, China.

Name From the Latin *auripigmentum*, meaning "golden paint," in allusion to its color.

Marcasite

Formula FeS_2	**Specific Gravity** 4.9
Crystal System orthorhombic	**Cleavage** {101} distinct
Space Group *Pnnm*	**Fracture** conchoidal; uneven
Hardness 6.0–6.5	**Tenacity** brittle

Habit Silvery yellow to pale brassy yellow, tending toward light green. Crystals common, typically tabular or pyramidal; also stalactitic, globular or reniform, with radiating internal structure. Metallic luster; opaque. Greenish to brownish black streak.

Environment Typically formed under low-temperature conditions in sedimentary environments (shales, limestones and low-ranked coals), often as concretions or replacing fossils, and in hydrothermal veins.

Notable Localities Canada: Nanisivik Mine, Nunavut. USA: Baxter Springs and Galena, Cherokee County, Kansas. Latin America: Santa Eulalia district, Chihuahua, Mexico; Llallagua, Bolivia. Europe: Tavistock, Devon, and Kent, England; several places in the Czech Republic.

Name Of Arabic or Moorish origin, from a word applied to minerals that resemble pyrite.

Marcasite, Frankfort, Ohio, USA • 13 x 11 x 7 cm

Pyrite

Formula FeS_2

Crystal System cubic

Space Group $Pa3$

Hardness 6.0–6.5

Specific Gravity 5.0

Cleavage {001} indistinct

Fracture conchoidal to uneven

Tenacity brittle

Pyrite sun (dollar) in laminated shale matrix, Illinois, USA • 22 x 10 x 1 cm

Iron is the fourth most abundant element in Earth's crust. While the majority goes into the manufacture of steel, it has other uses such as in magnets and transformer cores for electronics. Iron is also used as a pigment in cosmetics, inks and dyes.

Iron is a dark grey metallic element, although it's rarely found in that form. It is very reactive, easily combining chemically with other elements — hence its propensity to rust when in contact with moisture and oxygen.

Pyrite is a source of iron, but so are other minerals such as hematite, magnetite and ilmenite.

Habit Pale brassy yellow; sometimes tarnishes to iridescent. Cubic crystals common, but octahedral and pyritohedral (pentagonal dodecahedra) possible with striations; also commonly granular, globular, framboidal or stalactitic. Metallic luster; opaque. Greenish black streak.

Environment The most widespread and common sulfide mineral, occurring in almost all geological environments, including hydrothermal veins, contact metamorphic rocks and sedimentary rocks such as shale, coal and limestone.

Notable Localities Canada: Nanisivik Mine, Nunavut. USA: Butte, Montana; Park City and Bingham, Utah; Franklin, New Jersey. Latin America: Cananea, Sonora, and Naica and Santa Eulalia, Chihuahua, Mexico; Llallagua, Bolivia; Serra do Cabral, Minas Gerais, Brazil. Europe: Kovdor, Kola Peninsula, Russia; Brosso, Piedmont, and Elba Island, Italy; Kassandra, Greece.

Name From the Greek *pyr*, meaning "fire," because pyrite emits sparks when struck by iron.

Pyrite is perhaps better known by its informal name "fool's gold," because its similarity to gold often leads amateur prospectors astray.

ABOVE: Pyrite pseudomorph after pyrrhotite, Mont-Saint-Hilaire, Quebec, Canada • 6 x 7.5 x 4 cm
RIGHT: Pyrite, Boccheggiano Mines, Montieri, Tuscany, Italy • 8 x 9 x 4 cm

Polybasite

Formula $(Ag,Cu)_{16}(Sb,As)_2S_{11}$

Crystal System monoclinic

Space Group $C2/m$

Hardness 2.0–3.0

Specific Gravity 6.1

Cleavage imperfect on {001}

Fracture uneven

Tenacity very brittle

Habit Iron black. Tabular, pseudo-hexagonal crystals, often showing triangular striations; can be massive. Metallic luster; opaque except in thin fragments, which are transparent. Black to reddish black streak.

Environment Occurs in silver veins of low- to medium-temperature formation.

Notable Localities Canada: Husky Mine, Elsa, Yukon. USA: Red Mountain, Gilman and Ouray districts, Colorado. Latin America: Las Chiapas Mine, Arizpe, Sonora, Mexico; Sabana Grande, Honduras; Tres Puntas, near Copiapó, Atacama, Chile.

Name From the Greek for "many" and for "base," alluding to the many metallic bases present.

Polybasite sometimes occurs in sufficient quantities to be a significant ore mineral of silver.

Enargite, Quiruvilca Mine, Santiago de Chuco, La Libertad, Peru • 8 x 7 x 5 cm

Enargite

Formula Cu_3AsS_4

Crystal System orthorhombic

Space Group $Pmn2_1$

Hardness 3.0

Specific Gravity 4.4–4.5

Cleavage perfect on {110}; distinct on {100} and {010}; indistinct on {001}

Fracture uneven

Tenacity brittle

Habit Usually grayish black to iron black. Crystals are small, tabular or prismatic, typically striated parallel to c; also massive or granular. Metallic to dull luster; opaque. Black streak.

Environment Formed at moderate temperatures in veins and replacement deposits associated with chalcopyrite, covellite, galena, pyrite and sphalerite.

Notable Localities USA: Butte, Montana. Latin America: Morococha and Cerro de Pasco, Peru; Sierra de Famatina, La Rioja, Argentina. Europe: Alghero and Calabona, Sardinia, Italy; Bor, Serbia. Africa: Tsumeb, Namibia.

Name From the Greek *enarge*, meaning "distinct," referring to its perfect cleavage.

Polybasite, Husky Mine, Elsa, Yukon, Canada • 5.5 x 4 x 2.5 cm

Stephanite

Formula Ag_5SbS_4

Crystal System orthorhombic

Space Group $Cmc2_1$

Hardness 2.0–2.5

Specific Gravity 6.2–6.5

Cleavage imperfect on {010} and {021}

Fracture subconchoidal to uneven

Tenacity brittle

Habit Iron black. Short prismatic to tabular crystals; also massive. Metallic luster; opaque. Black streak.

Environment A late-stage mineral in hydrothermal silver deposits.

Notable Localities Canada: Husky Mine, Elsa, Yukon; Cobalt district, Ontario. USA: Comstock Lode, Nevada. Latin America: Arizpe, Sonora, Mexico; San Cristobal, Peru; Colquechaca, Potosí, Bolivia. Europe: Wheal Boys (Trewatha) Mine, St. Endellion, Cornwall, England; Freiberg, Saxony, Germany. Australia: Broken Hill, New South Wales.

Name Named for Archduke Victor Stephan of Habsburg-Lorena (1817–67), an engineer who was Austria's mining director.

Stephanite, Husky Mine, Elsa, Yukon, Canada • 5 x 3.5 x 3 cm

Tetrahedrite, Monte Romero Mine, Huilva, Andalusia, Spain • 6 x 13 x 6 cm

Tetrahedrite

Formula $Cu_{12}Sb_4S_{13}$

Crystal System cubic

Space Group $I\bar{4}3m$

Hardness 3.0–4.0

Specific Gravity 4.6–5.1

Cleavage none

Fracture subconchoidal to uneven

Tenacity somewhat brittle

Habit Flint gray to iron black to dull black. Tetrahedral crystals; massive, compact or granular. Metallic luster, commonly splendent; opaque except in very thin fragments. Black to brown streak.

Environment Occurs in hydrothermal veins and contact metamorphic deposits.

Notable Localities Canada: Nanisivik Mine, Nunavut. USA: Park City, Utah; Tombstone and Globe, Arizona. Latin America: Noche Buena and Concepcion del Oro, Zacatecas, Mexico. Europe: Herodsfoot Mine, Cornwall, England; Freiberg, Saxony, Germany; Tyrol region, Austria; Botes, Romania. Australia: Mount Isa, Queensland; Broken Hill, New South Wales.

Name From its tetrahedral crystal shape.

Tetrahedrite is probably the most common sulfosalt mineral.

Bournonite, Herodsfoot Mine, Liskeard, Cornwall, England • 14 x 21.5 x 11 cm

Bournonite

Formula $PbCuSbS_3$

Crystal System orthorhombic

Space Group $Pn2_1/m$

Hardness 2.5–3.0

Specific Gravity 5.8

Cleavage {010} imperfect

Fracture subconchoidal to uneven

Tenacity brittle

Habit Steel gray to black. Short prismatic to tabular crystals, forming cruciform or cogwheel aggregates; massive, granular or compact. Metallic luster; opaque. Black streak.

Environment Low- to medium-temperature hydrothermal veins associated with galena, sphalerite, pyrite and chalcopyrite.

Notable Localities Canada: Mineral King Mine, British Columbia. Latin America: Naica, Chihuahua, Mexico. Europe: Wheal Boys and Herodsfoot mines, Cornwall, England; Clausthal, Neudorf and Wolfsberg, Harz, and Westerwald, Germany; Saint-Laurent-le-Minier, Gard, France; Trepča, Kosovo. Australia: Broken Hill, New South Wales.

Name Named for the French mineralogist Jacques L. de Bournon (1751–1825).

Boulangerite

Formula $Pb_5Sb_4S_{11}$

Crystal System monoclinic

Space Group $P2_1/a$

Hardness 2.5–3.0

Specific Gravity 6.2

Cleavage {100} distinct

Fracture none

Tenacity brittle; flexible in thin crystals

Habit Dull, lead gray. Needlelike crystals to 1 cm, rarely as tiny rings; fibrous, compact masses. Metallic luster; opaque. Gray to brown streak.

Environment Occurs in hydrothermal veins formed at low to medium temperatures.

Notable Localities Canada: Madoc, Ontario. USA: Mt. Augusta, Colorado. Europe: Molières, Gard, France; Bottino Mine, Tuscany, Italy; Příbram, Czech Republic. Australia: Broken Hill, New South Wales.

Name Named after Charles Louis Boulanger (1810–49), the French mining engineer who called attention to the species.

Boulangerite, Trepča Valley, Kosovska Mitrovica, Kosovo • 8 x 14 x 4 cm

Zinkenite

Formula $Pb_9Sb_{22}S_{42}$

Crystal System hexagonal

Space Group $P6_3$

Hardness 3.0–3.5

Specific Gravity 5.3

Cleavage poor/indistinct on $\{11\bar{2}0\}$

Fracture irregular/uneven

Tenacity brittle

Habit Steel gray. Crystals thin, prismatic and striated, seldom distinct; columnar to radial fibrous aggregates, massive. Metallic luster; opaque. Steel gray streak.

Environment Associated with base metal and tin sulfides and sulfosalts in hydrothermal veins.

Notable Localities Canada: Bonanza Creek, Bridge River district, British Columbia. Latin America: Oruro, Bolivia. Europe: Carrock Fell, Cumbria, England; Saint-Pons, Haute-Provence, and Pontgibaud, Puy-de-Dôme, France; Wolfsberg, Harz, and Aldersbach, Bavaria, Germany. Australia: Magnet Mine, Dundas, Tasmania.

Name Named for J.K.L. Zincken (1798–1862), a German mineralogist and mining geologist.

Proustite, Keeley Mine, South Lorrain, Timiskaming District, Ontario, Canada • 3 x 2 x 2 cm

Proustite

Formula Ag_3AsS_3

Crystal System trigonal

Space Group $R3c$

Hardness 2.0–2.5

Specific Gravity 5.8

Cleavage distinct on $\{10\bar{1}1\}$

Fracture conchoidal to uneven

Tenacity brittle

Habit Scarlet or vermilion red. Crystals prismatic, commonly rhombohedral or scalenohedral; massive or compact. Adamantine luster; translucent, darkening with exposure to light. Red streak.

Environment A late-forming mineral in hydrothermal deposits; associated with other silver minerals and sulfides.

Notable Localities Canada: Cobalt-Gowganda district, Ontario. USA: Red Mountain and Georgetown, Colorado. Latin America: Chañarcillo, Atacama, Chile. Europe: Freiberg and Niederschöna, Saxony, Germany; Lengenbach Quarry, Binn Valley, Switzerland. Australia: Broken Hill, New South Wales.

Name Named in honor of Joseph Louis Proust (1754–1826), a French chemist.

Zinkenite, San José Mine, Oruro, Cercado, Bolivia • 10 x 9 x 9 cm

Cosalite

Formula $Pb_2Bi_2S_5$

Crystal System orthorhombic

Space Group *Pbnm*

Hardness 2.5–3.0

Specific Gravity 6.9–7.0

Cleavage indistinct

Fracture uneven

Tenacity flexible

Habit Lead gray to steel gray. Prismatic crystals, often acicular, with flexible capillary fibers; commonly massive in aggregates of radiating prismatic, fibrous or feathery forms. Metallic luster; opaque. Black streak.

Environment Occurs in hydrothermal deposits formed at medium temperatures; also found in contact metasomatic replacements, epithermal replacements and pegmatites.

Notable Localities Canada: Timiskaming District, Ontario. USA: Darwin, California; Red Mountain district, Colorado. Latin America: Nuestra Señora and Cosalá mines, Sinaloa, Mexico. Europe: Iilijärvi, Finland; Zlaté Hory, Czech Republic; Vaskő, Hungary. Asia: Kara-Oba, Kazakhstan. Australia: near Oberon, New South Wales.

Name Named for the Cosalá region in Mexico, where it is found.

Cosalite, Kara-Oba deposit, Karaganda Oblast, Kazakhstan • 5 x 6 x 3 cm

Andorite, San José Mine, Oruro, Cercado, Bolivia • 9 x 7 x 3 cm

Andorite IV

Formula $Ag_{15}Pb_{18}Sb_{47}S_{96}$

Crystal System monoclinic

Space Group *P2*

Hardness 3.5

Specific Gravity 5.4

Cleavage none

Fracture smooth conchoidal

Tenacity brittle

Habit Grayish yellow, dark gray or steel gray. Prismatic to columnar crystals up to 15 mm long; radial or massive aggregates. Metallic luster; opaque. Black streak.

Environment Occurs in subvolcanic hydrothermal silver- and tin-bearing veins.

Notable Localities Canada: near Takla Lake, British Columbia. USA: Darwin, California; Keyser Mine, Nevada. Latin America: Llallagua, Itos and San José mines, Oruro, Bolivia. Europe: Les Cougnasses Mine, Hautes-Alpes, Provence–Alpes–Côte d'Azur, France; Baia Mare, Romania.

Name Named for Andor von Semsey (1833–1923), an Austro-Hungarian mineral collector.

Andorite was originally considered a single mineral; it has since been split up into two separate species, andorite IV and andorite VI.

Miargyrite

Formula $AgSbS_2$

Crystal System monoclinic

Space Group $C2/c$

Hardness 2.0–2.5

Specific Gravity 5.24

Cleavage imperfect on {010}; indistinct on {100} and {101}

Fracture subconchoidal

Tenacity brittle

Habit Iron black to steel gray. Thick tabular crystals, often deeply striated; also massive. Metallic adamantine luster; nearly opaque, but translucent in thin fragments. Red streak.

Environment Occurs in hydrothermal veins of low-temperature origin.

Notable Localities Canada: Silver Tunnel (Van Silver Mine), Vancouver mining district, British Columbia. Latin America: El Quevar Mine, Salta, Argentina. Europe: Bräunsdorf, Freiberg district, Saxony, and Sankt Andreasberg district, Harz Mountains, Lower Saxony, Germany.

Name From the Greek words *meyon*, meaning "smaller," and *argyros*, meaning "silver."

Miargyrite was often mistaken for pyrargyrite, but it contains less silver.

Miargyrite, San Genaro Mine, Castrovirreyna, Huancavelica, Peru • 8 x 5 x 3.5 cm

Galkhaite, Getchell Mine, Humboldt County, Nevada, USA • 6 x 5 x 2 cm

Galkhaite

Formula $(Cs,Tl)(Hg,Cu,Zn)_6(As,Sb)_4S_{12}$

Crystal System cubic

Space Group $I\bar{4}3m$

Hardness 3.0

Specific Gravity 5.4

Cleavage none

Fracture uneven to fine conchoidal

Tenacity brittle

Habit Dark red orange. Cubic crystals; also massive. Vitreous to adamantine luster; opaque. Orange streak.

Environment Occurs in hydrothermal mercury-gold deposits.

Notable Localities Canada: Hemlo gold deposit, near Marathon, Ontario. USA: Getchell and Carlin mines, Nevada. Asia: Gal-Khaya, Yakutia, Russia; Khaidarkan, Kyrgyzstan.

Name Named for Gal-Khaya, the area in Yakutia where it was first described. Yakutia, also known as the Sakha Republic, is part of the Far Eastern Federal District of Russia.

CHAPTER 3
Oxides & Hydroxides

Oxides are oxygen-bearing minerals, combining oxygen (O) with one or more metals, while hydroxides are characterized by hydroxyl $(OH)^-$ groups. The oxide class of minerals is quite diverse: it includes minerals that are hard enough to be used as abrasives, such as corundum, and some that are quite soft, such as gibbsite. In this group there are also many gemstones in a variety of colors, such as corundum (rubies and sapphires), chrysoberyl and spinel. The large diversity of oxides can be partly attributed to the amount of oxygen in Earth's crust — 45 percent by weight. This means plenty of opportunities for single oxygen atoms or hydroxyl groups to combine with various elements in many different ways.

ABOVE: Cluster ring, Peter Kochuta (Toronto, Canada), ruby and diamonds set in platinum. This ring has 52 diamonds, with a total weight of 4.80 carats. The ruby is approximately 6.50 carats in weight and shows no detectable evidence of thermal enhancement.

RIGHT: Golden needles of rutile on hematite, Novo Horizonte, Bahia, Brazil • 5 x 3 x 0.6 cm

LEFT: Mixture of hematite and goethite, Graves Mountain, Georgia, USA. This iridescent mixture is sometimes referred to as turgite. • 20 x 14 x 12 cm

Ilmenite

Formula $Fe^{2+}TiO_3$

Crystal System hexagonal

Space Group $R\bar{3}$

Hardness 5.0–6.0

Specific Gravity 4.7

Cleavage none

Fracture conchoidal

Tenacity brittle

Habit Iron black. Usually thick tabular crystals; sometimes thin laminae, compact, massive, or disseminated grains. Submetallic luster; opaque. Non- or weakly magnetic. Brownish black streak.

Environment Occurs principally as a common accessory mineral in igneous rocks such as gabbros, diorites, kimberlites and anorthosites, as veins and disseminated deposits, and in high-grade metamorphic rocks. May attain economic concentration in layered mafic intrusions and "black sand" placer deposits.

Notable Localities Canada: Bancroft, Ontario; Allard Lake, Quebec. USA: Iron Mountain, Wyoming; Sanford Lake, Tahawus, New York. Asia: Ilmen Mountains, Chelyabinskaya Oblast, Russia; Travancore, southern India. Africa: Ambatofotsikely pegmatite, Betafo, Madagascar. Australia: Woodstock, Western Australia.

Name From an early noted location of the mineral in the Ilmen Mountains, part of the southern Ural Mountains, in Chelyabinskaya Oblast, Russia.

Ilmenite is a major source of titanium. The most important use of titanium is in alloys, which are mixtures of metals. It is commonly added to steel because it is lightweight and resistant to corrosion.

Ilmenite, Poudrette Quarry, Mont-Saint-Hilaire, Quebec, Canada • 1.5 x 3 x 1.5 cm

Perovskite, Achmatovsk Mine, Zlatoust, Chelyabinskaya Oblast, Russia • 9 x 13 x 7 cm

Perovskite

Formula $CaTiO_3$

Crystal System orthorhombic

Space Group *Pnma*

Hardness 5.5

Specific Gravity 4.0

Cleavage {001} imperfect

Fracture subconchoidal to uneven

Tenacity brittle

Habit Iron black, brown or reddish brown to yellow. Crystals cubic, sometimes highly modified; rarely massive, granular or reniform. Adamantine to metallic luster but may be dull as well; opaque, but transparent in thin fragments. White to gray streak.

Environment Occurs both as an accessory mineral of the magmatic stage and as a late-stage mineral.

Notable Localities Canada: Moose Creek, near Leanchoil, British Columbia. USA: Crestmore Quarries, Riverside County, and Diablo Range, San Benito County, California; Magnet Cove, Arkansas. Europe: Gardiner complex, Kangerlussuaq Fjord, eastern Greenland; Wildkreuzjoch, Pfitschtal, Trentino, Italy. Asia: Zlatoust district, Ural Mountains, Russia.

Name Named after L.A. Perovski (1792–1856), a Russian mineralogist from St. Petersburg.

Perovskite is thought to be a major constituent of the upper mantle of Earth. It is often rich in cerium, niobium, thorium, lanthanum, neodymium and other rare-earth metals, which are growing in value to industry. Titanium is also recovered from perovskite.

Zincite

Formula ZnO

Crystal System hexagonal

Space Group *C6mc*

Hardness 4.0

Specific Gravity 5.7

Cleavage {10$\bar{1}$0} perfect but difficult

Fracture conchoidal

Tenacity brittle

Habit Yellow orange to deep red; rarely yellow, green or colorless. Crystals rare; usually massive, irregular grains or rounded masses. Subadamantine to resinous luster; translucent, but transparent in thin fragments. Orange yellow streak.

Environment Occurs as a primary mineral in metamorphosed stratiform zinc ore bodies (in New Jersey, USA) or as a secondary mineral altered from other zinc minerals.

Notable Localities USA: Franklin and Sterling Hill, New Jersey. Europe: Bottino, near Saravezza, Tucsany, Italy; Olkusz and Kielce, Poland. Africa: Tsumeb, Namibia. Australia: Heazlewood Mine, Tasmania.

Name From the zinc in its chemical composition (zinc oxide).

Zincite, Sterling Hill, New Jersey, USA • 8 x 8 x 5 cm

Magnetite, Zinc Corporation of America No. 4 Mine, Balmat, New York, USA • 10 x 12 x 15 cm

Magnetite

Formula Fe$_3$O$_4$

Crystal System cubic

Space Group *Fd3m*

Hardness 5.5–6.5

Specific Gravity 5.1

Cleavage none

Fracture uneven

Tenacity brittle

Habit Iron black. Usually octahedral crystals, very rarely cubic; skeletal, granular or massive. Metallic to submetallic luster or may be dull; opaque, but translucent in thin flakes. Highly magnetic. Black streak.

Environment Found in diverse geological environments, sometimes in sufficient abundance to constitute an important iron ore. A high-temperature accessory mineral in igneous and metamorphic rocks and in sulfide veins; also occurs as a product of fumarolic activity and as a detrital mineral.

Notable Localities One of the most widespread oxide minerals. Canada: Bancroft, Ontario. USA: Iron Springs district, Utah. Latin America: Itabira, Minas Gerais, Brazil. Europe: Gardiner complex, Kangerlussuaq Fjord district, Greenland; Kiruna and Gellivare, Sweden; Zillertal, Tyrol, Austria; Alp Lercheltini, Binntal, Valais, Switzerland; Mt. Elba, Italy. Asia: Magnitogorsk, Ural Mountains, Russia.

Name Named after Magnes, a shepherd in ancient Greece, said to have first discovered the mineral on Mount Ida.

Magnetite is an ore of iron commonly used in making steel. Small crystals of magnetite have been found in bacteria and in the brains of insects and some birds and fish. They are thought to be used to sense the polarity of Earth's magnetic field, thus acting as a navigation aid.

Hematite

Formula Fe_2O_3

Crystal System hexagonal

Space Group $R\bar{3}c$

Hardness 5.0–6.0

Specific Gravity 5.3

Cleavage none

Fracture subconchoidal to uneven

Tenacity brittle in crystals; soft and unctuous in earthy varieties; elastic in thin laminae

Habit Steel gray to black; may tarnish to iridescent. Crystals thick to thin tabular, as rosettes, rarely prismatic or scalenohedral; sometimes micaceous to platy; also compact columnar or fibrous (pencil ore), frequently radiating, in reniform masses with smooth fracture (kidney ore), and in botryoidal and stalactitic shapes. Commonly earthy, frequently mixed with clay or other impurities; also granular, friable to compact, concretionary or oolitic. Metallic or submetallic to dull luster; opaque, but transparent on thin edges. Blood red to brownish red streak.

Environment The most important hematite deposits are sedimentary in origin, occurring either in sedimentary beds or in metamorphosed sediments.

Notable Localities USA: Quartzsite, Arizona. Latin America: Miguel Burnier iron mines and Dom Bosco, Ouro Preto, Minas Gerais, Brazil. Europe: Ulverstone, Lancashire, England; Framont, Alsace, France; Rio Marina, Elba, and the Vesuvius, Etna and Stromboli volcanoes, Italy; Saurüssel, Zillertal, Tyrol, Austria. Africa: Wessels Mine, Northern Cape, South Africa. Asia: Korshunovskoye, Siberia, Russia.

Name From the Greek *haimatitis*, meaning "blood red," alluding to its red color, especially in powder form.

Hematite is an important ore of iron. In its red powder form it can be used as a pigment.

ABOVE: Hematite, Dom Bosco, Minas Gerais, Brazil • 7 x 8 x 7 cm

RIGHT: Ring stone (Egypto-Roman, 100–400 CE), hematite, 1.7 x 1.3 x 0.2 cm. This flat oval stone, meant to be set in a ring, is carved on both sides. It depicts female themes and is inscribed around the rim with Greek letters.

Hematite has a number of different habits, many of which have descriptive names. For example, hematite rose (or iron rose) is a flower-like circular arrangement of bladed crystals, and pencil ore has a fibrous structure. Tiger iron is a 2.2-billion-year-old sedimentary rock consisting of alternating layers of silver gray hematite and red jasper, chert or even tiger's-eye quartz. Kidney ore is the massive botryoidal form (see opposite page) and specularite (specular hematite) has a micaceous, or flaky, habit that gives it a sparkling silver gray appearance.

RIGHT: Hematite, Frizington, Cumbria, England • 9 x 7 x 4 cm

Corundum

Formula Al_2O_3

Crystal System hexagonal

Space Group $R\overline{3}c$

Hardness 9.0

Specific Gravity 4.0

Cleavage none

Fracture uneven to conchoidal

Tenacity brittle, but very tough when compact

Corundum (ruby variety) surrounded by green zoisite, Mataba Mountains, Mt. Kilimanjaro region, Tanzania • 13 x 9 x 4 cm

Corundum, Ratnapura district, Sabaragamuwa, Sri Lanka • 7.5 x 2.5 x 2 cm

Habit Can be any color, but most notable are blue (sapphire) and pigeon-blood red (ruby). Commonly prismatic, often barrel-shaped crystals, as well as tabular or rhombohedral; massive or granular. Adamantine to vitreous luster; transparent to translucent. White streak.

Environment Characteristically found in silica-deficient rocks such as syenites and their associated pegmatites. Also occurs in mica schist, gneiss and some marbles in metamorphic terranes.

Notable Localities Canada: Bancroft, Ontario. USA: Yogo district, Montana; Hogback Mountain and Buck Creek, North Carolina; Laurel Creek Mine, Georgia. Europe: Naxos and Samos islands, Greece. Asia: Jegdalek marble near Sorobi, Laghman, Afghanistan; Zanskar district, Kashmir, India; Ratnapura district, Sri Lanka; Mogok district, Myanmar (Burma); Chanthaburi and Trat, Thailand; Bottambang and Pailin districts, Cambodia. Africa: Ampanihy, Madagascar; Merkestein, near Longido, and Morogoro district, Tanzania; Umba Valley, Tanzania. Australia: Anakie, Queensland.

Name Probably from the Sanskrit *kurivinda*, meaning "ruby," through the Tamil *kurundam*.

The principal use of corundum is as an abrasive, which is usually called alumina. It is also used as a gem, and synthetic crystals are used in bearings for watches and fine instruments, as well as for lasers.

Braunite

Formula $Mn^{2+}Mn^{3+}_6O_8SiO_4$

Crystal System tetragonal

Space Group $I4_1/acd$

Hardness 6.0–6.5

Specific Gravity 4.8

Cleavage {112} perfect

Fracture uneven to subconchoidal

Tenacity brittle

Habit Brownish black to steel gray. Pyramidal crystals; also granular or massive. Submetallic luster; opaque. Weakly magnetic. White streak (sometimes brownish).

Environment Formed by metamorphism of manganese silicates and oxides; also a product of weathering, associated with pyrolusite, hausmannite, jacobsite, bixbyite, rhodonite, spessartine and hematite.

Notable Localities USA: Spiller manganese mine, Texas; Cartersville, Georgia. Latin America: Miguel Burnier district, near Ouro Preto, Minas Gerais, Brazil. Europe: Långban and Jakobsberg, Värmland, Sweden; Ohrenstock and Elgersberg, near Ilmenau, Thuringia, Germany; St. Marcel, Piedmont, Italy. Asia: Kacharwali, Nagpur district, Maharashtra, and Tirodi, Madhya Pradesh, India.

Name Named for Kamerath Braun (1790–1872), a German mineralogist of Gotha, Germany.

Braunite, S.A. Minerals manganese mine, Otjiwarongo district, Namibia • 7 x 9 x 5.5 cm

Columbite-(Mn), Minas Gerais, Brazil • 5 x 4 x 1 cm

Columbite Group

Formula $(Fe^{2+},Mn^{2+},Mg)(Nb,Ta)_2O_6$

Crystal System orthorhombic

Space Group *Pbcn*

Hardness 6.0

Specific Gravity 5.0–6.5 (depending on Nb:Ta ratio)

Cleavage {010} distinct; less distinct on {010}

Fracture subconchoidal to uneven

Tenacity brittle

Habit Brownish black to black. Short, prismatic, equant crystals as well as flat tabular; massive. Submetallic luster; opaque, but translucent at thin edges. Brown to black streak.

Environment Accessory mineral of granitic pegmatites and elsewhere where niobium (Nb) more predominant than tantalum (Ta). Rarely found in alkalic pegmatites and as an alteration mineral of other niobium-rich minerals. An important ore of tantalum and niobium.

Notable Localities **Columbite-(Fe)** USA: New London, Connecticut; Keystone, South Dakota. Europe: Ivittuut, Greenland; Ånneröd, Tveit and elsewhere, Norway. Africa: Ambatofotsikely and Antsirabe, Madagascar. Asia: Miass, Ural Mountains, Russia; Ishikawa district, Fukushima, Japan. **Columbite-(Mn)** Canada: Tanco Mine, Bernic Lake, Manitoba. USA: Etta Mine, Keystone, and Helen Beryl Mine, South Dakota. Europe: Uto, Sweden. Africa: Morrua, Muiane and Marropino mines, Alto Ligonha, Mozambique. Asia: Kokoto Hai Mine, Xinjiang, China. **Columbite-(Mg)** USA: Old Mike Mine and Elk Creek, South Dakota. Australia: Londonderry Mine, Coolgardie, Western Australia.

Name Named after "Columbia," a poetical term for the United States, where the first specimens were found.

Franklinite, Sterling Hill, New Jersey, USA • 13 x 8 x 5 cm

Franklinite

Formula $ZnFe^{3+}_2O_4$

Crystal System isometric

Space Group *Fd3m*

Hardness 6.0

Specific Gravity 5.0–5.2

Cleavage none

Fracture uneven to subconchoidal

Tenacity brittle

Habit Black to reddish brown. Crystallizes as octahedrons, commonly with rounded edges; also granular or massive. Metallic to semi-metallic luster or may be dull; opaque but translucent in fine fragments. Slightly magnetic. Reddish brown streak.

Environment Occurs in beds and veins formed by high-temperature metamorphism of marine carbonate sediments, and as a minor mineral in some manganese and iron deposits.

Notable Localities USA: Franklin and Sterling Hill mines, Franklin, and Ogdensburg, New Jersey. Asia: Pereval marble quarry, near Slyudyanka, Sayan Mountains (south end of Lake Baikal), Siberia, Russia; Koduru manganese mine, Srikakulam district, Andhra Pradesh, India.

Name From Franklin, New Jersey, which was named after Benjamin Franklin (1706–90), a Founding Father of the United States.

Franklin and Ogdensburg, New Jersey, are well-known for their zinc mines. Franklin bills itself as "the fluorescent mineral capital of the world."

Spinel

Formula $MgAl_2O_4$

Crystal System cubic

Space Group *Fd3m*

Hardness 7.5–8.0

Specific Gravity 3.6

Cleavage none

Fracture conchoidal to uneven

Tenacity brittle

Habit Brown and black to red (ruby spinel), orange, yellow, green, blue, indigo, violet or colorless. Crystals usually octahedrons; also granular or massive. Vitreous, splendent to dull luster; transparent to nearly opaque. White streak.

Environment Formed at high temperatures as an accessory in igneous rocks, in regionally metamorphosed aluminum-rich schists and in regionally and contact-metamorphosed limestones. Also occurs as a detrital mineral

Notable Localities Canada: Burgess, Ontario; Wakefield, Quebec. USA: between Amity and Edenville, New York, to Andover, New Jersey. Europe: Bavaria, Germany; Monte Somma and Mt. Vesuvius, Campania, Italy. Asia: Mogok, Myanmar (Burma).

Name From the Latin *spinella*, meaning "little thorn," because of its spiny octahedral crystals.

Spinel, Bathurst, Ontario, Canada • 4 x 5 x 4 cm

Cuprite

Formula Cu_2O

Crystal System cubic

Space Group $Pn3m$

Hardness 3.5–4.0

Specific Gravity 6.0

Cleavage {111} interrupted; {001} rare

Fracture conchoidal to uneven

Tenacity brittle

Cuprite, Rubtsovskiy Mine, Altaiskiy Krai, Russia • 5.5 x 5 x 5 cm

Cuprite, Tsumeb, Namibia • 11.5 x 20 x 10.5 cm

The history of copper can be traced back far as the earliest civilizations. The ancient Egyptians discovered that copper could be combined with tin to create an alloy that was stronger than either metal, leading to the Bronze Age. In the fourth millennium BCE the ancient Greeks mined copper on the island of Cyprus, from where the metal got its name. They were drawn to its resistance to rust and its ease of use for fashioning objects, as well as its beauty.

The properties that made copper prized by the ancients hold true for us today, with a few additions. We know now that it is ductile, which allows it to be drawn into lengths, and also an excellent conductor of heat and electricity. These properties make copper ideal for manufacturing wire and pipes.

Habit Dark ruby red to purplish red to nearly black. Crystals octahedral or cubic, rarely dodecahedral; can occur in hair-like capillary forms with square section, reticulated, tufted or matted; also earthy, compact granular or massive. Adamantine submetallic luster; transparent to translucent. Brick red streak.

Environment Common in oxidized portions of many copper deposits, usually associated with native copper, malachite, azurite, tenorite, chrysocolla and limonite.

Notable Localities USA: common in several Arizona mines, especially at Bisbee. Latin America: Chuquicamata, Antofagasta, Chile. Europe: Cornwall, England; Rheinbreitbach, North Rhine–Westphalia, Germany. Africa: Tsumeb, Namibia. Asia: Ural Mountains, Russia. Australia: Broken Hill, New South Wales.

Name From the Latin *cuprum*, meaning "copper," for its chemical composition (cuprous oxide).

Cuprite has been a major ore of copper throughout history and is still mined in many places around the world. The biggest use of copper is in electrical wiring: it is an excellent conductor of electricity, corrodes very slowly, and can easily be formed into thin wires.

Spinel

Spinel (source unknown) • 10.2 x 12.5 x 7.4 mm, 6.30 ct

Spinel, Mogok, Myanmar (Burma) •
30.1 x 23 x 13 mm, 61.50 ct

Chrysoberyl

Chrysoberyl (source unknown) • 11.5 x 15.7 x 17.9 mm, 10.90 ct

(Ruby and Sapphire)

Sarpech (Uttar Pradesh, India, 19th century), gold, diamonds, rubies and emeralds, 9 x 16.6 cm. This stylish jewel for a turban would have been worn by a nobleman to demonstrate his rank. Such jewels were often given as gifts of political allegiance. Flanking the central flower are mythical creatures called makaras; these hybrid crocodile-elephant-fish symbolized good luck, fertility and the primal source of life. A ruby and diamond plume extends upward, a form once reserved exclusively for the emperor. Seven polished emerald pendants hang from the plume and the base.

"Star of Lanka" cabochon sapphire, Sri Lanka • 3 x 2.7 x 2.3 cm, 193.00 ct. A pure sapphire is colorless; it is the impurities within the mineral's structure that impart color. Trace amounts of iron and titanium create the blue of this sapphire. The asterism effect in the gem is also remarkable. The "star" is formed by rutile mineral inclusions; when polished, they reflect light back in radiating bands.

Cuprite

Cuprite, Onganja, Namibia • 26.2 x 18.8 x 10.3 mm, 66.30 ct. Some of the finest transparent red cuprite crystals known are from the Onganja Mine in Namibia. The surface of cuprite will undergo some alteration to malachite after long exposure to light, so these gemstones are typically stored in the dark.

Chromite, Tiébaghi Mine, Kaala-Gomen, New Caledonia • 12 x 12 x 8 cm

Chromite

Formula $FeCr_2O_4$

Crystal System chromite

Space Group *Fd3m*

Hardness 5.5

Specific Gravity 4.5–4.8

Cleavage none

Fracture uneven

Tenacity brittle

Habit Blackish brown to black. Crystals octahedral; commonly fine granular, compact or massive. Metallic to submetallic luster; translucent to opaque. Brown streak.

Environment Most commonly found as an accessory mineral in ultramafic igneous rocks or concentrated in sediments derived from them; occurs as layers in a few ultramafic bodies. The most important ore of chromium.

Notable Localities Canada: serpentine areas of Quebec. USA: Stillwater complex, Montana. Europe: Haroldswick and Swinaness, Unst, Shetland Islands, Scotland; Gassin, Var, France. Africa: Bushveld complex, Transvaal, South Africa; Great Dyke, Zimbabwe.

Name From the chromium in its chemical composition.

Adding chromium to iron creates an alloy that is highly resistant to corrosion and discoloration, hence its role in manufacturing stainless steel. It is also used for chrome plating.

Chrysoberyl

Formula $BeAl_2O_4$

Crystal System orthorhombic

Space Group *Pnma*

Hardness 8.5

Specific Gravity 3.7

Cleavage distinct on {110}; imperfect on {010}; poor on {001}

Fracture uneven to conchoidal

Tenacity brittle

Habit Various shades of green, yellow and brownish to greenish black; different types of lighting can produce dramatic changes of color, as in alexandrite. Crystals usually tabular, sometimes stout prismatic, prominently striated and twinned (the cyclic twins, called trillings, can be quite pronounced). Vitreous luster; transparent to translucent or may be opaque and chatoyant. White streak.

Environment Occurs in granites and granitic pegmatites, although alexandrites are found in mica schists.

Notable Localities USA: near Golden, Colorado. Brazil: Tancredo, Itaguaçu; Colatina, Espírito Santo; Faria Lemos, Santa Luzia de Carangola and Americana, Teófilo Otoni, Minas Gerais. Asia: Izumrudnye Mines, Tokovaya River, near Yekaterinburg (Sverdlovsk), and Mursinka, Ural Mountains, Russia. Asia: Ratnapura district, Sri Lanka.

Name From the Greek for "golden" and "beryl," although the latter is a misnomer.

Chrysoberyl, Espírito Santo, Brazil • 5 x 5 x 2 cm

Romanèchite, Romanèche-Thorins, Burgundy, France • 7.5 x 13 x 4 cm

Romanèchite

Formula $(Ba,H_2O)_2(Mn^{4+},Mn^{3+})_5O_{10}$

Crystal System monoclinic

Cleavage none

Space Group $C2/m$

Fracture uneven

Hardness 6.0

Tenacity brittle

Specific Gravity 4.7

Habit Iron black to gray. Massive, often botryoidal; also earthy. Submetallic to dull luster; opaque. Brownish black streak.

Environment A product of the weathering of manganese-bearing oxides, carbonates and silicates; also occurs in sedimentary deposits.

Notable Locality Romanèche, Saône-et-Loire, France.

Name From where it is found.

Romanèchite is an ore of manganese. Eighty-five to ninety percent of manganese is used in the steel industry, as small amounts improve the workability of steel at high temperatures. It is also mixed with aluminum to decrease corrosion and is used in beverage cans.

Samarskite-(Y)

Formula $(Y,Ce,U,Fe)_3(Nb,Ta,Ti)O_4$

Crystal System orthorhombic

Cleavage {010} indistinct

Space Group *Pbcn*

Fracture conchoidal

Hardness 5.0–6.0

Tenacity brittle

Specific Gravity 4.3–5.9

Habit Black or brownish black to brown to yellowish brown, due to alteration. Crystals usually rough, often massive, found in close association with columbite-group minerals. Vitreous to resinous luster, but may be submetallic or splendent; opaque, but transparent in thin fragments. Reddish brown streak.

Environment Found as an accessory mineral in granitic pegmatites rich in rare earths; occurs rarely as a detrital mineral.

Notable Localities Canada: Maisonneuve, Quebec. USA: Pelton's Quarry, Portland, Connecticut. Latin America: Divina de Uba, near Belo Horizonte, Minas Gerais, Brazil. Africa: Antanamalaza, Madagascar. Asia: Miass, Ural Mountains, Russia.

Name Named after Colonel Vasilii Evgrafovich von Samarskii-Bykhovets (1803–70) of the Russian Corps of Mining Engineers.

Samarskite, Arendal, Aust-Agder, Norway • 4 x 4 x 3 cm

Pyrolusite

Formula MnO_2

Crystal System tetragonal

Space Group $P4_2/mnm$

Hardness 6.0

Specific Gravity 4.4–5.1

Cleavage {110} perfect

Fracture irregular/uneven

Tenacity brittle

Habit Gray black or black; may have a bluish cast when massive. Crystals uncommon, long to short prismatic or equant; usually columnar or fibrous, botryoidal, granular, massive or earthy. Metallic to earthy luster; opaque. Black streak.

Environment Formed under highly oxidizing conditions in manganese-bearing hydrothermal deposits and rocks.

Notable Localities Canada: Bathurst, New Brunswick. USA: Ironwood, Michigan. Europe: Elgersburg, Friedrichroda and Öhrenstock, near Ilmenau, Thuringia, and Eibenstock, Saxony, Germany; Horní Blatná, Czech Republic.

Name From the Greek for "fire" and "to wash," because it was used to decolorize brown and green tints in glass.

Pyrolusite is the primary ore of manganese. Besides being a decolorizer in the making of glass, it is also used in manufacturing steel, in electric batteries and in coloring materials for bricks and pottery.

Pyrolusite, Steep Rock Lake, Rainy River District, Ontario, Canada • 9 x 11 x 5 cm

Rutile, Novo Horizonte, Bahia, Brazil • 19 x 14 x 6 cm

Rutile

Formula TiO_2

Crystal System tetragonal

Space Group $P4_2/mnm$

Hardness 6.0–6.5

Specific Gravity 4.2

Cleavage {110} distinct; {100} less distinct

Fracture conchoidal to uneven

Tenacity brittle

Habit Red, reddish brown, brown, yellow or black. Commonly prismatic, often slender to acicular, striated, rarely pyramidal or equant; also granular or massive, coarse to fine. Adamantine metallic luster; opaque, but transparent in thin fragments. Brown streak.

Environment A common high-temperature, high-pressure accessory mineral in igneous and metamorphic rocks. Also common in aluminous rocks and in alpine-type veins and fissures.

Notable Localities USA: Magnet Cove, Arkansas. Latin America: Conquista and Ibitiara, Bahia, Brazil. Europe: Cavradi, Tavetsch, Graübunden, and Lodrino, Tessin, Switzerland; Pfitschtal, Trentino–Alto Adige, Italy. Africa: Giftkuppe Mine, Omaruru, Namibia.

Name From the Latin *rutilus*, meaning "red," for its usual color.

Titanium dioxide is the most widely used white pigment because of its brightness. It is often used to whiten foods and drinks such as non-fat milk, cookies and frosting — even toothpaste! It is the physical blocking ingredient in most sunscreens because of its high refractive index, its strong UV-absorbing capability and its resistance to discoloration under ultraviolet light.

Anatase

Formula TiO_2

Crystal System tetragonal

Space Group $I4_1/amd$

Hardness 5.5–6.0

Specific Gravity 3.9

Cleavage {001} and {011} perfect

Fracture subconchoidal

Tenacity brittle

Habit Brown, indigo blue, green, gray or black. Crystals pseudo-octahedral, less commonly prismatic. Adamantine to metallic luster; transparent when light colored and nearly opaque when deeply colored. White streak.

Environment Usually secondary, derived from other titanium-bearing minerals. Typically found in veins or crevices of the alpine type in gneiss and schists, associated with brookite, quartz, hematite, chlorite and titanite.

Notable Localities Canada: Sherbrooke, Nova Scotia; Henvey, Ontario. USA: Placerville, California. Latin America: Minas Gerais and Pará, Brazil. Europe: Tysse, Hardangervidda, Norway; Maronne, Le Bourg-d'Oisans, Isère, France; many localities in Switzerland; Monte Cervandone, Ossola, Italy.

Name From the Greek *anatasis*, meaning "extension," alluding to the greater length of the common pyramidal faces compared to other tetragonal minerals.

Anatase, brookite and rutile are polymorphs, meaning they all have the same chemical composition (TiO_2) but differ in crystal structure.

Anatase, Valdres, Oppland, Norway • 7 x 5 x 5 cm

Brookite, Dodo Mine, Khanty-Mansi, western Siberia, Russia • 3 x 9 x 3 cm

Brookite

Formula TiO_2

Crystal System orthorhombic

Space Group *Pbca*

Hardness 5.5–6.0

Specific Gravity 4.0–4.1

Cleavage {120} indistinct

Fracture subconchoidal

Tenacity brittle

Habit Various shades of brown to black. Crystals commonly pyramidal and pseudo-hexagonal; typically tabular, elongated and striated. Adamantine luster; opaque to translucent, and transparent in thin fragments. Light brown to white streak.

Environment An accessory mineral in fissures and veins of alpine-type rocks in gneiss and schist with anatase, rutile, titanite and albite; also in contact metamorphic zones.

Notable Localities USA: Magnet Cove, Arkansas. Europe: Prenteg, Tremadog, Gwynedd, Wales; Le Plan du Lac, St. Christophe-en-Oisans, Isère, France; Tête Noir and Finhaut, Mont Blanc Massif, Wallis, Switzerland. Asia: Miass, Ilmen Mountains (southern Urals), Russia.

Name Named for Henry James Brooke (1771–1857), an English crystallographer and mineralogist.

Cassiterite

Formula SnO_2

Crystal System tetragonal

Space Group $P4_2/mnm$

Hardness 6.0–7.0

Specific Gravity 7.0

Cleavage {100} imperfect; {110} indistinct

Fracture subconchoidal to uneven

Tenacity brittle

Cassiterite, San Luis Potosí, Mexico • 6 x 6 x 4 cm

ABOVE: Cassiterite, Horní Slavkov, Karlovy Vary region, Bohemia, Czech Republic • 5.5 x 4 x 4 cm
LEFT: Cassiterite, Veta Honda Mine, San Felipe, Guanajuato, Mexico • 6.5 x 9 x 5 cm

Cassiterite is the main source for tin, an essential component of many solders and corrosion-resistant coatings for other metals. Commercial metal food containers are commonly referred to in North America as "tin cans," and in Britain simply as "tins." However, none of the cans currently in use are composed primarily of tin. "Tin" cans are actually made of steel with a thin coating of tin or aluminum, and in the future they will probably contain no tin at all. A similar thing has happened with metal foil — some people still refer to it as "tinfoil," but in reality foil is now made of aluminum.

Habit Black, brown, yellow gray, colorless or white; rarely red. Crystals short to long prismatic, terminated by steep pyramidal forms; radially fibrous botryoidal crusts and concretionary masses, fine to coarse granular or massive. Adamantine to adamantine metallic, splendent luster; transparent when light colored, but dark material nearly opaque. Brownish white streak.

Environment Characteristic of deep-seated high-temperature veins and association with highly acidic igneous rocks such as granites; also in pegmatites. Important placer deposits are derived from the weathering of stockworks of cassiterite-bearing veins in granite.

Notable Localities Latin America: Fazenda do Funil, Ferros, Minas Gerais, Brazil. Europe: Panasqueira and Cabreiros, Portugal; San Piero, Campo, Elba, Italy. Africa: Otjimbojo, Namibia. Australia: Greenbushes and Pilbara, Western Australia; Mt. Bischoff and Mt. Zeehan, Tasmania.

Name From the Greek *kassiteros*, meaning "tin," for its chemical composition.

A concretionary form of cassiterite combined with quartz and hematite is known as "wood tin."

Gahnite, Alto Mirador Mine, Ermo, Rio Grande do Norte, Brazil • 5.5 x 7 x 4 cm

Gahnite

Formula $ZnAl_2O_4$

Crystal System isometric

Space Group *Fd3m*

Hardness 7.5–8.0

Specific Gravity 4.5–4.6

Cleavage none

Fracture conchoidal

Tenacity brittle

Habit Dark green, bluish green or blue to indigo; also yellow to brown. Octahedral crystals; also irregular grains or massive. Vitreous luster; translucent to nearly opaque. Gray streak.

Environment Found in crystalline schists, lithium-rich granitic pegmatites and contact-metamorphosed limestones. Also in high-temperature replacement ore deposits in schists or marbles or quartzose rocks.

Notable Localities Canada: Geco Mine, Manitouwadge, Ontario; Hudson, Quebec. USA: Franklin and Sterling Hill, New Jersey; Mineral Hill and Patapsco mines, Maryland. Europe: Nafversberg and Eric Matts mines, Falun, Sweden; Träskböle, Perniö parish, Finland. New Zealand: Victoria Range, Nelson.

Name Named for Johann Gottlieb Gahn (1745–1818), the Swedish chemist and mineralogist who discovered manganese.

Uraninite

Formula UO_2

Crystal System isometric

Space Group *Fm3m*

Hardness 5.0–6.0

Specific Gravity 7.0–10.0

Cleavage none

Fracture uneven to conchoidal

Tenacity brittle

Habit Black, brownish black, grayish or greenish; green gray in thin fragments. Octahedral crystals, less commonly cubes or combination of the two. Greasy submetallic to dull luster; opaque. Brownish black streak.

Environment Occurs in granite and syenite pegmatites, as colloform crusts in high-temperature hydrothermal veins, and in quartz-pebble conglomerates.

Notable Localities Canada: Wilberforce, Ontario; Great Bear Lake, Northwest Territories. USA: Branchville, Connecticut; Grafton, New Hampshire. Europe: Jáchymov and Horní Slavkov, Czech Republic.

Name From the uranium in its chemical composition (uranium oxide).

Uraninite is the principal ore of uranium, which has many uses, most notably for generating nuclear power and in the military sector for nuclear weapons and high-density penetrators. "Pitchblende" is a massive, often globular, possibly impure, variety of uraninite.

Uraninite, Cardiff, Haliburton County, Ontario, Canada • 2.5 x 3 x 2 cm

Fergusonite, Gole Quarry, Murchison, Nippissing District, Ontario, Canada • 6 x 3.5 x 3 cm

Fergusonite-(Y)

Formula $YNbO_4$

Crystal System tetragonal

Space Group $I4_1/a$

Hardness 5.5–6.5

Specific Gravity 4.2–5.7

Cleavage {111} in traces

Fracture subconchoidal

Tenacity brittle

Habit Black to brownish black, brown, gray or yellow. Crystals prismatic to pyramidal, as irregular masses or grains; typically metamict. Dull vitreous luster; opaque but transparent on thin edges. Brown streak.

Environment Typical of rare earth–bearing granite pegmatites; occurs in placers.

Notable Localities Canada: Madawaska, Ontario. USA: Spruce Pine, North Carolina; Champion and Rutherford pegmatite deposits, Texas. Europe: Qeqertaussaq, Julienhåb district, Greenland; Laurinmäki, Finland; Iveland district, Norway; Ytterby, Sweden. Asia: Blum Mine, Ilmen Mountains (southern Urals), Russia; gem gravels in Sri Lanka.

Name Named for Robert Ferguson (1767–1840), a Scottish advocate (lawyer), politician and mineralogist.

Pyrochlore Group

Formula $(Ca,Na)_2Nb_2O_6(O,OH,F)$

Crystal System cubic

Space Group $Fd3m$

Hardness 5.0–5.5

Specific Gravity 3.5–4.6

Cleavage octahedral {111} (may be a parting) sometimes distinct but usually not distinguishable

Fracture irregular/uneven, splintery, subconchoidal

Tenacity brittle

Habit Brown, yellow brown, reddish brown, orange or black. Crystals usually octahedral, sometimes modified by cube faces. Vitreous, resinous luster; transparent. Pale yellow to brown streak.

Environment Occur in pegmatites in nepheline syenites, granitic pegmatites and greisens, and carbonatites.

Notable Localities Canada: Oka, Quebec. USA: St. Peter's Dome area, Colorado. Europe: Fredricksvärn, Norway; Alnö region, Sweden.

Name From the Greek for "fire" and "green," because some specimens of the mineral turn green when ignited.

Pyrochlore was formerly the name of a single mineral; it was recently changed to include a group of minerals.

Pyrochlore, St. Lawrence Columbium, Oka, Quebec, Canada • 6.5 x 8 x 4 cm

Baddeleyite

Formula ZrO_2

Crystal System monoclinic

Space Group $P2_1/c$

Hardness 6.5

Specific Gravity 5.5–6.0

Cleavage {001} nearly perfect; {010} and {110} less perfect

Fracture subconchoidal to uneven

Tenacity brittle

Habit Colorless to yellow, green, greenish or reddish brown, brown or black. Crystals short to long, prismatic, usually flattened; sometimes radially fibrous or botryoidal masses. Vitreous to greasy luster; transparent. White streak.

Environment An accessory mineral in carbonatites and kimberlites, in syenites, diabases, gabbros and anorthosites, and in gem gravels; also in lunar basalt, tektites and meteorites.

Notable Localities USA: Bozeman, Montana. Latin America: Jacupiranga, São Paulo, Brazil. Europe: Monte Somma, Italy. Africa: Phalaborwa, Limpopo, South Africa. Asia: Rakwana and Balangoda, Sri Lanka.

Name Named for Joseph Baddeley, who first called attention to the Sri Lankan material.

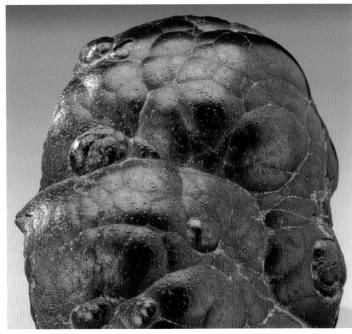

Baddeleyite, Brazil • 6 x 8 x 4 cm

Minium, Broken Hill Mine, New South Wales, Australia • 3.5 x 5.5 x 4 cm

Minium

Formula Pb_3O_4

Crystal System tetragonal

Space Group $P4_2/mbc$

Hardness 2.5

Specific Gravity 8.9–9.2

Cleavage {110} perfect; {010} perfect

Fracture uneven

Tenacity dull, clay-like fractures

Habit Scarlet to brownish red; may have a yellowish tint. Scaly; commonly earthy, pulverulent or massive. Dull to slightly greasy luster; semitransparent. Yellowish orange streak.

Environment A rare secondary alteration mineral in some highly oxidized lead-bearing mineral deposits; can form as a product of mine fires.

Notable Localities USA: Jay Gould Mine, Idaho. Europe: Minius River, northwest Spain; Leadhills, Lanarkshire, Scotland. Asia: Altai Mountains, Russia. Australia: product of a mine fire, Broken Hill, New South Wales.

Name From the Latin *minium*, which is derived from an Iberian word for cinnabar, a red pigment.

Tapiolite Group

Formula (Fe,Mn)(Ta,Nb)$_2$O$_6$

Crystal System tetragonal

Space Group $P4_2/mnm$

Hardness 6.0–6.5

Specific Gravity 8.0

Cleavage {110} imperfect

Fracture uneven to subconchoidal

Tenacity brittle

Habit Black. Short prismatic or equant crystals. Subadamantine to submetallic, brilliant luster; opaque, but transparent on thin edges. Brown streak.

Environment Found in pegmatites and alluvial deposits.

Notable Localities Canada: Tanco Mine, Bernic Lake, Manitoba. Europe: Kulmala pegmatite, Sukula, Tammela, and Viitaniemi, Eräjärvi, Orivesi, Finland; Chanteloube, Limoges, France. Australia: Strelley, Pilbara, Western Australia.

Name Originally both forms were simply called tapiolite, for Tapio, the god of the forest in Finnish mythology. Later renamed ferrotapiolite and manganotapiolite, they are now referred to as tapiolite-(Fe) and tapiolite-(Mn).

Tapiolite, Jabuti Mine, São Geraldo do Baixio, Minas Gerais, Brazil • 5.5 x 5.5 x 3 cm

Tantalite-(Mn), São José da Safira, Minas Gerais, Brazil • 7.0 x 7.0 x 7.5 cm

Tantalite Group

Formula (Fe,Mn,Mg)(Ta,Nb)$_2$O$_6$

Crystal System cubic

Space Group $Fd3m$

Hardness 6.0–6.5

Specific Gravity 8.0

Cleavage none

Fracture uneven

Tenacity brittle

Habit Black, brownish black or orange red. Typically octahedral crystals, less commonly dodecahedral or cubic; skeletal, granular or massive. Metallic to submetallic luster, but may be dull; opaque. Brownish red to black streak.

Environment An accessory mineral in igneous and metamorphic rocks, in which magmatic segregation or contact metamorphism may produce economic deposits. Also occurs as extensive deposits in sedimentary banded iron formations and as an important detrital mineral.

Notable Localities Canada: Tanco Mine, Bernic Lake, Manitoba. USA: Etta Mine, Keystone, and Helen Beryl Mine, Custer, South Dakota. Europe: Utö, Sweden. Africa: Morrua, Muiane and Marropino mines, Alto Ligonha, Mozambique. Asia: Kokoto Hai Mine, Xinjiang, China. Australia: Parelhas and Carnauba dos Dantas, Greenbushes, Western Australia.

Name Named for Tantalus, who in Greek myth was punished in the underworld by food and drink that was always just out of reach, in allusion to the tantalizing difficulties encountered in making a solution of the mineral in acids.

Hercynite, Franklin Quarry, Sussex County, New Jersey, USA • 5 x 5.5 x 3.5 cm

Hercynite

Formula $FeAl_2O_4$	**Specific Gravity** 4.0
Crystal System isometric	**Cleavage** {111} indistinct
Space Group *Fd3m*	**Fracture** conchoidal
Hardness 7.5–8.0	**Tenacity** brittle

Habit Dark blue green, yellow or brown. Massive; also rounded black grains. Vitreous luster; translucent. Dark grayish green to dark green streak.

Environment In high-grade metamorphosed ferruginous argillaceous sediments and in some mafic and ultramafic igneous rocks. Also occurs in placers.

Notable Localities USA: near Colton, New York. Latin America: near Cuauhtémoc, Chihuahua, Mexico. Europe: Le Prese, Veltlin, Switzerland; Načetiń and Hoslau, near Ronsberg, Czech Republic.

Name From the Latin name — Silva Hercynia — for the ancient Bohemian Hercynian Forest, where the mineral was first found.

Stibiconite

Formula $Sb_3O_6(OH)$	**Specific Gravity** 3.5–5.9
Crystal System isometric	**Cleavage** none
Space Group *Fd3m*	**Fracture** none
Hardness 4.0–5.5	**Tenacity** earthy

Habit White to yellow or brown. Massive, botryoidal or incrustations; may be concentrically zoned to several centimeters thick; typically powdery and compact. Pearly, opaline, glassy to earthy luster; transparent to translucent. Yellow streak.

Environment A secondary mineral in hydrothermal mineral deposits, formed by the oxidation of other antimony-bearing minerals, commonly stibnite, which it may entirely replace.

Notable Localities Canada: Wolfe County, Quebec. USA: Antimony Peak, California. Latin America: El Antimonio, Sonora, and Catorce and Charcas, San Luis Potosí, Mexico; Cochabaniba, Bolivia. Europe: Goldkronach, Germany. Asia: Derekdy, Gonyuh, Turkey; Hunan, China.

Name From the Latin for antimony, *stibium*, and the Greek for "powder" or "dust," referring to a common form of the substance.

Stibiconite has now been discredited as a mineral.

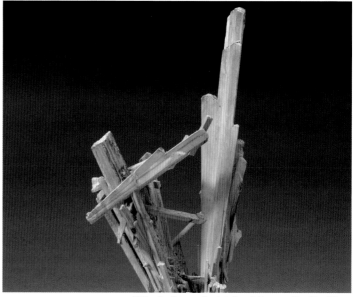

Stibiconite, Catorce, San Luis Potosí, Mexico • 34 x 15 x 8.5 cm

Bauxite

Bauxite is formed by a combination of several aluminum-rich minerals, so it is a valuable source of aluminum ore. It is named after Baux (or Beaux), which is near St. Reny, Bouches-du-Rhône, in France.

Bauxite, Tikhvin, Leningradskaya Oblast, Russia • 8 x 6 x 4 cm

Limonite

The term "limonite" is most often used for the mineral species goethite, which is composed of hydrated iron oxides. Its name comes from the Greek for "meadow," because it occurs in bogs.

Limonite, Utah, USA • 7 x 11 x 9 cm

Goethite

Formula FeO(OH)

Crystal System orthorhombic

Space Group *Pnma*

Hardness 5.0–5.5

Specific Gravity 3.3–4.3

Cleavage {010} perfect; {100} less so

Fracture uneven fracture

Tenacity brittle

Habit Blackish brown, or yellow to reddish brown in massive aggregates; may be banded. Crystals prismatic and striated, also flattened into tablets or scales; usually massive, as reniform, botryoidal or stalactitic masses with radial fibrous structure. Adamantine to metallic luster, sometimes dull and earthy, also silky; opaque, but transparent on thin edges. Brown to brownish yellow streak.

Environment A common weathering product derived from iron-bearing minerals in oxygenated environments, especially siderite, pyrite, magnetite and glauconite. Widespread in bogs and springs ("bog iron ore").

Notable Localities USA: Superior Mine, Marquette, Michigan; Pikes Peak district and Florissant, Colorado. Latin America: Diamantina, Minas Gerais, Brazil. Europe: Cornwall, England; Chaillac, Vienne, France; Siegen, Eiserfeld Horhausen and Oberstein, Germany. Asia: Lake Onega and Bakal, southern Ural Mountains, Russia.

Name Named for Johann Wolfgang von Goethe (1749–1832), the German poet, philosopher and naturalist.

Goethite, Old Helen Mine, Chabanel, Algoma District, Ontario, Canada • 26 x 20 x 16 cm

ABOVE: Goethite pseudomorph after gypsum, Laurium, Greece • 50 x 41 x 25 cm

RIGHT: Goethite, Tern Islands, New Zealand • 25 x 22 x 6 cm

Goethite is a source of iron, which is rarely found in nature in its elemental form. Thus goethite and other iron-containing minerals must be smelted to separate the iron from the oxygen and other elements in them.

Brucite

Formula Mg(OH)$_2$

Crystal System hexagonal

Space Group $P\bar{3}m1$

Hardness 2.5

Specific Gravity 2.4

Cleavage {0001} perfect

Fracture uneven

Tenacity sectile; separable plates flexible and fibers elastic

---

Habit White, pale green, gray or blue. Crystals tabular, often subparallel aggregates of plates; massive, foliated or fibrous, rarely fine granular. Waxy to vitreous/pearly luster; transparent. White streak.

Environment Typically forms as a low-temperature hydrothermal vein mineral in serpentine and chlorite and dolomite schists.

Notable Localities Canada: Asbestos and Wakefield, Quebec. USA: Hoboken, New Jersey. Europe: Mt. Vesuvius, Campania, and Teulada, Sardinia, Italy. Africa: Phalaborwa, Limpopo, South Africa. Asia: Yekaterinburg, Ural Mountains, Russia.

Name Named for Archibald Bruce (1777–1818), an American mineralogist.

Brucite has such a high melting point that it is used to line kilns.

Brucite, Cross Quarry, Wakefield, Quebec, Canada • 5 x 5 x 3 cm

Manganite, Ilfeld, Harz Mountains, Thuringia, Germany • 7 x 8 x 5 cm

Manganite

Formula Mn^{3+}O(OH)

Crystal System monoclinic

Space Group $P2_1/c$

Hardness 4.0

Specific Gravity 4.3

Cleavage {010} perfect; {110} and {001} good

Fracture uneven

Tenacity brittle

Habit Typically dark steel grey to iron black. Crystals pseudo-orthorhombic, short to long prismatic, with striations parallel to their length, often grouped in bundles or markedly composite; rarely massive or stalactitic. Submetallic luster; opaque, but transparent on thin edges. Reddish to brownish black streak.

Environment Occurs in low-temperature hydrothermal deposits associated with barite (baryte), calcite and siderite; in replacement deposits with goethite; and in shallow marine deposits, lakes and bogs.

Notable Localities Canada: Caland Mine, Atikokan, Ontario. USA: Negaunee and Marquette districts, Michigan. England: Botallack Mine, St. Just, Cornwall; Egremont, Cumbria; Upton Pyne, Exeter, Devonshire. Africa: Kuruman, Cape Province, South Africa.

Name From the manganese in its chemical composition.

Diaspore

Formula AlO(OH)

Crystal System orthorhombic

Space Group *Pnma*

Hardness 6.5–7.0

Specific Gravity 3.4

Cleavage {010} perfect; {110} distinct; {100} in traces

Fracture conchoidal

Tenacity very brittle

Habit White, grayish white or colorless; also greenish gray, brown, yellowish, lilac or pink. As crystals, platy, elongated, sometimes prismatic or acicular, rarely tabular; also massive, foliated or thin scales. Vitreous to brilliant luster; transparent to translucent. White streak.

Environment Forms in metamorphic rocks, such as schists and marbles, where it is often associated with corundum, manganite and spinel. It is also found in hydrothermally altered rocks and in sediments.

Notable Localities USA: Culsagee Mine, Franklin, North Carolina. Europe: Banská Belá, Slovakia; Jordansmühl, Silesia, Poland; Sivec, near Prilep, Macedonia. Asia: Mugula, eastern Anatolia, Turkey; Kyshtym, Ural Mountains, Russia; Shokozan Mine, Honshu, Japan.

Name From the Greek for "to scatter," a reference to the way diaspore crackles when strongly heated.

Diaspore, Postmasburg, Northern Cape, South Africa • 7.5 x 9 x 5 cm

Gibbsite, Bisbee, Arizona, USA • 10 x 7 x 3 cm

Gibbsite

Formula Al(OH)$_3$

Crystal System monoclinic

Space Group *P*2$_1$/*c*

Hardness 2.5–3.5

Specific Gravity 2.4

Cleavage {001} perfect

Fracture none

Tenacity tough

Habit White, grayish, blue green to gray green or reddish white; rarely blue. Crystals tabular with a hexagonal aspect; concretions, massive stalactitic or compact/earthy. Vitreous to pearly luster; transparent. White streak.

Environment Most gibbsite is a secondary product resulting from the weathering, leaching and alteration of aluminous minerals. Also forms as a low-temperature hydrothermal mineral in veins or cavities in alkaline or other igneous rocks.

Notable Localities USA: Richmond, Massachusetts; Champion Mine, White Mountains, California. Latin America: Saramenha district, Ouro Preto, Minas Gerais, Brazil. Europe: Eikaholmen and Lille-Arø islands, Langesundsfjord, and Tredalen, near Larvik, Norway. Asia: Kodikanal, Madras, and Talevadi, near Mumbai, Maharashtra, India. Australia: Dundas, Tasmania.

Name Named for Colonel George Gibbs (1777–1834), the original owner of the Gibbs mineral collection, which was acquired by Yale College early in the nineteenth century.

Gibbsite is one of the principal ores of aluminum, which is used for a variety of purposes from aircraft and rockets to aluminum foil. Since it is highly reactive, aluminum doesn't form by itself in nature; it combines with other elements to form more than 270 different minerals.

CHAPTER 4
Halides

The halides form a group of minerals whose principal anions are halogens — such as fluorine, chlorine, iodine or bromine — which usually have a charge of minus 1 when chemically combined. Halides tend to have rather simply ordered structures and therefore a high degree of symmetry.

The typical halide mineral is soft, transparent and not very dense. It also has good cleavage and often occurs in bright colors. There are only a few common halide minerals. One is ordinary table salt (NaCl), which is mined as the mineral halite. Fluorite (CaF_2) is popular with collectors because of its beautiful crystals; it is also used in paint pigments and in the chemical, plastics and ceramics industries.

ABOVE: Fluorite, Mexico •
20 x 18.5 x 14 mm, 37.60 ct

RIGHT: Fluorite, Madoc, Ontario,
Canada • 16 x 16 x 16 cm

LEFT: Fluorite, Kongsberg, Norway •
10 x 9 x 4 cm

Halite

Formula NaCl

Crystal System cubic

Space Group *Fm3m*

Hardness 2.0–2.5

Specific Gravity 2.1–2.6

Cleavage {001} perfect

Fracture conchoidal

Tenacity brittle

Halite, Wieliczka, Poland • 9 x 12 x 9 cm

Habit Colorless or white when pure; otherwise gray, blue, purple or reddish (red from inclusions of hematite). Cubic crystals, sometimes hopper or skeletal shape; massive, rarely stalactitic, granular or compact. Vitreous luster; transparent to translucent. White streak.

Environment Typically in sedimentary rocks of evaporite association; may form beds a kilometer (0.6 mile) or more thick. Also occurs as volcanic sublimates and cave deposits associated with sylvite, carnallite, gypsum, anhydrite and dolomite.

Notable Localities Canada: massive deposits in Saskatchewan. USA: Permian Basin, Texas and New Mexico (e.g., Potash Corporation of America mine, Carlsbad potash district, New Mexico); Michigan Basin, underlying Ohio, Michigan and New York; salt domes along the Gulf Coast, Louisiana and Texas, including Louann salt formation, Alabama; Restof, New York. Europe: Hallstadt, Salzburg, Austria; Stassfurt-Leopoldshall, Saxony-Anhalt, Germany; Sicily, Italy. Asia: Salt Range, Punjab, Pakistan; numerous places in Russia and China.

Name From the Greek *hals*, meaning "salt."

Halite is better known as common salt. Besides its culinary use, it is a preservative; a source of sodium carbonate (soda ash), which is used in manufacturing soap and glass; and the source of sodium bicarbonate, or baking soda. It is also used as a source of chlorine for hydrochloric acid and other chlorine compounds, particularly PVC (polyvinyl chloride) plastics.

Halite, PCS Mine, Rocanville, Saskatchewan, Canada • 11.5 x 24 x 6 cm

Sylvite, Buggingen, Baden-Württemberg, Germany • 9 x 7 x 6 cm

Sylvite

Formula KCl

Crystal System cubic

Space Group $Fm3m$

Hardness 2.0

Specific Gravity 2.0

Cleavage {001} perfect

Fracture uneven

Tenacity brittle; ductile under low strain

Habit Colorless to white, pale blue, pale blue gray; yellowish red to red when included with hematite. Cubic, cubo-octahedral and octahedral crystals; may be columnar, in crusts, coarse granular to compact, or massive. Vitreous luster; transparent. White streak.

Environment Occurs in sedimentary basins, forming thick bedded deposits with halite; also as a sublimate in volcanic fumaroles and cave deposits.

Notable Localities Canada: Smoky Hills, Peace River, Alberta; Esterhazy and Rocanville, Saskatchewan. USA: Permian salt basin, New Mexico and Texas; Louann salt formation, Alabama. Latin America: Tarapacá, Chile. Europe: Westeregeln and Stassfurt, Germany; Mt. Etna, Sicily, and Mt. Vesuvius, Italy; Kalusz, Ukraine. Asia: Solikamsk-Berezniki region, Ural Mountains, Russia.

Name From *sal disgestivus sylvii*, or "digestive salt," an old chemical term for the substance. It was named for François Sylvius de le Boe (1614–72), a Dutch physician and chemist.

Cryolite

Formula Na_3AlF_6

Crystal System monoclinic

Space Group $P2_1/c$

Hardness 2.5

Specific Gravity 3.0

Cleavage none

Fracture uneven

Tenacity brittle

Habit Colorless to white; also brown, red, brownish red or rarely black. Equant pseudo-cubic crystals; usually massive or coarsely granular. Vitreous to greasy luster; transparent to translucent. White streak.

Environment Occurs as a late-stage mineral in some granite pegmatites, in tin-bearing alkalic granites, as a vapor-phase mineral along fractures and in the groundmass of some fluorine-rich topaz-bearing rhyolites, and in pods in carbonatite veins.

Notable Localities Canada: Mont-Saint-Hilaire and Francon Quarry, Montreal, Quebec. USA: St. Peter's Dome, Pikes Peak area, Colorado; Morefield Mine, Amelia, Virginia. Europe: Ivittuut (Ivigtut), Greenland. Asia: Miass, Ural Mountains, Russia.

Name Named from the Greek words for "ice" and "stone," because of its ice-like appearance.

Cryolite is an essential ingredient in aluminum production. It is also used to make glass and enamel and in the manufacture of insecticides.

Cryolite, Ivittuut (Ivigtut), Kitaa, Greenland • 17 x 24 x 27 cm

Fluorite

Formula CaF_2

Crystal System cubic

Space Group *Fm3m*

Hardness 4.0

Specific Gravity 3.0–3.3

Cleavage {111} perfect

Fracture splintery to subconchoidal

Tenacity brittle

ABOVE: Fluorite, Westmoreland, New Hampshire, USA • 7 x 8 x 7 cm
RIGHT: Fluorite, Elmwood Mine, Carthage, Tennessee, USA • 22 x 16 x 9 cm

ABOVE: Fluorite, Wölsendorf, Bavaria, Germany • 28 x 17.5 x 7.5 cm

RIGHT: Fluorite, Annabel Lee Mine, Ozark-Mahoning County, Illinois, USA • 30 x 24.5 x 19.5 mm, 78.10 ct

Habit Colorless, white, bluish black or virtually any color. Cubes, octahedra or rarely dodecahedra; many other forms possible, such as nodular, botryoidal or massive; columnar, granular or fibrous rare. White streak.

Environment An accessory mineral in granite, granitic pegmatites and syenites; uncommon as a late hydrothermal product in cavities and joints in granite. Also occurs in carbonatites and alkaline intrusives.

Notable Localities Canada: Rock Candy Mine, near Grand Forks, British Columbia; Madoc, Ontario. USA: Fort Wayne, Indiana; Elmwood Mine, near Carthage, Tennessee; Westmoreland, New Hampshire. Latin America: Naica, Chihuahua, Mexico; Huanzala, Peru. Europe: Cumbria, Yorkshire and Derbyshire, England; Argentières, Mont Blanc Massif, France; Aar Massif, Switzerland. Africa: Orongo Mountains, Namibia; Zeerust district, North West Province, South Africa. Asia: Tormiq area, Pakistan; Chiang Mai, Thailand.

Name From the Latin *fluere*, meaning "to flow," in allusion to its low melting point.

Fluorite is used as a flux in the manufacture of steel, in the production of hydrofluoric acid, and in the manufacture of opalescent glass, enamels and cooking utensils.

Atacamite

Formula $Cu_2Cl(OH)_3$

Crystal System orthorhombic

Space Group *Pnam*

Hardness 3.0–3.5

Specific Gravity 3.8

Cleavage {010} perfect; {101} fair

Fracture conchoidal

Tenacity brittle

Habit Bright green or dark emerald green to dark green. Crystals slender, prismatic or tabular. Adamantine to vitreous luster; transparent to translucent. Apple green streak.

Environment An oxidation product of other copper minerals, especially in arid or saline conditions.

Notable Localities USA: Bisbee, Arizona; San Manuel Mine and Tintic district, Utah. Latin America: Boleo, Baja California, Mexico; Atacama Desert, Chile. Europe: Cumbria and Cornwall, England. Africa: Tsumeb, Namibia. Asia: Bogoslovsk, Ural Mountains, Russia; Kara-Kamys, Kazakhstan.

Name Named for the Atacama Desert in Chile.

Atacamite is an alteration product on corroded bronze and copper objects, including the USA's Statue of Liberty.

Atacamite, Copiapó, Chile • 13 x 11 x 7 cm

Villiaumite, Poudrette Quarry, Mont-Saint-Hilaire, Quebec, Canada • 3 x 4 x 3 cm

Villiaumite

Formula NaF

Crystal System cubic

Space Group *Fm3m*

Hardness 2.0–2.5

Specific Gravity 2.8

Cleavage {001} perfect

Fracture none

Tenacity brittle

Habit Carmine red or pink red to light orange. Crystals rare, but can be cubic; commonly granular or massive. Vitreous luster; transparent. Pinkish white streak.

Environment Occurs in nepheline syenite and nepheline syenite pegmatites.

Notable Localities Canada: Mont-Saint-Hilaire, Quebec. USA: Point of Rocks, New Mexico; Porphyry Mountain, Colorado. Europe: Kvanefjeld, Ilímaussaq intrusion, Greenland; Khibiny Massif, Kola Peninsula, Russia.

Name Named in honor of Maxime Villiaume, a French explorer whose collection of rocks from Guinea contained the first identified occurrence of the mineral.

Although this mineral is beautiful to look at, it is extremely soft and soluble in water, so it's not well suited for jewelry.

Pachnolite

Formula $NaCaAlF_6 \cdot H_2O$

Crystal System monoclinic

Space Group *F2/d*

Hardness 3.0

Specific Gravity 2.98

Cleavage {001} poor to indistinct

Fracture uneven

Tenacity brittle

Habit Colorless to white. Prismatic crystals. Vitreous luster; transparent to translucent. White streak.

Environment Most commonly occurs in pegmatites, as an alteration product of cryolite and other alkaline aluminum fluorides.

Notable Localities USA: St. Peter's Dome, near Pikes Peak, and Goldie carbonatite, Colorado; Zapot pegmatite, Fitting district, Nevada. Latin America: El Criollo pegmatite, Córdoba, Argentina. Europe: Ivittuut (Ivigtut) deposit, southwestern Greenland; Lake Gjerdingen, Nordmarka, Norway; Hagendorf Süd pegmatite, Bavaria, Germany.

Name From the Greek words for "frost" and "stone," in allusion to its appearance.

Pachnolite, Ivigtut cryolite mine, Ivittuut, Kitaa, Greenland • 6.5 x 7 x 3 cm

Mendipite, Torr Works Quarry, Cranmore, Somerset, England • 7 x 5 x 3 cm

Mendipite

Formula $Pb_3O_2Cl_2$

Crystal System orthorhombic

Space Group $P2_12_12_1$

Hardness 2.5

Specific Gravity 7.2

Cleavage {110} perfect; {100} and {010} distinct to fair

Fracture conchoidal to uneven

Tenacity brittle

Habit Colorless to white or gray, often tinged with pink or other colors. Fibrous or columnar masses, often radiated. Pearly to silky luster on cleavages, resinous to adamantine luster across fractures; translucent, rarely transparent. White streak.

Environment Occurs in nodules in manganese oxide ores.

Notable Localities Europe: Långban, Värmland, Sweden; Mendip Hills, Somerset, England; Kunibert Mine, Brilon, Westphalia, Germany; Tarnowitz, Silesia, Poland; Laurium, Greece (in slag).

Name Named for where it was first described, the Mendip Hills in England.

CHAPTER 5

Carbonates

ABOVE: Calcite, Egremont, Cumbria, England •
9 x 10.5 x 3.5 cm

LEFT: Rhodochrosite, Catamarca, Argentina •
8 x 8 x 0.5 cm

The carbonate minerals, which contain the anion $(CO_3)^{2-}$, comprise an important group of minerals in the crust of Earth. Carbonates are commonly deposited in oceans and seas, where the shells of dead marine life settle and accumulate on the seafloor. They also form deposits where seas have evaporated, leaving behind carbonates and salt. Spectacular cave formations such as stalactites and stalagmites are mostly made of carbonates that crystallized from underground waters.

Calcite ($CaCO_3$), one of the most common minerals in Earth's crust, occurs in an amazing number of beautiful crystal shapes. Calcite is used in animal feed and antacids and for waste treatment, as well as in the food, glass, paper, optical and photographic industries. Limestone and marble, which are carbonate rocks, are used in the building industry for both construction and decoration.

Smithsonite, Otavi Mine, Tsumeb, Namibia • 13 x 10 x 7 cm

Azurite, Copper Queen Mine, Bisbee, Arizona, USA • 14.5 x 16 x 9 cm

Calcite

Formula CaCO$_3$

Crystal System hexagonal

Space Group $R\overline{3}c$

Hardness 3.0

Specific Gravity 2.96

Cleavage $\{10\overline{1}1\}$ perfect

Fracture conchoidal

Tenacity brittle

Habit Colorless and transparent to white when pure, but occurs in virtually every color, including blue and black. Hundreds of different crystal faces and forms, commonly rhombohedral or scalenohedral prismatic crystals, thin to thick tabular, and a variety of shapes created by twinning; also as fibers, aggregates or earthy (chalk), and nodular and stalactitic forms. Vitreous, sometimes pearly, to iridescent luster; transparent to opaque. White streak.

Environment Found in most geologic settings and as a later-forming replacement mineral in most other environments, commonly in thick and massive sedimentary rocks such as limestones, chalk, marl, oolitic limestone and marbles. Also forms earthy crusts and efflorescences on soil, stalactites in caves or cementing material in sedimentary rocks. Can be regionally or contact-metamorphosed into marbles, rarely forms igneous rocks (carbonatites) and is a common gangue mineral in hydrothermal deposits.

ABOVE: Calcite, Tsumeb Mine, Tsumeb, Namibia • 3 x 5 x 2 cm
RIGHT: Calcite, Tsumeb Mine, Tsumeb, Namibia • 5 x 6 x 4 cm

Notable Localities Found almost everywhere; a few exceptional examples are listed here. USA: Keweenaw Peninsula, Michigan; Tri-State Mining District; Mammoth Cave, Kentucky (stalactites and stalagmites); Elmwood and Gordonsville mines, near Carthage, Tennessee. Europe: Kongsberg, Norway; White Cliffs of Dover, England (massive); Sankt Andreasberg and Elbingerode, Harz Mountains, Germany; La Collada and La Viesca, Spain; Příbram, Czech Republic. Africa: Tsumeb, Namibia. Asia: Sarbay-Sokolov, Kazakhstan; Guilin, China (stalactites and stalagmites). Australia: Garibaldi Mine, Lionville, New South Wales.

Name After a Greek root meaning "to reduce to a powder by heat." The Latin *calx*, from the same root, means "burnt lime."

Iceland spar, a variety of calcite, has the optical property of double refraction: light passing through it is split into two components, creating a double image of any object viewed through it. Limestone is a sedimentary rock composed primarily of calcite; marble is a metamorphic rock that forms when limestone is subjected to heat and pressure. Both limestone and marble have been used as building materials for centuries, including for the pyramids of Egypt.

Calcite (cave formation), Bisbee, Arizona, USA • 26 x 14.5 x 14 cm

Magnesite, Mt. Brussilof magnesite mine, Radium Hot Springs, British Columbia, Canada • 16 x 11 x 7 cm

Magnesite

Formula $MgCO_3$

Crystal System hexagonal

Space Group $R\bar{3}c$

Hardness 3.5–4.5

Specific Gravity 3.0

Cleavage {$10\bar{1}1$} perfect

Fracture conchoidal

Tenacity brittle

Habit Colorless, white, pale yellow, pale brown, faintly pink or lilac rose. Uncommon as crystals; typically earthy, chalky, porcelaneous, fibrous, coarse to fine granular, compact or massive. Vitreous luster; transparent to translucent. White streak.

Environment A primary mineral in igneous or sedimentary rocks, formed by metamorphism or alteration of serpentine and peridotite. Uncommon in marine evaporites and hydrothermal veins and rare in carbonatites.

Notable Localities Canada: Mt. Brussilof Mine, near Radium Hot Springs, British Columbia; Del Oro deposits, Timmins, Ontario. USA: commercial deposits in California; Gabbs, Nevada. Europe: Snarum, Norway; Baldissero Canavese, Piedmont, Italy; Magnesia, Greece. Asia: Liaoning district, Liaoning, China.

Name Named for the magnesium in its composition.

An ore of magnesium commonly used as a refractory material, magnesite has a very high melting point, making it ideal for lining furnaces. It is also used as a catalyst and filler in the production of synthetic rubber and in the preparation of magnesium chemicals for fertilizers.

ABOVE: Magnesite (mesitite variety), Traversella, Piedmont, Italy • 7 x 8 x 5 cm

LEFT: Magnesite, Brumado district, Bahia, Brazil • 34 x 29 x 23 mm, 132.80 ct

Witherite

Formula $BaCO_3$

Crystal System orthorhombic

Space Group *Pmcn*

Hardness 3.0–3.5

Specific Gravity 4.22

Cleavage {010} distinct; {110} imperfect

Fracture uneven

Tenacity brittle

Habit Colorless to milky white or gray; also tinted yellow, brown or green. Crystals always twinned, most commonly in pseudo-hexagonal trillings that are bipyramidal, and also short prismatic, tabular to lenticular; also globular, botryoidal, granular or coarse fibrous. Vitreous luster, resinous on fractures; transparent to translucent. White streak.

Environment Usually occurs in small amounts in low-temperature hydrothermal veins, typically as an alteration product of barite (baryte).

Notable Localities Canada: Gun Claim, MacMillan Pass, Yukon; Porcupine Mine, Ontario. USA: Cave-in-Rock, Illinois; Pigeon Roost, Arkansas. Europe: Alston Moor, Cumbria, England; Příbram, Czech Republic. Asia: Hasei Mine, Akita, Japan.

Name Named after Dr. William Withering (1741–99), an English physician and mineralogist who first described the mineral.

Witherite, Cave-in-Rock, Hardin, Illinois, USA • 18 x 13 x 9 cm

Strontianite, Oberdorf, Styria, Austria • 19 x 15 x 6 cm

Strontianite

Formula $SrCO_3$

Crystal System orthorhombic

Space Group *Pmcn*

Hardness 3.5

Specific Gravity 3.76

Cleavage {110} nearly perfect; {021} poor

Fracture uneven to subconchoidal

Tenacity brittle

Habit Colorless, gray, pale yellow, pale green, yellowish brown or pale red. Crystals typically short to long prismatic but may be acicular or pseudo-hexagonal; also columnar, fibrous, rounded, granular, powdery or massive. Vitreous luster, resinous on breaks; transparent to translucent. White streak.

Environment Mainly found as a low-temperature mineral in limestone; also as a gangue mineral in sulfide veins.

Notable Localities Canada: Nepean, Ontario; Oka complex, Quebec. USA: Homestake Mine, Lead, South Dakota; Cave-in-Rock, Illinois. Latin America: Sierra Mojada district, Coahuila, Mexico. Europe: Khibiny and Lovozero massifs, Kola Peninsula, Russia; Strontian, Highland, Scotland; Clausthal and Bad Grund, Harz Mountains, Germany; Oberdorf, Styria, Austria.

Name Named after where it was discovered, Strontian, in the Lochaber district of Scotland.

Aragonite

Formula CaCO$_3$

Crystal System orthorhombic

Space Group *Pmcn*

Hardness 3.5–4.0

Specific Gravity 2.9

Cleavage {010} distinct; {110} and {011} imperfect

Fracture subconchoidal

Tenacity brittle

ABOVE: Aragonite (flos ferri variety), Eisenerz, Styria, Austria • 23.5 x 18 x 21 cm

LEFT: Aragonite (korite variety), St. Mary River, Lethbridge, Alberta, Canada • 18 x 14 x 5 cm

Aragonite is a polymorph of calcite, which means that it has the same chemistry as calcite (CaCO$_3$) but forms in a different crystal system, and more important, it has different symmetry and crystal shapes. The specimen on page 110 is a piece of fossilized ammonite shell. Ammonites were squid-like marine creatures that became extinct 65.5 million years ago. The beautiful iridescent color seen here is known in the gem world as ammolite or korite. It is found primarily along the eastern slopes of the Rocky Mountains.

Habit Colorless or white; also gray, pale shades of yellow, blue, violet, green or red. Short to long prismatic isolated crystals or acicular, dipyramidal or thick tabular; also as columnar crystal aggregates and crusts, globular, reniform, pisolitic, coralloidal, stalactitic, internally fibrous or banded. Vitreous luster, resinous on fracture surfaces; transparent to translucent. White streak.

Environment Typically forms in low-temperature environments and near the surface; relatively unstable and can alter to calcite. Also occurs as speleothemes in limestone caves, as pisolites, sinters and massive lamellar deposits at geysers and hot springs, and as a replacement mineral in various rock types and ore deposits.

Notable Localities USA: Bisbee, Arizona; Santa Rosa, New Mexico; Passaic Mine, Sterling Hill, Ogdensburg, New Jersey. Europe: Frizington and Cleator Moor, Cumbria, England; Molina, Guadalajara, Spain; Agrigento, Sicily, Italy; Spitzberg, Hořenz, near Bílina, Czech Republic. Africa: Tazouta, near Sefrou, Morocco; Tsumeb, Namibia.

Name Named for where it was first described from, Molina de Aragón, Spain.

When aragonite occurs as coral-like aggregates in iron ore deposits in association with siderite (its iron carbonate counterpart), it is called *flos ferri*, meaning "flowers of iron."

Aragonite, Podrečany, Banskobystrický, Slovakia • 25 x 23 x 6 cm

Rhodochrosite

Formula $MnCO_3$

Crystal System hexagonal

Space Group $R\bar{3}c$

Hardness 3.5–4.0

Specific Gravity 3.7

Cleavage $\{10\bar{1}1\}$ perfect

Fracture uneven to subconchoidal

Tenacity brittle

Habit Pink, rose red, cherry red, yellow, yellowish gray or cinnamon brown; may be banded. Crystals rhombohedral or scalenohedral, may be rounded or saddle-shaped; commonly in bladed aggregates, columnar, stalactitic, botryoidal, compact granular or massive. Vitreous luster, pearly in aggregates; transparent to translucent. White streak.

Environment A primary mineral in low- to moderate-temperature hydrothermal veins and in metamorphic deposits; common in carbonatites and authigenic and secondary in sediments.

Notable Localities Canada: Mont-Saint-Hilaire, Quebec. USA: Emma Mine, Butte, Montana; Sweet Home Mine, Alma, Colorado. Latin America: Cananea, Sonora, and Santa Eulalia, Chihuahua, Mexico; Las Capillitas Mine, San Luis, Catamarca, Argentina. Africa: N'Chwaning Mines, near Kuruman, Cape Province, South Africa.

Name From the Greek *rhodon*, meaning "rose," and *chrosis*, meaning "coloring."

ABOVE: Rhodochrosite, Sweet Home Mine, Alma, Colorado, USA • 15 x 13 x 7 cm
BELOW: Rhodochrosite, Las Capillitas Mine, Catamarca, Argentina • 29 x 9 x 2 cm
RIGHT: Rhodochrosite, N'Chwaning Mines, Kuruman, Northern Cape, South Africa • 5 x 3 x 2.5 cm

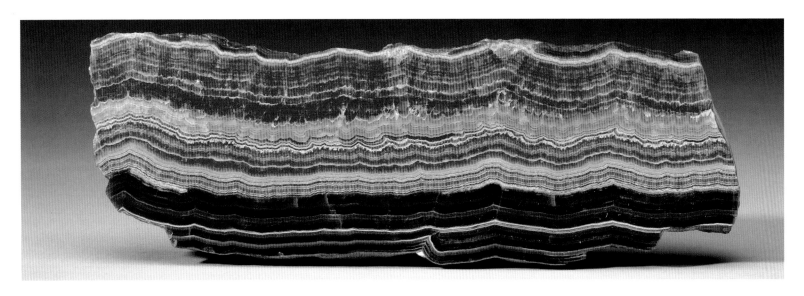

Dolomite

Formula $CaMg(CO_3)_2$

Crystal System hexagonal

Space Group $R\bar{3}$

Hardness 3.5–4.0

Specific Gravity 2.86

Cleavage $\{10\bar{1}1\}$ perfect

Fracture subconchoidal

Tenacity brittle

Habit Colorless, white, yellow, brown or pale pink. Crystals tabular and may exhibit curved faces; also columnar, stalatitic, granular or massive. Vitreous to pearly luster; transparent to translucent. White streak.

Environment An important sedimentary and metamorphic mineral, the principal mineral in dolostones and metadolostones and an important mineral in limestones and marbles where calcite is the principal mineral present. Also found as a gangue in hydrothermal veins, forming crystals in cavities, and in serpentinites and similar rocks.

Notable Localities A major rock-forming mineral. Canada: Nanisivik Mine, Baffin Island, Nunavut. USA: Tri-State Mining District, Oklahoma; Mississippi Valley. Latin America: Naica, Chihuahua, Mexico; Brumado, Bahia, and Morro Velho gold mine, Nova Lima, Minas Gerais, Brazil. Europe: Vuoriyarvi carbonatite complex, Kola Peninsula, Russia; Frizington, Cumbria, England; Tyrol, Austria; Piedmont, Italy.

Name Named after Dieudonné Sylvain Guy Tancrède de Gratet de Dolomieu, usually known as Déodat de Dolomieu (1750–1801), a French geologist and naturalist who contributed to early descriptions of the species in dolostone.

Dolomite, Tsumeb, Namibia • 16 x 12 x 10 cm

Siderite, Mont-Saint-Hilaire, Quebec, Canada • 16.5 x 11.5 x 13 cm

Siderite

Formula $FeCO_3$

Crystal System hexagonal

Space Group $R\bar{3}c$

Hardness 3.75–4.25

Specific Gravity 3.96

Cleavage perfect on $\{10\bar{1}1\}$

Fracture uneven to conchoidal

Tenacity brittle

Habit Yellowish brown, brown, white, ash or yellowish gray, pale green or colorless. Commonly crystallized, typically rhombohedral to steep scalenohedral prismatic; also fibrous, stalactitic, spherulitic and fine-grained to massive. Vitreous luster, but may be pearly or silky; translucent. White streak.

Environment A common component of bedded sedimentary iron ores and metamorphic iron formations. Also occurs in hydrothermal metallic veins.

Notable Localities USA: Bisbee and Antler Mine, Arizona; Leadville, Colorado. Latin America: Mosojllacta, Colavi, Bolivia; Morro Velho gold mine, Nova Lima, Minas Gerais, Brazil. Europe: Ivittuut (Ivigtut), Greenland; Virtuous Lady Mine, Tavistock, Devon, and many mines in Cornwall, England; Panasqueira, Portugal; Freiberg and Neudorf, Harz Mountains, and Siegerland district, Westphalia, Germany; Erzberg, near Eisenerz, Styria, and Hüttenberg-Lölling, Carinthia, Austria.

Name From the Greek word for iron, *sideros*, because of the iron in its composition.

Siderite is used as a minor ore of iron, and also as a pigment when a red or brown color is desired.

Ankerite

Formula $CaFe^{2+}(CO_3)_2$

Crystal System hexagonal

Space Group $R\bar{3}$

Hardness 3.5–4.0

Specific Gravity 3.11

Cleavage {1011} perfect

Fracture subconchoidal

Tenacity brittle

Habit Brown, yellow or white. Crystals rhombohedral with curved or saddle-shaped faces, prismatic to tabular or pseudo-octahedral columnar; also stalactitic, granular or massive. Vitreous to pearly luster; translucent to transparent. White streak.

Environment Formed in low-grade metamorphosed ironstones and sedimentary banded iron formations, in carbonatites or as a product of hydrothermal alteration of carbonate sediments, and in hydrothermal sulfide veins.

Notable Localities Canada: Sokoman iron formation, Howells River area, Quebec. USA: Eagle Mine, Gilman district, and many other places in Colorado; Jeffrey Quarry, near Little Rock, Arkansas. Latin America: Muzo, Boyacá, Colombia. Europe: Styrian Erzberg, Eisenerz, Styria, and Gollrad, Steiermark, Austria. Australia: Dales Gorge member, Hamersley Group, Western Australia.

Name Named after Professor Matthias Joseph Anker (1772–1843), an Austrian mineralogist.

Ankerite, Sterling Mine, Antwerp, New York, USA • 9 x 6 x 5 cm

Bastnäsite-(Ce), Warsak, Mohmand Agency, North West Frontier, Pakistan • 3 x 5 x 2 cm

Bastnäsite-(Ce)

Formula $CeCO_3F$

Crystal System hexagonal

Space Group $P\bar{6}2c$

Hardness 4.0–4.5

Specific Gravity 5.12

Cleavage {1010} indistinct

Fracture uneven

Tenacity brittle

Habit Wax or honey yellow or reddish brown. Commonly tabular to equant crystals, horizontally striated, but may be elongated, or in syntaxic intergrowth with röntgenite-(Ce), synchysite-(Ce), parisite-(Ce) or cordylite-(Ce); also granular or massive. Vitreous to greasy luster, pearly on basal partings; transparent to translucent. White streak.

Environment Typically hydrothermal, though primary igneous occurrences are known. Found in granite and alkali syenites and pegmatites, carbonatites and contact metamorphic deposits; rarely as detrital mineral in placers.

Notable Localities Canada: Mont-Saint-Hilaire, Quebec. USA: Crystal Park, near Pikes Peak, Colorado; Red Cloud fluorite mine, Gallinas Mountains, New Mexico. Europe: Bastnäs Mine, near Riddarhyttan, Västmanland, Sweden. Asia: Zegi Mountain, Fata, Pakistan; Bayan Obo iron/niobium/rare-earth deposit, north of Baotou, Inner Mongolia, China.

Name Named for its first noted occurrence, in the Bastnäs Mine in Sweden.

Bastnäsite is the most abundant rare earth–bearing mineral.

Cerussite

Formula PbCO$_3$

Crystal System orthorhombic

Space Group *Pmcn*

Hardness 3.0–3.5

Specific Gravity 6.55

Cleavage {110} and {021} good; {010} and {012} poor

Fracture conchoidal

Tenacity very brittle

ABOVE: Cerussite, Broken Hill, New South Wales, Australia • 7 x 6 x 6 cm

LEFT: Cerussite ("Light of the Desert"), Tsumeb Mine, Tsumeb, Namibia. The rough material before cutting weighed 1,030 grams (5,150.00 carats). • 48 x 48 x 32 mm, 898.00 ct

At just under 900 carats, the "Light of the Desert" is the largest faceted piece of cerussite in the world. This gem was named for its intense light dispersion (also known as fire) and for the deserts where it was found and faceted, in Namibia and Arizona respectively. Cerussite's dispersion, in which white light is split into its spectral colors, is even greater than that of diamond. Until this specimen was found in the 1960s, no cerussite of more than 200 carats had ever been faceted. The mineral is extremely sensitive to heat and vibration — even the warmth of your hand can damage it — so great care was taken during polishing and grinding that the heat generated didn't shatter the gemstone.

Habit Colorless, white, pale yellow, smoky to dark gray or black, with inclusions. Crystal morphology extremely varied: simple crystals often tabular and elongated, also equant or dipyramidal and then pseudo-hexagonal; rarely acicular or very thin tabular. Also massive, granular, dense or compact; stalactitic at times or pulverulent to earthy; fibrous rare. Adamantine luster tending toward vitreous or resinous; transparent to translucent. White streak.

Environment Usually found in oxidized zones of lead ore deposits; a very common weathering product of galena and other lead ore minerals.

Notable Localities USA: Stevenson-Bennett Mine, Organ district, New Mexico; Leadville, Colorado. Europe: Leadhills, South Lanarkshire, Scotland; Schletzenburg, Haut-Rhin, Alsace, France. Africa: Tsumeb and Kombat copper/lead/silver mine, south of Tsumeb, Namibia. Asia: Nakhlak Mine, Anarak district, Iran; Nerchinsk, Siberia, Russia. Australia: Broken Hill, New South Wales.

Name From the Latin *cerussa*, meaning "white lead."

Cerussite, Tsumeb, Namibia • 17 x 11 x 13 cm

Smithsonite

Formula $ZnCO_3$

Crystal System hexagonal

Space Group $R\bar{3}c$

Hardness 4.0–4.5

Specific Gravity 4.43

Cleavage {1011} nearly perfect

Fracture uneven to conchoidal

Tenacity brittle

Habit White, pale to dark gray, pale brown or brown; more rarely pale shades of red, pink, orange, yellow, green, apple green, emerald green, blue or bluish gray. Uncommon as crystals, rhombohedral and scalenohedral; typically botryoidal, reniform, spherulitic, stalactitic, earthy, friable, granular to porous or compact massive. Vitreous luster or may be pearly; transparent to translucent. White streak.

Environment A secondary mineral formed in oxidized zones of zinc-bearing deposits and replacing adjacent carbonate rocks, where it may constitute an ore.

Notable Localities USA: Mammoth–St. Anthony Mine, Tiger, Arizona; Kelly Mine, Magdalena, New Mexico; Friedensville, Pennsylvania. Europe: Chessy, near Lyon, Rhône, France; Moresnet, Belgium; Iglesias, Sardinia, Italy; Bleiberg, Carinthia, Austria; Tarnowitz and Beuthen, Poland; Laurium, Greece.

Name Named in honor of James Lewis Smithson (1754–1829), the British chemist and mineralogist whose bequest founded the Smithsonian Institution in Washington, DC.

Smithsonite, Tsumeb, Namibia • 16 x 5.5 x 6 cm

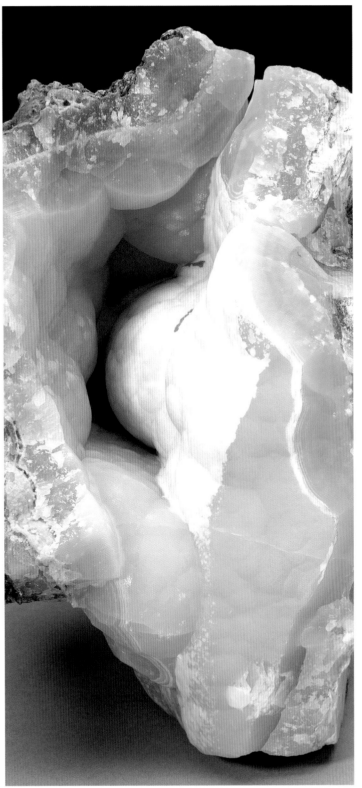

Smithsonite, Kelly Mine, Magdalena, New Mexico, USA • 14 x 19 x 17 cm

Phosgenite

Formula $Pb_2CO_3Cl_2$

Crystal System tetragonal

Space Group *P4/mbm*

Hardness 2.0–3.0

Specific Gravity 6.12

Cleavage {001} and {110} distinct; {100} indistinct

Fracture conchoidal

Tenacity sectile; flexible

Habit Pale yellow to yellowish brown, light brown or smoky violet; also colorless, pale rose, gray, yellowish gray or pale green. Crystals short prismatic to prismatic, rarely thick tabular; also granular or massive. Adamantine luster; transparent to translucent. White streak.

Environment Formed in the oxidation zone of lead ore deposits, especially where seawater or other sources of chlorine are present.

Notable Localities USA: Terrible Mine, Isle, Colorado; Mammoth–St. Anthony Mine, Tiger, Arizona; Stevenson-Bennett Mine, New Mexico. Latin America: Boleo, near Santa Rosalia, Baja California, Mexico. Europe: Tarnowitz, Poland. Africa: Touissit Mine, near Oujda, Morocco; Tsumeb, Namibia. Asia: Syzjanov Mine, Altai district, Siberia, Russia. Australia: Broken Hill, New South Wales; Comet Mine, Dundas, Tasmania.

Name From the gas phosgene, or carbonyl dichloride ($COCl_2$), because the mineral also contains carbon, oxygen and chlorine.

Phosgenite, Monteponi, Carbonia-Iglesias, Sardinia, Italy • 5 x 8 x 5 cm

Shortite, Mont-Saint-Hilaire, Quebec, Canada • 3 x 1.5 x 1.5 cm

Shortite

Formula $Na_2Ca_2(CO_3)_3$

Crystal System orthorhombic

Space Group *Amm*2

Hardness 3.0–4.5

Specific Gravity 2.62

Cleavage distinct on {010}

Fracture conchoidal

Tenacity brittle

Habit Colorless, pale yellow or dark yellow. Crystals typically wedge-shaped, tabular to short prismatic. Vitreous luster; transparent. White streak.

Environment Occurs in kimberlite dikes and carbonatite and in differentiated alkalic massifs. Also associated with intrusive alkalic gabbro-syenite complexes.

Notable Localities Canada: Upper Canada gold mine, Kirkland Lake district, Ontario; Mont-Saint-Hilaire, Quebec. USA: Green River formation, Wyoming; Uintah Basin, northeastern Utah. Europe: Vuoriyarvi carbonatite complex, Kola Peninsula, Russia.

Name Named after Dr. Maxwell Naylor Short (1889–1952), a professor of mineralogy at the University of Arizona in Tucson.

Malachite

Formula $Cu_2CO_3(OH)_2$

Crystal System monoclinic

Space Group $P2_1/a$

Hardness 3.5–4.0

Specific Gravity 4.05

Cleavage perfect on $\{\overline{2}01\}$; fair on $\{010\}$

Fracture subconchoidal to uneven

Tenacity brittle

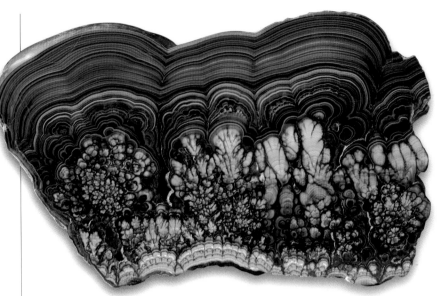

ABOVE: Malachite, Katanga, Democratic Republic of the Congo • 24 x 15 x 10 cm
RIGHT: Malachite, Bisbee, Arizona, USA • 6.5 x 8.5 x 1.5 cm

Malachite, Bisbee, Arizona, USA • 26 x 23 x 17 cm

Habit Bright green, with crystals deeper shades of green or very dark to nearly black. Crystals uncommon, usually short or long prismatic or acicular, often in rosettes, sprays or tufts; botryoidal to mammillary aggregates of radiating fibrous crystals more common; also massive, compact or stalactic. Adamantine to vitreous luster, silky if fibrous or dull to earthy if massive; transparent to translucent. Light green streak.

Environment A common secondary mineral formed in the oxidation zone of copper deposits.

Notable Localities USA: Copper Queen Mine, Czar, Bisbee and Morenci, Arizona; Santa Rita, New Mexico. Europe: Chessy, near Lyon, Rhône, France. Africa: Mashamba West Mine, Katanga (Shaba), Democratic Republic of the Congo (Zaire); Onganja Mine, northeast of Windhoek, and Tsumeb, Namibia. Australia: Broken Hill and Cobar, New South Wales; Burra, South Australia.

Name Named in antiquity after the Greek word for mallows, alluding to the similarity of the mineral's green color to that of mallow leaves.

Malachite is a minor ore of copper but is mainly employed as an ornamental material or cut to make gemstones. It has also been used as a green artist's pigment and as a cosmetic, from as early as 3000 BCE.

Azurite, Chessy-les-Mines, Rhône-Alpes, France • 9.5 x 7 x 9 cm

Azurite

Formula $Cu_3(CO_3)_2(OH)_2$

Crystal System monoclinic

Space Group $P2_1/c$

Hardness 3.5–4.0

Specific Gravity 3.78

Cleavage {011} perfect but interrupted; {100} fair; {110} poor

Fracture conchoidal

Tenacity brittle

Habit Azure blue or very dark to pale blue. Crystals typically complex, with more than 100 forms recorded: tabular short to long prismatic, with wedge-like terminations, or as rhomboidal, lenticular or spherical subparallel aggregates, which may form rosettes; also internally radial stalactitic or columnar aggregates, botryoidal, drusy, earthy or massive. Vitreous to subadamantine luster; transparent to translucent. Light blue streak.

Environment Occurs in oxidized zones of copper deposits associated with carbonate rocks, and may constitute an ore of copper.

Notable Localities USA: Apex Mine, St. George, and Big Indian Mine, near La Sal, Utah; Copper Queen and other mines, Warren district, Bisbee, and Mammoth–St. Anthony Mine, Morenci, Arizona; New Cornelia Mine, Ajo, and Kelly and Graphic mines, Magdalena, New Mexico.

Name From the Persian *lazhward*, for its characteristic blue color.

Bisbee, Arizona, was founded in 1880 as a copper-, gold- and silver-mining town. Copper carbonate deposits in the region eventually produced millions of kilograms of copper, as well as thousands of remarkably beautiful specimens of malachite and azurite, such as the one below.

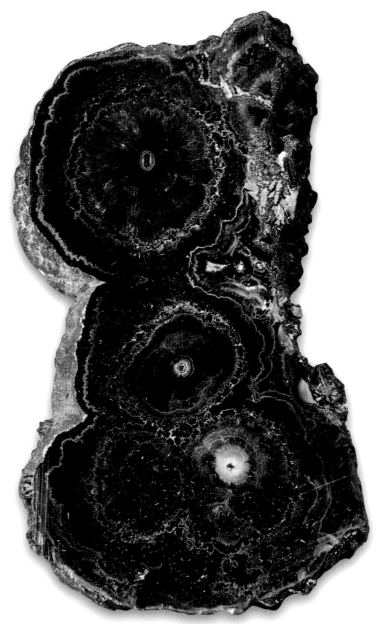

Azurite, Bisbee, Arizona, USA • 13 x 7.5 x 1.5 cm

Remondite-(Ce)

Formula $Na_3(Ca,Ce,La,Na,Sr)_3(CO_3)_5$

Crystal System monoclinic

Space Group $P2_1$

Hardness 3.0–3.5

Specific Gravity 3.4

Cleavage imperfect

Fracture conchoidal

Tenacity brittle

Habit Orange red to brown. Crystals rare; typically massive or filling veinlets. Vitreous luster; transparent to translucent. White streak.

Environment Occurs only in a nepheline syenite and associated with an intrusive alkalic gabbro-syenite complex.

Notable Localities Canada: Mont-Saint-Hilaire, Quebec. Africa: Ebounja, near Kribi, Cameroon.

Name Named after Guy Remond (b. 1935), a French mineral physicist.

Remondite-(Ce), Mont-Saint-Hilaire, Quebec, Canada • 14 x 9 x 9 mm, 7.30 ct

Remondite-(Ce), Poudrette Quarry, Mont-Saint-Hilaire, Quebec, Canada • 2 x 2 x 2 cm

Mont-Saint-Hilaire, in the Canadian province of Quebec, formed about 150 million years ago, when magma of a rare composition rose up from Earth's interior and solidified. Rich in uncommon elements such as zirconium, cerium and beryllium, to name only a few, the magma intruded into 445-million-year-old shales, siltstones and limestones. Complex interactions, both within the magma and between it and the surrounding sedimentary rocks, resulted in a distinctive suite of minerals, many extremely rare — such as remondite-(Ce). More than 360 mineral species have so far been found in a single place on the mountain, a rock quarry. Few other localities worldwide are so diverse in mineral species.

CHAPTER 6
Phosphates, Arsenates & Vanadates

Phosphate, arsenate and vanadate minerals are grouped together because of their similar crystal structures. Phosphates contain phosphorus and oxygen in PO_4 groups. The phosphate class of minerals is large and diverse, with more than 200 species, but only a few species are relatively common. Arsenates contain arsenic (As) as AsO_4 groups, and vanadates contain vanadium (V) as VO_4 groups.

These minerals can form colorful and well-crystallized specimens. The PO_4, AsO_4 and VO_4 anions have the same charge and are roughly the same size, so they can usually substitute for each other in the structures of minerals.

ABOVE: Vanadinite, Mibladen Mine, Oued Adeghoual, Morocco • 3.5 x 5.5 x 5.5 cm

RIGHT: Gormanite, Crosscut Creek (near Rapid Creek), Yukon, Canada • 4 x 4.5 x 3 cm

LEFT: Vivianite, Big Fish River, Dawson Mining District, Yukon, Canada • 5 x 4.5 x 3 cm

Monazite, Ilímaussaq complex, Kitaa, Greenland • 12 x 8 x 7 cm

Monazite Group

Formula $(Ce,La,Nd,Th)PO_4$

Crystal System monoclinic

Space Group $P2_1/n$

Hardness 5.0–5.5

Specific Gravity 4.6–5.4

Cleavage {100} distinct; {010} poor

Fracture conchoidal to uneven

Tenacity brittle

Habit Yellowish or reddish brown to brown, pale yellow, pink or gray to nearly white. Crystals typically tabular or may be prismatic, equant or wedge-shaped; also granular or massive. Resinous to waxy luster, vitreous to adamantine, or can be dull to earthy; translucent to opaque. Grayish white streak.

Environment An accessory mineral in granites, syenites and pegmatites and high-grade metamorphic rocks; also occurs in detrital river and beach sands. Associated with zircon, xenotime, titanite, thorite and columbite.

Notable Localities Canada: Parry Sound, Ontario; Villeneuve, Quebec. USA: Himalaya Mine, California; Petaca district, New Mexico; Pikes Peak batholith, Platte district, Wyoming; Amelia, Virginia. Europe: Norde Stromfjord, Greenland; Tveit Farm pegmatites, Iveland, Norway; Prince of Wales Quarry, Tintagel, Cornwall, England. Africa: Ambatofotsikely and Ampangabé, Madagascar. Asia: Zlatoust, Ilmen (Ural) Mountains, Russia; Bayan Obo iron/niobium/rare-earth elements deposit, near Baotou, Inner Mongolia, China. Australia: Mt. Weld carbonatite, near Laverton, Western Australia.

Name From the Greek for "solitary," for its apparent rarity in its first known localities.

Xenotime-(Y)

Formula YPO_4

Crystal System tetragonal

Space Group $I4_1/amd$

Hardness 4.0–5.0

Specific Gravity 4.4–5.1

Cleavage {100} good

Fracture uneven to splintery

Tenacity brittle

Habit Yellowish brown, reddish brown, red, gray, white, pale yellow or greenish. Short to long prismatic crystals, may be pyramidal or equant; also radial or rosette-like aggregates of coarse crystals. Vitreous to resinous luster; translucent to opaque. White streak.

Environment An accessory mineral in alkalic to granitic rocks, well-developed in associated pegmatites. Also a very common detrital mineral in placers.

Notable Localities Canada: Gunter Quarry, near McKenzie Lake, Ontario; Evans-Lour Mine, Quebec. USA: placers in Polk, McDowell and Bruke counties, North Carolina. Latin America: Urubu pegmatite, Minas Gerais, Brazil. Europe: Tavetschtal, Graubunden, Switzerland. Africa: Cape Province, South Africa. Asia: Manbhum district, Bihar and Orissa, India. New Zealand: North Westland.

Name From the Greek words for "vain" and "honor," because when it was first described, the yttrium in xenotime was mistakenly believed to be a new element.

Xenotime-(Y), Novo Horizonte, Bahia, Brazil • 1.5 x 0.7 x 0.7 cm

Vivianite, Morococala Mine, Santa Fé Mining District, Oruro, Bolivia • 10 x 3.5 x 2.5 cm

Vivianite

Formula $Fe^{2+}_3(PO_4)_2 \cdot 8H_2O$

Crystal System monoclinic

Space Group $C2/m$

Hardness 1.5–2.0

Specific Gravity 2.7

Cleavage perfect on {010}

Fracture fibrous

Tenacity sectile

Habit Colorless or very pale green when freshly exposed; turns dark blue, dark greenish blue, indigo blue, then black with exposure. Prismatic crystals, either flattened or somewhat elongated, may be rounded or corroded; also as incrustations, concretionary, earthy or powdery. Vitreous to pearly luster or dull to earthy; transparent to translucent. Bluish white streak.

Environment A secondary mineral associated with metallic ore deposits and complex granite pegmatites. Also occurs in clays, recent alluvial and glauconitic sediments and other organic sediments such as lignite, peat and bog iron.

Notable Localities USA: Big Chief, Bull Moose and Tip Top pegmatites, South Dakota; Palermo No. 1 Mine, North Groton, New Hampshire. Latin America: Siglo XX Mine, Llallagua, Potosí, Bolivia; Telido Mine and Larada Ilha, Taquaral, São Paulo, Brazil. Europe: Millersdale, Derbyshire, and Cornwall, England; Hagendorf, Bavaria, Germany.

Name Named in honor of John Henry Vivian (1785–1855), a Welsh-Cornish mineralogist from Truro, England, who discovered the species.

Wavellite

Formula $Al_3(PO_4)_2(OH,F)_3 \cdot 5H_2O$

Crystal System orthorhombic

Space Group $Pcmn$

Hardness 3.5–4.0

Specific Gravity 2.4

Cleavage {110} perfect; good on {101}; distinct on {010}

Fracture uneven to subconchoidal

Tenacity brittle

Habit White, greenish white, green, yellow, brown, bluish brown or brownish black; can be zoned. Commonly radial aggregates or prismatic crystals, elongated and striated; euhedral crystals uncommon. Vitreous to resinous, pearly luster; translucent. White streak.

Environment A secondary mineral in low-grade metamorphic rocks and phosphate deposits.

Notable Localities USA: Mineral Park Mine, Arizona; Amity, New York. Latin America: Llallagua, Potosí, and Oruru, Bolivia. Europe: Tipperary, Ireland; High Down Quarry, Devonshire, England. Africa: Katanga (Shaba), Democratic Republic of the Congo (Zaire). Australia: Iron Monarch Quarry, Iron Knob, South Australia.

Name Named for William Wavell, a physician from Horwood parish in Devon, England, who discovered the mineral.

Wavellite, Mount Ida, Arkansas, USA • 10 x 13 x 8 cm

Torbernite

Formula $Cu(UO_2)_2(PO_4)_2 \cdot 8-12H_2O$

Crystal System tetragonal

Space Group $I4/mmm$

Hardness 2.0–2.5

Specific Gravity 3.2

Cleavage {001} perfect; indistinct on {100}

Fracture none

Tenacity brittle

Habit Emerald green, grass green or apple green. Thin to thick tabular crystals, typically in subparallel aggregates, foliated or micaceous. Vitreous, subadamantine or waxy luster, becoming dull on dehydration; transparent to translucent. Pale green streak.

Environment An uncommon secondary mineral formed in the oxidized zones of some uranium-rich copper deposits; associated with metatorbernite, autunite and uraninite.

Notable Localities USA: Majuba Hill Mine, Nevada; Chalk Mountain, North Carolina. Europe: a number of mines in Cornwall, England; Schneeberg and Johanngeorgenstadt, Germany; Sabugal, Portugal. Africa: Shinkolobwe, Democratic Republic of the Congo (Zaire). Australia: Mt. Painter, Flinders ranges, South Australia.

Name Named after Torbern Olof Bergmann (1735–84), a chemist and mineralogist at Uppsala University in Sweden.

Torbernite, Katanga (Shaba), Democratic Republic of the Congo • 8 x 13 x 10 cm

Variscite, Fairfield, Utah, USA • 18 x 21 x 6 cm

Variscite

Formula $AlPO_4 \cdot 2H_2O$

Crystal System orthorhombic

Space group $Pbca$

Hardness 4.5

Specific Gravity 2.57

Cleavage {010} good; poor on {001}

Fracture uneven to splintery; conchoidal when glassy

Tenacity brittle

Habit Pale green, emerald green, bluish green or colorless. Uncommon in crystals; may be lathlike but usually fine-grained and massive, in nodules, stalactites, crusts and veinlets. Vitreous to waxy luster; transparent to translucent. White streak.

Environment Typically deposited from phosphate-bearing waters in contact with aluminous rocks.

Notable Localities USA: Champion Mine, White Mountains, California; Little Green Monster Mine, Fairfield, Utah. Europe: Messbach Plauen, Voigtland, Thuringia, Germany; Zeleznik, Trenic, Bohemia, Czech Republic. Australia: Iron Knob and Iron Monarch mines, South Australia.

Name From Variscia, the ancient name of the Voigtland district in Germany, where the mineral was discovered.

Herderite

Formula $CaBe(PO_4)F$

Crystal System monoclinic

Space Group $P2_1/a$

Hardness 5.0–5.5

Specific Gravity 3.0

Cleavage irregular

Fracture subconchoidal

Tenacity brittle

Habit Light green or colorless to pale yellow. Crystals euhedral, stout prismatic or thick tabular; also in botryoidal or spheroidal radiating aggregates. Vitreous luster; transparent. White streak.

Environment Forms principally in granitic pegmatites in association with quartz, albite, topaz and tourmaline.

Notable Localities Latin America: Brazil. Europe: possibly Ehrenfriedersdorf, Saxony, Germany (samples at the boundary between herderite and hydroxylherderite). Africa: probably Erongo, Namibia. Asia: Mogok stone tract, Myanmar (Burma); Yichung, China.

Name Named after Siegmund August Wolfgang von Herder (1776–1838), a mining official from Freiberg, Saxony, in Germany.

Hydroxylherderite, Golconda district, Governador Valaderes, Minas Gerais, Brazil • 3.5 x 5 x 3.5 cm

Triplite, Skrumpetorp, Godegård, Östergötland, Sweden • 6 x 4 x 3 cm

Triplite

Formula $(Mn^{2+},Fe^{2+},Mg)_2(PO_4)(F,OH)$

Crystal System monoclinic

Space Group $I2/a$

Hardness 5.0–5.5

Specific Gravity 3.5–3.9

Cleavage {001} good; {010} fair; {100} poor

Fracture uneven to subconchoidal

Tenacity brittle

Habit Chestnut to reddish brown or salmon pink; brownish black to black if altered. Crystals typically very rough but have many indistinct forms; usually nodular or massive. Vitreous to resinous luster; translucent to opaque. Yellowish gray streak.

Environment A principal primary phosphate or one that has replaced earlier species.

Notable Localities USA: Pala, California; Elk Ridge Mine, South Dakota. Latin America: Sierra de Zapata, Catamarca, Córdoba, Argentina. Europe: Horrsjöberg, Värmland, Sweden; Limoges near Chanteloube, Haute-Vienne, France. Asia: Tigrinoye, Sikhote-Alin Range, Ural Mountains, Russia.

Name From the Greek for "threefold," probably for its three cleavage directions.

Fluorapatite

Beryllonite

Fluorapatite-(CaF), Madagascar • 13.8 x 15.8 x 9.6 mm, 15.20 ct. Fluorapatite is fairly uncommon as a gemstone because it is quite soft and heat sensitive, but it is a nice collector's stone. It can be found in a wide range of colors, with blue, violet and yellow being notably attractive. Gemstones of a vibrant saturated electric blue to blue green color, resembling and rivaling the bright blue copper-rich tourmalines from Paraíba, Brazil, were discovered in Madagascar in the 1980s.

Beryllonite, Maine, USA • 11.9 x 7.4 x 6 mm, 2.75 ct. Beryllonite is a rare beryllium mineral and a very rare collector's gem. It lacks fire and color and is quite difficult to cut into gemstones because of its perfect basal cleavage. Beryllonite was once found only at Stoneham, Maine, USA; the adjacent town of Lovell was named as its source in order to maintain secrecy among collectors and competing dealers. The mineral has since been discovered at several localities worldwide, including Brazil, Canada and Afghanistan.

Turquoise

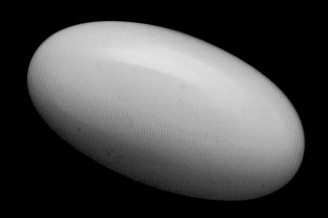

Turquoise, Iran • 2 x 4 x 2 cm, 76.18 ct. The region once known as Persia is an important source of turquoise that dates back thousands of years, and it still sets the standard for quality. Over the centuries many mines have been established on the slopes of the Al-Mirsah-Kuh Mountains, in present-day Iran. The material from this deposit is a rich turquoise blue, with less matrix than that mined elsewhere, and is usually harder. It is thought that much of the turquoise taken to Europe for use in jewelry was traded from this region through Turkey, hence its name.

Fluorapatite, Aldeia do Eme Mine, Conselheiro Pena, Minas Gerais, Brazil • 9 x 13 x 7 cm

Fluorapatite

Formula $Ca_5(PO_4)_3F$

Crystal System hexagonal

Space Group $P6_3/m$

Hardness 5.0

Specific Gravity 3.1–3.2

Cleavage poor on {0001} and {10$\bar{1}$0}

Fracture conchoidal to uneven

Tenacity brittle

Habit Sea green, violet, purple, blue, pink, yellow, brown, white or colorless. Prismatic hexagonal crystals; also granular, globular to reniform, nodular or massive. Vitreous to subresinous luster; transparent to translucent. White streak.

Environment Very common, occurring in all types of igneous rocks, marbles and skarns, especially in calcium-rich regional and contact metamorphic rocks. An essential component of sedimentary phosphorites.

Notable Localities Canada: Mont-Saint-Hilaire and several other localities in Quebec; Ontario. USA: Tip Top Mine, Custer, South Dakota; Newry and Mt. Apatite, Auburn, Maine. Latin America: Cerro de Mercado, Durango, Mexico; Jacupiranga Mine, São Paulo, and Tapira, Minas Gerais, Brazil. Europe: Khibiny and Kovdor massifs, Kola Peninsula, Russia; Ehrenfriedersdorf, Saxony, Germany; Untersulzbachtal, Salzburg, Austria; Panasqueira, Portugal. Africa: Onganja Mine, Namibia; Phalaborwa, Limpopo, South Africa. Australia: Mt. Weld carbonatite, near Laverton, Western Australia.

Name From the Greek *apate*, meaning "deceit," referring to its similarity to crystals of other minerals such as aquamarine, amethyst and olivine.

Beryllonite

Formula $NaBePO_4$

Crystal System monoclinic

Space Group $P2_1/n$

Hardness 5.5–6.0

Specific Gravity 2.8

Cleavage {010} perfect; {100} good; {101} indistinct

Fracture conchoidal

Tenacity brittle

Habit Colorless or white to pale yellow. Tabular to short prismatic crystals; also spherical aggregates and fibrous or massive. Vitreous to adamantine luster; transparent to translucent. White streak.

Environment A rare secondary mineral in granitic and alkalic pegmatites.

Notable Localities Canada: Mont-Saint-Hilaire, Quebec. USA: Dunton Quarry and Bell Pit, Sugarloaf Mountain, Maine. Europe: Viitaniemi pegmatite, Eräjärvi, Finland; Norrö pegmatite, Rånö Island, Sweden. Asia: Paprok, Nuristan, Afghanistan.

Name From one of the major constituents of the mineral, beryllium.

Beryllonite, Paprok Mine, Kamdesh District, Nuristan, Afghanistan • 11 x 10 x 9 cm

Turquoise, Mohave County, Arizona, USA • 23.5 x 12 x 4 cm

Turquoise

Formula $CuAl_6(PO_4)_4(OH)_8 \cdot 4H_2O$

Crystal System triclinic

Space Group $P\bar{1}$

Hardness 5.0–6.0

Specific Gravity 2.6–2.8

Cleavage {001} perfect

Fracture conchoidal to smooth when massive

Tenacity brittle

Habit Sky blue, bluish green, apple green or green gray when massive; bright blue as crystals. Crystals rare, short and prismatic; normally massive, also cryptocrystalline, stalactitic, concretionary or as crusts or veinlets. Waxy luster, but vitreous as crystals; opaque, but transparent as crystals. Pale bluish streak.

Environment A secondary mineral found with chalcedony, iron oxides, kaolin and oxyhydroxides in the potassic alteration zone of hydrothermal copper deposits. Also occurs as a vein-filling mineral in volcanic rocks and phosphate-rich sediments.

Notable Localities USA: Mineral Park, Globe-Miami district, and Morenci, Arizona; Bishop Mine, Lynch Station, Virginia. Latin America: Itatiaiuçu iron mine, Minas Gerais, Brazil; Chuquicamata, Antofagasta, Chile. Europe: several localities in Cornwall, England; Ottré, near Vielsalm, Belgium. Asia: Ma'dan, Iran. Australia: Narooma, New South Wales.

Name From Turquie, the French name for Turkey, as turquoise from Iran was imported to Europe from there.

Amblygonite

Formula $LiAl(PO_4)(F,OH)$

Crystal System triclinic

Space group $C\bar{1}$

Hardness 5.5–6.0

Specific Gravity 3.11

Cleavage {100} perfect; {110} good; {0$\bar{1}$1} distinct

Fracture uneven to subconchoidal

Tenacity brittle

Habit Milk white, pale yellow, beige, salmon pink, pale green, pale blue or gray; may be colorless. Crude crystals, typically equant with complex form development; massive. Vitreous to greasy luster; transparent to translucent. White streak.

Environment An uncommon accessory mineral in zoned lithium-bearing granitic pegmatites; associated with spodumene, lithiophilite-triphyllite, apatite-group minerals, lepidolite, petalite, pollucite and tourmaline-group minerals.

Notable Localities Canada: Tanco pegmatite, Manitoba. USA: Custer district, South Dakota; New Pit, Newry, Maine. Latin America: many localities in Minas Gerais, Brazil. Europe: Montebras, Creuse, France; Saxony, Germany.

Name From the Greek words for "blunt" and "angle," for its approximately 90-degree cleavage angle.

Amblygonite, Ademar pegmatite, Rio Jequitinhonha, Itinga, Minas Gerais, Brazil • 10 x 6 x 5 cm

Augelite

Formula $Al_2PO_4(OH)_3$

Crystal System monoclinic

Space Group $C2/m$

Hardness 4.5–5.0

Specific Gravity 2.69

Cleavage {110} perfect; {$\overline{2}$01} good; {001} and {$\overline{1}$01} imperfect

Fracture uneven

Tenacity brittle

Habit Colorless to white; may be yellowish or pale rose. Thick tabular, prismatic to acicular crystals or thin triangular plates; also massive. Vitreous to pearly luster on cleavage planes; transparent. White streak.

Environment Formed by hydrogen metamorphism of phosphate-bearing rocks in aluminum-rich sediments. Also occurs in some high-temperature hydrothermal ore deposits.

Notable Localities Canada: Big Fish River, Yukon. USA: Champion Mine, White Mountains, California; Hugo pegmatite, Keystone, South Dakota; Palermo No. 1 Mine, North Groton, New Hampshire. Latin America: Tatasi and Portugalete, Potosí, Bolivia. Europe: Westanå iron mine, Näsum, Kristianstad, Sweden. Africa: Buranga pegmatite, Rwanda; Mbale, Uganda. Asia: Ural Mountains, Russia. Australia: Mount Perry, southwest of Bundaberg, Queensland.

Name From the Greek word for "luster," for its pearly luster on cleavage planes.

Augelite, Rapid Creek, Yukon, Canada • 3.5 x 3 x 3 cm

Augelite, Rapid Creek, Yukon, Canada • 5 x 6 x 4 cm

Prospectors searching for iron deposits in the remote Rapid Creek–Big Fish River region, Yukon, Canada, encountered some well-crystallized but unfamiliar minerals in phosphate-rich sedimentary rocks. Mountain-building in the region had folded the layered rocks, and the more brittle layers had fractured, creating open spaces. Water moving through the rocks dissolved various minerals, resulting in solutions that were especially rich in phosphate. These solutions trickled into the fractures, where conditions were favorable for crystallization of rare phosphate minerals that included augelite.

Pyromorphite

Formula $Pb_5(PO_4)_3Cl$

Crystal System hexagonal

Space Group P_63/m

Hardness 3.5

Specific Gravity 7.04

Cleavage $\{10\bar{1}1\}$ in traces

Fracture uneven to subconchoidal

Tenacity brittle

Habit Dark grass green, green, yellow, yellow orange, reddish orange, yellow brown, brown, tan or grayish; may be colorless. Crystals prismatic, generally simple; also equant, barrel shaped, rarely tabular or pyramidal, globular or granular. Resinous to subadamantine luster; transparent to translucent. White streak.

Environment Occurs as a secondary mineral in the oxidized zone of lead deposits, and rarely as a volcanic sublimate.

Notable Localities Canada: Moyie Mines, British Columbia; Mont-Saint-Hilaire, Quebec. USA: Coeur d'Alene district, Idaho; Loudville Mine, Massachusetts. Latin America: San Juan Guazapares, Chihuahua, Mexico; Boquira Mine, Bahia, Brazil. Europe: El Horcajo, Castilla, and Ciudad Real, Spain; Bad Ems, Rhineland-Palatinate, Germany; Horcajo Mines, south of Brazatortas, Příbram, Czech Republic. Africa: Touissit Mine, Oujda, Morocco; Kabwe Mine, Zambia.

Name From the Greek *pyros*, meaning "fire," and *morphos*, meaning "form," because when a sample is melted into a globule, a crystalline shape forms on cooling.

Pyromorphite, Saint-Salvy-de-la-Balme, Midi-Pyrénées, France • 4 x 3 x 2.5 cm

Pyromorphite is a lead phosphate — its formula is $Pb_5(PO_4)_3Cl$ — found around the oxidized edges of lead deposits. It is occasionally used as an ore of lead. One of the classic localities for pyromorphite is the Broken Hill Mine in New South Wales, Australia. Broken Hill's massive ore body, which formed about 1,800 million years ago, is among the world's largest silver-lead-zinc mineral deposits.

ABOVE: Pyromorphite, Les Farges Mine, Limousin, France • 9.5 x 7.5 x 4.5 cm

RIGHT: Pyromorphite, Yangshuo Mine, Guilin, Guangxi Zhuang Autonomous Region, China • 11 x 9 x 6 cm

Gormanite, Rapid Creek, Yukon, Canada • 10 x 6 x 4 cm

Gormanite

Formula $Fe^{2+}_3Al_4(PO_4)_4(OH)_6 \cdot 2H_2O$

Crystal System triclinic

Space Group $P\bar{1}$

Hardness 4.0–5.0

Specific Gravity 3.10

Cleavage {001} poor

Fracture none

Tenacity brittle

Habit Blue green. Radiating aggregates and blades elongated up to 3 mm. Vitreous luster; semitransparent. Pale green streak.

Environment Occurs as low-temperature fracture fillings in phosphate-ironstones (in Yukon Territory, Canada) and in fractures in tonalite (Bisbee, Arizona, USA).

Notable Localities Rapid Creek and Big Fish River, Yukon, Canada.

Name Named for Dr. Donald Herbert Gorman (b. 1922), a former professor of mineralogy in the Department of Geology, University of Toronto.

Kulanite

Formula $BaFe^{2+}_2Al_2(PO_4)_3(OH)_3$

Crystal System monoclinic

Space Group $P2_1/m$

Hardness 4.0

Specific Gravity 3.91

Cleavage fair to good on {010} and {100}

Fracture none

Tenacity brittle

Habit Green to blue. Thin, flattened tablets forming rosettes of up to 3 mm. Vitreous luster; transparent to translucent. Greenish white streak.

Environment Occurs in fractures in sideritic iron formations (Cross Cut Creek, Yukon Territory, Canada) and found as disseminations and veinlets in a granitic pegmatite (Xiyuantou, China).

Notable Localities Rapid Creek (Cross Cut Creek), Big Fish River, Yukon, Canada.

Name Named for Alan Kulan (1921–77), a prospector who was co-discoverer of the Rapid Creek phosphate occurrences in Yukon.

Kulanite, Crosscut Creek (near Rapid Creek), Yukon, Canada • 9 x 5 x 3 cm

Lazulite, Rapid Creek, Yukon, Canada • 7 x 8 x 4 cm

Lazulite

Formula $MgAl_2(PO_4)_2(OH)_2$

Crystal System monoclinic

Space Group $P2_1/c$

Hardness 5.5–6.0

Specific Gravity 3.12

Cleavage poor to good on {110}; indistinct on {101}

Fracture brittle

Tenacity uneven to splintery

Habit Azure blue, sky blue, bluish white, yellow green or blue green; rarely green. Crystals acute pyramidal; also tabular, massive compact or granular. Vitreous luster; transparent to translucent, and may be nearly opaque. White streak.

Environment Found in aluminous high-grade metamorphic rocks with quartz as disseminated grains, in quartz veins or dikes in these rocks, or in granitic pegmatites.

Notable Localities Canada: Blow River, Yukon. USA: White Mountains, California; Palermo No. 1 Mine, North Groton, New Hampshire; Chubbs Mountain and Chowders Mountain, North Carolina; Graves Mountain, Georgia. Latin America: Real Socavaon, Potosí, Bolivia; Dattas, Minas Gerais, Brazil. Europe: Westanå, Sweden; Werfen Salzburg, Austria; near Zermatt, Valais, Switzerland.

Name From the German *lazurstein*, meaning "blue stone."

Erythrite

Formula $Co_3(AsO_4)_2·8H_2O$

Crystal System monoclinic

Space Group $C2/m$

Hardness 1.5–2.5

Specific Gravity 3.06

Cleavage perfect on {010}; poor on {100} and {$\bar{1}$02}

Fracture none

Tenacity sectile

Habit Crimson to peach red, pale rose or pink. Rarely well crystallized, typically flattened; as aggregates, fibrous, drusy, powdery or massive. Subadamantine luster; transparent to translucent. Pinkish red streak.

Environment A secondary mineral associated with some cobalt/nickel/arsenic-bearing mineral deposits.

Notable Localities Canada: Cobalt, Ontario. USA: Blackbird Mine, Idaho. Latin America: Sara Alicia Mine, Sonora, Mexico. Europe: Chalanches, near Allemont, Isère, France; Schneeberg, Saxony, Germany; Jáchymov (Joachimsthal), Czech Republic. Africa: Bou Azzer district, Morocco. Australia: Mt. Cobalt, south of Cloncurry, Queensland.

Name From the Greek word for red, its characteristic color.

Erythrite, Bou Azzer District, Souss-Massa-Draâ, Morocco • 8 x 12 x 8 cm

Scorodite

Formula $Fe^{3+}AsO_4\cdot2H_2O$

Crystal System orthorhombic

Space Group *Pcab*

Hardness 3.5–4.0

Specific Gravity 3.2

Cleavage {201} imperfect; {001} and {100} in traces

Fracture subconchoidal

Tenacity brittle

Habit Pale leek green or gray green to brown, colorless, bluish, violet or yellow. Crystals pyramidal, tabular or prismatic; commonly crystalline crusts or may be porous, sinterlike, earthy or massive. Vitreous to subadamantine or subresinous luster; semitransparent to transparent in crystals. Greenish white streak.

Environment A secondary mineral formed by oxidation of arsenic-bearing sulfides.

Notable Localities USA: Grandview Mine, Arizona; Sterling Hill Mine, Ogdensburg, New Jersey. Latin America: El Cobre Mine, Aranzazú, Zacatecas, Mexico; Doce Valley, Minas Gerais, Brazil. Europe: Schwarzenberg, Saxony, Germany; Kamereza Mine, Attica, Greece. Africa: Tsumeb Mine, Tsumeb, Namibia. Asia: Rajasthan, India. Australia: Preamimma Mine, Callington, South Australia.

Name From the Greek word for "garlic-like," in reference to its odor when heated.

Scorodite, Tsumeb, Namibia • 4 x 6 x 5 cm

Legrandite, Ojuela Mine, Mapimí, Durango, Mexico • 4.5 x 6 x 4 cm

Legrandite

Formula $Zn_2(AsO_4)(OH)\cdot H_2O$

Crystal System monoclinic

Space Group $P2_1/c$

Hardness 4.5

Specific Gravity 4.0

Cleavage fair to poor on {100}

Fracture uneven

Tenacity brittle

Habit Bright yellow, wax yellow or colorless. Prismatic crystals, typically in sprays. Vitreous luster; transparent to translucent. White streak.

Environment A secondary mineral in the oxidized zones of zinc/arsenic-bearing deposits.

Notable Localities USA: Sterling Hill, New Jersey. Latin America: Flor de Peña Mine, Lampazos, Nuevo León, and Potosí Mine, Santa Eulalia, Mexico; Boa Vista, near Galiléia, Minas Gerais, Brazil. Africa: Tsumeb, Namibia. Asia: Ogibira Mine, near Osa, Okayama, and Toroku Mine, Miyazaki, Japan.

Name Named after M. Legrand, a Belgian mine manager who collected the first specimen.

Mimetite

Formula $Pb_5(AsO_4)_3Cl$

Crystal System hexagonal

Space Group $P6_3/m$

Hardness 3.5–4.0

Specific Gravity 7.28

Cleavage $\{10\bar{1}1\}$ in traces

Fracture subconchoidal

Tenacity brittle

Habit Pale yellow to yellowish brown, orange yellow, orange red, white or colorless. Crystals simple barrel shapes; also botryoidal, globular, reniform or granular, and rarely tabular or acicular. Resinous to subadamantine luster; translucent. White streak.

Environment Occurs as a secondary mineral in the oxidized zone of arsenic-bearing lead deposits.

Notable Localities USA: Centennial Eureka Mine, Tintic district, Utah; Mammoth–St. Anthony Mine, Tiger, and Rowley Mine, Arizona; Red Cloud copper mine, New Mexico; Phoenixville, Pennsylvania. Latin America: Santa Eulalia, Chihuahua, Mexico. Europe: Millers Dale, Derbyshire, and Merehead Quarry, Somerset, England; Les Farges Mine, France; Kamareza Mine, Attica, Greece. Africa: Tsumeb, Namibia. Asia: She Changi Mine, Iran. Australia: Broken Hill, New South Wales.

Name From the Greek word for "imitator," because of its resemblance to pyromorphite.

Mimetite, Bilbao Mine, Ojo Caliente, Zacatecas, Mexico • 7 x 8.5 x 4 cm

Carnotite, Caspar, Wyoming, USA • 7 x 5 x 3 cm

Carnotite

Formula $K_2(UO_2)_2(V_2O_8)\cdot1–3H_2O$

Crystal System monoclinic

Space Group $P2_1/a$

Hardness 2.0

Specific Gravity 4.7

Cleavage $\{001\}$ perfect, micaceous

Fracture uneven

Tenacity unknown

Habit Bright yellow to lemon yellow or slightly greenish. Rarely as crystals, with a diamond-shaped outline; typically fine aggregates or powdery to massive. Dull, earthy; semitransparent. Light yellow streak.

Environment Occurs in sandstones, typically in paleochannels and in calcretes and near playas. It is an alteration product of uraninite, montroseite or davidite.

Notable Localities USA: Uravan district, Colorado; San Rafael Swell, Utah; Grants district, New Mexico; Monument Valley, Arizona. Asia: Tyuya-Muyum and Uigursai, Fergana Valley, Alai Range, Kyrgyzstan. Australia: El Sherana, Northern Territories.

Name Named for Marie-Adolphe Carnot (1839–1920), a French mining engineer and chemist.

Vanadinite

Formula $Pb_5(VO_4)_3Cl$

Crystal System hexagonal

Space Group $P6_3/m$

Hardness 2.5–3.0

Specific Gravity 6.88

Cleavage none

Fracture uneven

Tenacity brittle

Habit Orange red, ruby red, brownish red or brown yellow to pale straw yellow. Crystals short to long prismatic with smooth faces and sharp edges; acicular to hair-like, occasionally hollow prism crystals with rounded domes in parallel grouping. Subresinous to admantine luster; subtransparent to nearly opaque. Brownish yellow streak.

Environment A secondary mineral found in the oxidized zone of lead deposits.

Notable Localities USA: Hillsboro and Lake Valley district, Nevada; Red Cloud, Mammoth–St. Anthony and Apache mines, Arizona. Latin America: Ahumada Mine, Los Lamentos, Chihuahua, Mexico; Itacarmbi Mine, Minas Gerais, Brazil. Europe: Leadhills, Scotland. Africa: Kabwe Mine, Zambia; Tsumeb, Namibia. Australia: Proprietary Mine, Broken Hill, New South Wales.

Name From the vanadium in its composition.

ABOVE: Vanadinite, Mibladen, Meknès-Tafilalet, Morocco • 4 x 4 x 3 cm
RIGHT: Vanadinite, Mibladen, Meknès-Tafilalet, Morocco • 8 x 12 x 6 cm

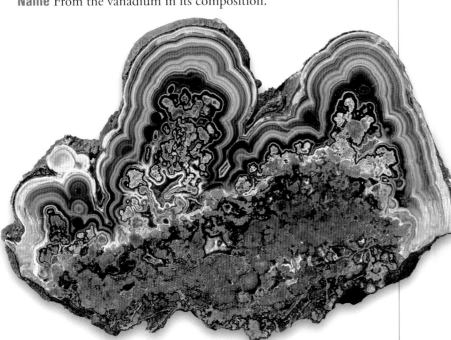

Vanadinite, Broken Hill, New South Wales, Australia • 18 x 8 x 2 cm

Along with carnotite and roscoelite, vanadinite is one of the main industrial ores of the element vanadium. Small amounts of vanadium can significantly improve the properties of certain ferrous (iron-containing) alloys. Vanadium steel is particularly strong and hard, with considerable shock resistance. Vanadium and aluminum are used together to give the required strength to titanium alloys used in jet engines and high-speed airframes.

CHAPTER 7

Borates & Nitrates

Borate minerals are naturally occurring compounds of boron (B) and oxygen. Most borate minerals are rare, but some form large deposits that are mined commercially. Boron is a component of many detergents, cosmetics and enamel glazes. It is also used as a fire retardant, an antifungal compound in fiberglass, an insecticide and a flux in metallurgy, as well as in many other aspects of the chemical industry.

Nitrate minerals are a small group of naturally occurring compounds composed of one atom of nitrogen (N) and three atoms of oxygen; the chemical symbol for nitrate is NO_3. They are very soluble and unstable, so they are more or less confined to arid regions. The only major deposit of nitrates is in the Atacama Desert of northern Chile.

ABOVE: Colemanite, Ryan, California, USA • 20 x 4 x 18 cm

RIGHT: Rhodizite, Antsirabe, Antananarivo, Madagascar • 5 x 3 x 2 cm. Rhodizite is a rare borate mineral.

LEFT: Ulexite, Boron, California, USA • 6.5 x 14 x 6 cm

Borax, West Baker Mine, Boron, California, USA • 11 x 8 x 6 cm

Borax

Formula $Na_2B_4O_5(OH)_4 \cdot 8H_2O$

Crystal System monoclinic

Space Group $C2/c$

Hardness 2.0–2.5

Specific Gravity 1.7

Cleavage {100} perfect; {110} less perfect; {010} in traces

Fracture conchoidal

Tenacity brittle

Habit Colorless, grey, white or yellowish; seldom bluish or greenish. Crystals commonly short prismatic, often tabular and striated, often malformed by abnormal development of part of one or more zones. Vitreous to resinous luster, but may be earthy; translucent to opaque. White streak.

Environment Occurs in evaporite deposits, salt lakes and playas, usually well crystallized; also found as efflorescence on soils in arid regions.

Notable Localities United States: Borax Lake and Kramer borate deposit, Boron, California; Alkali Flat, New Mexico. Latin America: Loma Blanca deposit, near Coranzuli, Jujuy, Argentina. Asia: Kirka borate deposit, Eskişehir, Turkey; Xiao Qaidam salt lake, Qinghai, China.

Name From the Arabic *bauraq*, meaning "white."

Borax has a wide variety of uses, including as a component of many detergents, as an insecticide and in cosmetics.

Ulexite

Formula $NaCaB_5O_6(OH)_6 \cdot 5H_2O$

Crystal System triclinic

Space Group $P\bar{1}$

Hardness 2.5

Specific Gravity 1.95

Cleavage {010} perfect; {1$\bar{1}$0} good; {110} poor

Fracture uneven across fiber groups

Tenacity brittle

Habit Colorless, white in aggregates or gray if included in clays. Distinct crystals rare; can be small nodular, rounded or lens-like masses; typically elongated to acicular, forming fibrous cotton-ball-like masses, in compact parallel fibrous veins, or in radiating and compact nodular groups. White streak.

Environment Found in arid regions, particularly salt playas and desiccated saline lakes.

Notable Localities Canada: Saskatchewan; Penobsquis evaporite deposit, near Sussex, and other occurrences in New Brunswick; Windsor, Nova Scotia. Latin America: more than 60 deposits in Jujuy, Salta and Catamarca provinces, Argentina; Iquique, Tarapaca, Chile. Europe: Niederellenbach, Hesse, Germany. Asia: Kirka borate deposit, Eskişehir, and Bigadiç borate district, Balıkesir, Turkey; Inder boron deposit, Kazakhstan.

Name Named after George Ludwig Ulex (1811–83), a German chemist who first correctly analyzed the species.

Ulexite is called "TV rock" or "television stone" because it can transmit images through its fibers.

Ulexite, Boron, California, USA • 2.5 x 3 x 2 cm

Howlite, Lang, California, USA • 11 x 12 x 7 cm

Howlite

Formula $Ca_2B_5SiO_9(OH)_5$

Crystal System monoclinic

Space Group $P2_1/c$

Hardness 3.5

Specific Gravity 2.58

Cleavage none

Fracture for porcelaneous types, nearly even and smooth

Tenacity brittle

Habit White. Tabular crystals rare; usually nodular masses. Subvitreous, glimmering luster; translucent in thin fragments. White streak.

Environment Found in borate deposits.

Notable Localities Canada: near Windsor, Iona and other localities in Nova Scotia; Flat Bay, Newfoundland. USA: Lang, Furnace Creek, Boron and Calico Mountains, California. Latin America: Magdalena, Sonora, Mexico. Europe: Rehden Borehole, Emsland, Germany. Asia: Susurkuk, Turkey; southern Ural Mountains, Russia.

Name Named after Henry How (1828–79), a Canadian chemist, geologist and mineralogist at the University of King's College, Windsor, Nova Scotia, who first described the mineral.

Ludwigite

Formula $Mg_2Fe^{3+}O_2(BO_3)$

Crystal System orthorhombic

Space Group *Pbam*

Hardness 5.0–5.5

Specific Gravity 3.8

Cleavage none

Fracture fibrous

Tenacity brittle

Habit Dark green to brown and black. Prismatic crystals; radiating plates or massive, fibrous or granular. Submetallic luster; opaque. Greenish black streak.

Environment A high-temperature mineral occurring in contact metamorphic deposits.

Notable Localities Canada: near Bancroft, Ontario; Outaouais, Quebec. USA: Philipsburg, Montana; Big and Little Cottonwood districts, Utah. Latin America: Toro Mocho, Morococha, Peru; Aguilar Mine, Jujuy, Argentina. Europe: Brosso Mine, northwest of Ivrea, Turin, Italy; Tyrol, Austria; Moravicza, Banat, Romania; Krumovo, Yambol Oblast, Bulgaria. Asia: Hol Kol Mine, Suan, Korea; Liaoning, northeastern China; Haneyama Mine, Fukushima, Japan.

Name Named in honor of Ernst Ludwig (1842–1915), an Austrian professor of chemistry at the University of Vienna, who analyzed the original material.

Ludwigite, Brosso, Piedmont, Italy • 7 x 6 x 2.5 cm

Colemanite

Formula $CaB_3O_4(OH)_3 \cdot H_2O$

Crystal System monoclinic

Space Group $P2_1/a$

Hardness 4.5

Specific Gravity 2.42

Cleavage {010} perfect; {001} distinct

Fracture uneven to subconchoidal

Tenacity brittle

Habit Colorless to white or gray. Complex crystals; also massive or granular to compact. Adamantine to vitreous luster; transparent to translucent. White streak.

Environment A common constituent of borate deposits formed in arid alkaline lacustrine environments that are deficient in sodium and carbonate, typically under warm conditions.

Notable Localities Canada: Penobsquis and Salt Springs, near Sussex, New Brunswick. USA: Furnace Creek area, Boron, California; Anniversary Mine, Nevada. Latin America: El Torreon and La Tinaja del Oso, near Magdalena, Sonora, Mexico; Ijes, Argentina. Asia: Bigadiç borate district, Balıkesir, Turkey; Inder borate deposit, Kazakhstan.

Name Named for William T. Coleman (1824–93), pioneer developer of the California borate industry and owner of the mine where the mineral was first found.

ABOVE: Colemanite, Boron, California, USA • 11x 17 x 8 cm
RIGHT: Colemanite, Thomson Mine, Death Valley National Park, California, USA • 42 x 29 x 28 cm

Elemental boron is not found naturally but is extracted from borate minerals such as borax, colemanite and kernite. Boron is used in glass and ceramics to give them resistance to thermal shock, including the glass in LCD screens. It is also a key component in fiberglass insulation and is widely used as a fertilizer additive, a water softener, a disinfectant and even a component in some mouthwashes.

Colemanite, Thomson Mine, Death Valley National Park, California, USA • 20 x 20 x 15 cm

Boracite

Formula $Mg_3B_7O_{13}Cl$

Crystal System orthorhombic

Space Group $Pca2_1$

Hardness 7.0–7.5

Specific Gravity 2.97

Cleavage none

Fracture conchoidal to uneven

Tenacity brittle

Habit Green, blue, colorless, grey or white. Pseudo-cubic crystals. Adamantine to vitreous luster; transparent to translucent. White streak.

Environment Found in evaporite deposits, usually associated with gypsum, anhydrite and/or halite.

Notable Localities Canada: Penobsquis and Salt Springs, New Brunswick. USA: Wichita Mountains, Oklahoma; Choctaw salt dome, Louisiana. Latin America: Alto Chapare, Cochabamba, Bolivia. Europe: Aislaby, Yorkshire, England; Luneville, France; Lüneberg, Hannover and Stassfurt, Saxony, Germany; Inowrocław salt dome, Poland. Asia: Inder, Kazakhstan; Khorat Plateau, Thailand.

Name From the boron in its composition.

Boracite, Sehnde, Lower Saxony, Germany • 1 x 1 x 1 cm

Kernite, Kern County, California, USA • 7 x 10 x 3.5 cm

Kernite

Formula $Na_2B_4O_6(OH)_2 \cdot 3H_2O$

Crystal System monoclinic

Space Group $P2_1/c$

Hardness 2.5

Specific Gravity 1.91

Cleavage {100} and {001} perfect; {$\overline{2}01$} fair

Fracture splintery

Tenacity flexible and elastic in cleavage fragments

Habit Colorless to white. Crystals nearly equant, commonly slightly elongated and deeply striated, with irregular form development, wedge-shaped at times or rounded because of repetition of faces; also as cleavable masses or massive. Vitreous luster, satiny on fibrous cleavages; transparent. White streak.

Environment An important ore mineral of borax, found in sedimentary borate deposits deposited under warm conditions or formed by metamorphism.

Notable Localities USA: Kramer borate deposit, Boron, California. Latin America: Tincalayu Mine, Salta, Argentina. Asia: Kirka borate deposit, Central Anatolia region, Turkey.

Name Named for one of the localities where it is found, Kern County, California.

Gerhardtite

Formula $Cu_2NO_3(OH)_3$
Crystal System orthorhombic
Space Group $P2_12_12_1$
Hardness 2.0
Specific Gravity 3.4
Cleavage {001} perfect; {100} good
Fracture none
Tenacity flexible

Habit Emerald green to dark green. Thick tabular crystals. Vitreous luster; transparent. Light green streak.

Environment A rare secondary mineral in oxidized portions of copper deposits.

Notable Localities USA: United Verde Mine, Jerome, and Daisy shaft, Mineral Hill Mine, Arizona. Europe: Roua copper mines, north of Nice, Alpes Maritimes, France. Africa: Likasi, Katanga (Shaba), Democratic Republic of the Congo (Zaire). Asia: Dzhezkazgan, Kazakhstan. Australia: Great Australia and Monakoff mines, near Cloncurry, Queensland.

Name Named in honor of Charles Frederic Gerhardt (1816–56), an American chemist who first prepared the artificial compound.

Gerhardtite, Copper Mountain distrinct, Greenlee County, Arizona, USA • 7 x 9 x 3 cm

Nitratine, Antofogasta, Chile • 9 x 12 x 4.5 cm

Nitratine

Formula $NaNO_3$
Crystal System hexagonal
Space Group $R\bar{3}c$
Hardness 1.5–2.0
Specific Gravity 2.25
Cleavage perfect on {10$\bar{1}$1}; imperfect on {01$\bar{1}$2} and {0001}
Fracture conchoidal
Tenacity sectile

Habit Colorless to white, tinged reddish brown or lemon yellow; gray with impurities. Rare as rhombohedral crystals; stalactitic, cotton-like, typically granular or in massive incrustations. Vitreous luster; transparent. White streak.

Environment Principally occurs in bedded deposits formed in playas or in caves, deposited by seeping groundwater leaching nitrates from overlying rocks, especially in very dry and cold climates.

Notable Localities USA: Death Valley and along the Armagosa River, California; Jornada del Muerto lava tubes, near Socorro, New Mexico; Aqua Fria Mountain, Texas. Latin America: Tarapacá district, Chile.

Name From the nitrogen in its composition.

CHAPTER 8

Sulfates, Chromates, Tungstates & Molybdates

Sulfates, chromates, tungstates and molybdates are grouped together because of their similar crystal structures and chemical behavior. Sulfate minerals contain the sulfate ion $(SO_4)^{2-}$, chromates have the chromate ion $(CrO_4)^{2-}$ and tungstates have the tungstate ion $(WO_4)^{2-}$. The sole molybdate in this section, wulfenite, contains the molybdate ion $(MoO_4)^{2-}$.

Sulfate minerals form in hydrothermal veins and as secondary minerals in sulfide deposits. About 200 sulfate minerals are known, but many are quite rare. Chromate and tungstate minerals are also rare, but when found in concentration they are important ores of the metals they contain.

ABOVE: Gypsum (selenite variety), Kingdon Mine, Galetta, Ontario, Canada • 12 x 13 x 5 cm

RIGHT: Wulfenite, Los Lamentos Mountains, Ahumada, Chihuahua, Mexico • 9 x 11 x 5 cm

LEFT: Crocoite, Dundas mineral field, Zeehan district, Tasmania, Australia • 2.5 x 5.5 x 6 cm

Glauberite, Lake Bumbunga, South Australia, Australia • 5 x 5 x 3 cm

Glauberite

Formula $Na_2Ca(SO_4)_2$

Crystal System monoclinic

Space Group $C2/c$

Hardness 2.5–3.0

Specific Gravity 2.78

Cleavage {001} perfect; {110} imperfect

Fracture conchoidal

Tenacity brittle

Habit Gray, yellowish or colorless. Prismatic, tabular or dipyramidal crystals. Vitreous, waxy or pearly luster; transparent to translucent. White streak.

Environment A common constituent of continental and marine evaporite deposits. Also occurs as sublimates around fumaroles, in mineral-filled cavities in basaltic lava and in nitrate deposits in arid climates.

Notable Localities Canada: Gypsumville, Manitoba. USA: Searles Lake, Borax Lake and Salton Sea, California; Great Salt Lake, Utah. Latin America: Taltal nitrate district, Antofagasta, Chile. Europe: Grillid volcanic cave, Surtsey Island, Iceland; Varangeville, near Nancy, Meurthe-et-Moselle, France; Villarrubia de Santiago, near Ocaña, Toledo, Spain; Douglashall, near Westeregeln, Saxony-Anhalt, Germany.

Name From its similarity in composition to Glauber's salt, which was named after Johann Rudolph Glauber (1603–68), a German alchemist.

Anhydrite

Formula $CaSO_4$

Crystal System orthorhombic

Space Group *Amma*

Hardness 3.0–3.5

Specific Gravity 2.98

Cleavage {010} perfect; {100} nearly perfect; {001} good to imperfect

Fracture irregular/uneven; splintery

Tenacity brittle

Habit Colorless to pale blue or violet if transparent; white, mauve, rose, pale brown or gray from included impurities. Crystals tabular or equant with large pinacoidal faces; typically granular, nodular, fibrous or massive. Pearly to vitreous luster; transparent to translucent. White streak.

Environment Commonly formed by dehydration of gypsum, occurring in sedimentary evaporite deposits and as caprock in salt domes, in igneous rocks, fumarolic deposits and seafloor hydrothermal chimneys. Also found as an alteration product in hydrothermal mineral deposits.

Notable Localities Canada: Faraday Mine, Bancroft, Ontario. USA: Carlsbad potash district, New Mexico; Boiling salt dome, Texas; Paterson, New Jersey; Fairfax Quarry, Centreville, Virginia. Latin America: Naica, Chihuahua, Mexico; Morococha, Peru. Europe: Hall, Tyrol, Ischl and Hallein, Salzburg, and Aussee, Styria, Austria; Simplon Tunnel, Valais, Switzerland; Campiano Mine, Boccheggiano district, Tuscany, and Mt. Vesuvius, Campania, Italy. Asia: Salt Range, Punjab, India; Mt. Pinatubo, Philippines.

Name From the Greek *anhydrous*, meaning "without water," in contrast to gypsum, which does contain water.

Anhydrite, Di Campiano Mine, Grosseto, Tuscany, Italy • 26 x 18 x 8.5 cm

Anglesite

Formula $PbSO_4$

Crystal System orthorhombic

Space Group *Pnma*

Hardness 2.5–3.0

Specific Gravity 6.36

Cleavage {001} good; {210} distinct; {010} less distinct

Fracture conchoidal

Tenacity brittle

Anglesite, Tsumeb, Namibia • 20.5 x 17 x 13.5 mm, 51.33 ct

Anglesite, North Broken Hill Mine, Broken Hill, New South Wales, Australia • 6 x 5 x 2.5 cm

Anglesite is a rare lead mineral. The typical high luster associated with lead minerals makes them beautiful gemstones, intensifying their "fire." Anglesite has a very high density but is quite soft and fragile, so it is not a good stone for jewelry. Found in lead deposits where the sulfide mineral galena is oxidized, it is also called lead spar.

Habit Colorless to white, commonly tinted gray; also orange, yellow, green, blue or rarely violet. Variable habit, with thin to thick tabular crystals, also equant or pyramidal and often striated; usually massive, granular to compact, often with concentric banding and enclosing an unaltered core of galena; may form epitaxial overgrowths on galena or barite (baryte). Adamantine, resinous to vitreous luster; transparent to opaque. White streak.

Environment Common in the oxidized zone of lead deposits, where it may constitute an important ore.

Notable Localities USA: Grand Reef Mine, Arizona; Wheatley Mine, Phoenixville, Pennsylvania; Bunker Hill Mine, Coeur d'Alene district, Hypotheek Mine, south of Kingston, and Last Chance and Tyler mines, Wardner, Idaho. Latin America: Los Lamentos, Chihuahua, Mexico. Europe: Leadhills, Lanarkshire, and Wanlockhead, Dumfries and Galloway, Scotland; Matlock and Cromford, Derbyshire, and Caldbeck Fells, Cumbria, England; Müsen, Littlefeld, Siegen and other places in Siegerland, Germany. Africa: Souss-Massa-Draâ, Morocco. Australia: Broken Hill, New South Wales; Dundas, Tasmania.

Name From its occurrence on the island of Anglesey, in Wales.

Celestine

Formula SrSO$_4$

Crystal System orthorhombic

Space Group *Pnma*

Hardness 3.0–3.5

Specific Gravity 3.97

Cleavage {001} perfect; {210} good; {010} poor

Fracture uneven

Tenacity brittle

Habit Colorless, white, pale blue, pink, pale green, pale brown or black. Well-formed crystals common, typically thin to thick tabular, lathlike or with equant cross-sections, or pyramidal; also fibrous, lamellar, earthy or massive granular forms. Vitreous luster, pearly on cleavages; transparent to translucent. White streak.

Environment The most common strontium mineral. Of primary sedimentary origin, precipitated by migrating strontium-bearing groundwater or basinal brines in carbonate rocks, concretions and nodules. Also occurs in hydrothermal veins and mafic volcanic rocks.

Notable Localities Canada: Dundas, Ontario. USA: Adamsville, Texas; Scofield Quarry, Maybee, Michigan; Cave-in-Rock, Illinois; Crystal Cave, Put-in Bay, South Bass Island, and Clay Center, Ohio; Bellwood, Pennsylvania. Latin America: near Matehuala, San Luis Potosí, and Muzquiz and Ramos Arizpe, Coahuila, Mexico. Europe: Bamle, Norway; Yate, near Bristol, England; Konrad Mine, near Salzgitter, Lower Saxony, Germany; Girgenti (Agrigento), Caltanissetta and elsewhere in Sicily, Italy. Africa: Jebel Mokattam, near Cairo, Egypt; Sakoany, near Mahajanga (Majunga), Madagascar.

Name From the Latin *caelestis*, meaning "celestial," in allusion to its typical bluish color.

Celestine, Dundas Quarry, near Hamilton, Ontario, Canada • 8 x 9.5 x 5 cm

Celestine geodes up to 11 meters (35 ft.) in diameter formed near the village of Put-in-Bay, Ohio, USA. The geode crystals can be as wide as 46 cm (18 in.) across and are estimated to weigh 135 kg (300 lb.) each. The geode cave was exposed when workers were digging a well for a winery.

Celestine, Madagascar • 15 x 14.5 x 11.4 mm, 21.00 ct

Chalcanthite, Planet Mine, La Paz County, Arizona, USA • 6 x 4 x 7 cm

Chalcanthite

Formula $CuSO_4 \cdot 5H_2O$

Crystal System triclinic

Space Group $P\bar{1}$

Hardness 2.5

Specific Gravity 2.29

Cleavage perfect on $\{1\bar{1}0\}$; interrupted on $\{110\}$

Fracture conchoidal

Tenacity brittle

Habit Dark blue to sky blue or greenish blue. Uncommonly short prismatic to thick tabular crystals; commonly stalactitic to reniform crusts, cross-vein fibrous, massive or granular. Vitreous to resinous luster; translucent. White streak.

Environment A secondary mineral in the oxidized portions of copper sulfide deposits, commonly of post-mining formation; found rarely as a fumarolic deposit.

Notable Localities USA: Bluestone Mine, Yerington district, Nevada; United Verde Mine and Clifton-Morenci district, Arizona; Bluebird Mine, Fierro-Hanover district, New Mexico. Latin America: Chuquicamata, Quetena, near Calama, and Copaquire, Antofagasta, Chile. Europe: Rio Tinto, Huelva, Spain; Mt. Vesuvius, Campania, Italy; Rammelsberg and Goslar, Harz Mountains, Germany.

Name From *chalcanthum*, its old Latin name, which means "flowers of copper."

Chalcanthite is used as an ore of copper.

Brochantite

Formula $Cu_4SO_4(OH)_6$

Crystal System monoclinic

Space Group $P2_1/a$

Hardness 3.5–4.0

Specific Gravity 3.97

Cleavage {100} perfect

Fracture uneven to conchoidal

Habit Green, emerald green, greenish black or light green. Crystals stout prismatic to acicular, also tabular; loosely coherent aggregates of acicular crystals, groups and drusy crusts, massive or granular. Vitreous luster, somewhat pearly on cleavages; transparent to translucent. Pale green streak.

Environment Common in the oxidized zone of copper deposits. Forms in conditions of low acidity, principally in arid regions.

Notable Localities USA: Mammoth–St. Anthony Mine, Arizona; Tintic district, Utah. Latin America: Chuquicamata and Atacama Desert region, Chile. Europe: Roughten Gill, Cumberland, England; Rio Tinto, Huelva, Spain; Hesse-Nassau, Germany; Rosas, Sardinia, Italy. Africa: Aïn Barbar, Constantine, Algeria; Tsumeb, Namibia. Asia: Gumeshevsk, near Yekaterinburg (Sverdlosk), Ural Mountains, Russia. Australia: Broken Hill, New South Wales.

Name Named for A.J.M. Brochant de Villiers (1772–1840), a French geologist and mineralogist.

Brochantite, Bisbee, Arizona, USA • 14 x 10 x 6 cm

Gypsum

Formula $CaSO_4 \cdot 2H_2O$

Crystal System monoclinic

Space Group *C2/c*

Hardness 2.0

Specific Gravity 2.3

Cleavage {010} perfect; {100} distinct

Fracture splintery

Tenacity flexible

ABOVE: Gypsum (selenite variety), Portman, Murcia, Spain • 14 x 11 x 5 cm
RIGHT: Gypsum (selenite variety), Santa Eulalia, Chihuahua, Mexico • 10.5 x 10.5 x 7.5 cm

Gypsum (selenite variety), Australia • 6 x 10 x 3 cm

Habit Colorless or white; yellow, tan, blue, pink, brown, reddish brown, gray or black if colored by impurities. Acicular to stubby prismatic or thin to thick tabular crystals, coarsely striated, also lenticular in rosettes and may be curved or bent; may be fibrous, earthy, concretionary, granular or massive. Subvitreous, pearly luster, silky if fibrous; transparent, translucent or opaque. White streak.

Environment As the most prevalent sulfate mineral, a common constituent of sedimentary rocks, occurring in marine evaporites, caves where the air is dry enough to allow it to be deposited and remain, and fumaroles. Also occurs sometimes in oxidized zones of sulfide deposits through evaporation or by later hydration of anhydrite.

Notable Localities Canada: Red River floodway and Gypsumville, Manitoba. USA: South Wash, Utah; Great Salt Plains, Oklahoma; exceptional speleothems in Lechuguilla Cave, Carlsbad Caverns National Park, New Mexico. Latin America: huge crystals in cave complexes in Naica lead/silver mine and in San Antonio Mine, Santa Eulalia, Chihuahua, Mexico; El Teniente Mine, west of Rancagua, O'Higgins, Chile. Europe: Montmartre district, Paris, France; Zaragoza, Spain; Eisleben-Mansfeld-Sangershausen district, Saxony-Anhalt, and near Königslutter, Lower Saxony, Germany; Bex, Valais, Switzerland; Aussee, Styria, and Hall, Tyrol, Austria.

Name Named in antiquity from the Greek *gypsos*, meaning "plaster."

White Sands National Monument is located in the United States, in the southern part of New Mexico. Here, great wavelike dunes of gypsum sand have engulfed 275 square miles (710 sq km) of desert, creating the world's largest gypsum dune field. Gypsum is rarely found in the form of sand because it is water soluble. Normally rain would dissolve this mineral and it would be carried to the sea, but in this geological basin there is no outlet to the sea, so the gypsum is trapped. The sand is very cool to the touch, even on the hottest of days.

Gypsum is used in gypsum board, more commonly known as drywall, and in plaster of Paris, which is used for surgical casts and by artists for modeling. It is also a component in foot creams, shampoos and many other hair products.

Epsomite, Stassfurt, Saxony, Germany • 3 x 2.5 x 2.5 cm

Epsomite

Formula $MgSO_4 \cdot 7H_2O$

Crystal System orthorhombic

Space Group $P2_12_12_1$

Hardness 2.0–2.5

Specific Gravity 1.68

Cleavage {010} perfect; {101} distinct

Fracture conchoidal

Tenacity brittle

Habit Colorless or white; also pink or green. Crystals rare; usually fibrous to acicular crusts, elongated botryoidal masses or stalactitic. Vitreous luster, but also silky or earthy; transparent to translucent. White streak.

Environment Found as efflorescence or crusts on the walls of mines, caves and outcrops of sulfide-bearing magnesian rocks or as a product of evaporation at mineral springs and saline lakes; rarely occurs as a fumarolic sublimate.

Notable Localities Canada: Claytonia Mine, Ashcroft, British Columbia; Dundas Quarry, near Hamilton, Ontario. USA: Mt. Princeton Hot Springs, Chalk Creek, Colorado; Mammoth Cave, Kentucky. Europe: Epsom, Surrey, England; Mt. Vesuvius, Campania, Italy; Sedlitz and Saidschitz, Czech Republic. Asia: Kamchatka Peninsula, Russia.

Name From its occurrence at Epsom, in England.

Epsomite is the same as common household Epsom salts, which are traditionally used for muscle-soothing baths and as a component of bath products.

Barite (Baryte)

Formula $BaSO_4$

Crystal System orthorhombic

Space Group *Pnma*

Hardness 2.5–3.5

Specific Gravity 4.5

Cleavage {001} perfect; {210} less perfect; {010} imperfect

Fracture uneven

Tenacity brittle

Habit Colorless or white; also brown, yellow, gray, reddish or blue. Often aggregates of tabular crystals with projecting crests or forming rosettes; also massive, compact, concretionary, fibrous, stalactitic, earthy or laminated. Vitreous to pearly luster; transparent to translucent. White streak.

Environment A common accessory mineral in lead and zinc low-temperature hydrothermal veins. Also occurs in residual deposits from weathered barite-bearing limestones, as an accessory mineral in igneous rocks, in carbonatites, and as a primary component of submarine volcanogenic massive sulfide deposits.

Notable Localities Canada: Rock Candy Mine, British Columbia. United States: Miekle Mine, Elko County, Nevada; Elk Creek, South Dakota; Norman, Oklahoma; Cheshire, Connecticut. Latin America: El Solar Mine, Taxco, Guerrero, Mexico. Europe: Alston Moor, Frizington, Cleator Moor and elsewhere in Cumbria, England; Beihilfe Mine, near Freiberg, and Pöhla Mine, Schwarzenberg, Saxony, Germany; Příbram, Czech Republic. Africa: Elandsrand gold mine, Carletonville, South Africa.

Name From the Greek word for "weight," referring to its high specific gravity.

Barite, Rock Candy Mine, Grand Forks, British Columbia, Canada • 10.5 x 8 x 8 cm

Cyanotrichite, Peacock Mine, Lemhi County, Idaho, USA • 8 x 4.5 x 3 cm

Cyanotrichite

Formula $Cu_4Al_2SO_4(OH)_{12}\cdot2H_2O$

Crystal System orthorhombic

Space Group undetermined

Hardness 1.0–3.0

Specific Gravity 2.76

Cleavage good

Fracture uneven

Tenacity undetermined

Habit Sky blue to azure blue. Velvet-, wool- or cotton-like aggregates and coatings composed of minute acicular crystals; also radial-fibrous or tufted. Silky luster; transparent to translucent. Pale blue streak.

Environment A secondary copper mineral found sparsely in the oxidation zones of copper-bearing ore bodies.

Notable Localities Canada: Eastern Metals Mine, Quebec. USA: Grandview (Last Chance) Mine, Grand Canyon National Park, Maid of Sunshine Mine, Courtland, and Bisbee, Morenci and Jerome, Arizona. Latin America: Mina la Vieja, near Potrerillos, Atacama, Chile. England: Wheal Gorland, St. Day; Phoenix United Mine, Linkinhorne; Lanivet and elsewhere — all in Cornwall; Old Potts Gill Mine, Caldbeck Fells, Cumbria. Europe: Sa Duchessa Mine, Sardinia, Italy; Laurium, Greece. Africa: Springbok Mine, Namaqualand, South Africa. Asia: Mednorudyanskoye copper deposit, near Nizhni Tagil, Ural Mountains, Russia.

Name From the Greek words for "blue" and for "hair," in allusion to its color and habit.

Sturmanite

Formula $Ca_6Fe^{3+}_2(SO_4)_{2.5}[B(OH)_4](OH)_{12}\cdot25H_2O$

Crystal System hexagonal

Space Group $P31c$

Hardness 2.5

Specific Gravity 1.85

Cleavage perfect on $\{10\bar{1}0\}$

Fracture uneven

Tenacity brittle

Habit Bright yellow to amber. Dipyramidal tabular to elongated hexagonal crystals; may be stacked in parallel aggregates. Greasy luster on fracture faces; transparent to translucent. Yellow white streak.

Environment An uncommon secondary mineral in cavities in metamorphosed bedded manganese deposits.

Notable Localities Africa: Kuruman district, with large crystals in the Wessels and N'Chwaning II mines, Northern Cape, South Africa.

Name Named for B. Darko Sturman (b. 1937), a mineralogist at the Royal Ontario Museum, Toronto.

Sturmanite, N'Chwaning Mine, Kuraman, Northern Cape, South Africa • 3.5 x 3.5 x 3 cm

Linarite

Formula $PbCuSO_4(OH)_2$

Crystal System monoclinic

Space Group $P2_1/m$

Hardness 2.5

Specific Gravity 5.35

Cleavage {100} perfect; {001} interrupted

Fracture conchoidal

Habit Bright to dark azure blue. Crystals elongated, typically tabular; crusts and aggregates. Vitreous to subadamantine luster; transparent to translucent. Light blue streak.

Environment An uncommon secondary mineral in the oxidized zone of lead/copper deposits.

Notable Localities USA: Blue Bell Claims, near Baker, California; Mammoth–St. Anthony Mine, Tiger, and Grand Reef Mine, Santa Teresa Mountains, Arizona; Blanchard and Mex-Tex mines, near Bingham, New Mexico; Tintic district, Utah. Europe: Leadhills, Lanarkshire, Scotland; Red Gill and other mines, Caldbeck Fells, Cumbria, England; Linares, Jaén, Spain; Arenas and San Giovanni, Sardinia, Italy. Africa: Tsumeb, Namibia.

Name From its occurrence at Linares, in Spain.

Linarite, Grand Reef Mine, Graham County, Arizona, USA • 3 x 5 x 2 cm

Crocoite, Dundas, Tasmania, Australia • 18 x 16 x 14 cm

Crocoite

Formula $PbCrO_4$

Crystal System monoclinic

Space Group $P2_1/n$

Hardness 2.5–3.0

Specific Gravity 6.0

Cleavage distinct on {110}; indistinct on {001} and {100}

Fracture small conchoidal to uneven

Tenacity sectile

Habit Orange red to yellow. Prismatic to acicular crystals with nearly square outline, elongated and striated, or short prismatic to pseudo-octahedral; may be highly modified, with terminations commonly hollow or incomplete; typically radial sprays to randomly intergrown aggregates. Adamantine to vitreous luster; transparent to translucent. Yellowish orange streak.

Environment A secondary mineral found in the oxidized zone of lead deposits, especially those associated with ultrabasic rocks.

Notable Localities USA: mines at Darwin, California; south of Wickenburg, Arizona. Latin America: Goyabeira, Congonhas do Campo, Minas Gerais, Brazil. Europe: Greystone Quarry, Lezant, Cornwall, England; Cantonniers Mine, Nontron, Dordogne, France. Africa: Old West and Proprietary mines, Penhalonga, Zimbabwe. Asia: Beresov, Yekaterinburg (Sverdlosk), Ural Mountains, Russia. Australia: Dundas district, Tasmania.

Name From the Greek word for saffron, an allusion to its distinctive red-orange color.

Hübnerite

Formula $MnWO_4$

Crystal System monoclinic

Space Group $P2/c$

Hardness 4.0–4.5

Specific Gravity 7.12

Cleavage perfect on {010}; partings on {100} and {102}

Fracture uneven

Tenacity brittle

Habit Yellowish to reddish brown, blackish brown or black; rarely red. Crystals typically prismatic and striated, also tabular to bladed; in radiating groups and in parallel. Adamantine, resinous or metallic luster; transparent to translucent. Reddish brown streak.

Environment Occurs in high-temperature hydrothermal veins and pneumatolytically altered granites yielding greisen, in granite pegmatites and in alluvial and eluvial deposits.

Notable Localities Canada: Brandywine Creek, British Columbia. USA: Ellsworth (Mammoth) and Manhattan districts, Nevada; Little Dragoon Mountains, Arizona; Nogal and White Oaks districts, New Mexico; Blue Wing district, Idaho. Latin America: Pasto Bueno Mine, Ancash, Peru. Europe: Wheal Gorland, Gwennap, and Hingston Down Quarry, Cornwall, England; Valcroze, Lozère, and Adervielle, Hautes-Pyrénées, France; Baia Sprie (Felsőbánya), Romania. Asia: Duoluoshan Mine, Huaiji, Guangdong, China.

Name Named in honor of Adolph Hübner, a mining engineer and metallurgist of Freiberg, Germany.

Hübnerite, Pasto Bueno, Ancash, Peru • 10.5 x 4 x 1 cm

Ferberite, Panasqueira Mines, Castelo Branco district, Fundão, Portugal • 10 x 9 x 6.5 cm

Ferberite

Formula $Fe^{2+}WO_4$

Crystal System monoclinic

Space Group $P2/c$

Hardness 4.0–4.5

Specific Gravity 7.58

Cleavage {010} perfect; partings on {100} and {102}

Fracture uneven

Tenacity brittle

Habit Black. Wedge-shaped crystals, typically flattened and elongated, with faces striated; occurs in groups of bladed crystals or massive. Submetallic to metallic adamantine luster; nearly to entirely opaque. Brownish black streak.

Environment Found in greisen or quartz-rich veins and pegmatites immediately associated with granitic intrusive rocks. Occurs in high-temperature hydrothermal veins, greisens and granitic pegmatites as well as in alluvial and eluvial deposits.

Notable Localities Canada: Mayo mining district, Yukon. USA: Elizabethtown district, New Mexico; Boulder County tungsten district, Colorado; Corral Creek, near Soldier Mountain, Idaho. Latin America: Mundo Nuevo and Junin, Peru. Europe: Panasqueira Mines, Castelo Branco district, Portugal.

Name Named in honor of Moritz Rudolph Ferber (1805–75), a factory owner and amateur mineralogist in Gera, Germany.

Wulfenite

Formula $PbMoO_4$

Crystal System tetragonal

Space Group $I4_1/a$

Hardness 2.8–3.0

Specific Gravity 6.7–7.0

Cleavage {011} distinct; {001} and {013} indistinct

Fracture subconchoidal to uneven

Tenacity not very brittle

Wulfenite, Glove Mine, Amado, Arizona, USA • 9 x 7.5 x 6.5 cm

The US state of Arizona is a noted locality for wulfenite. At the Red Cloud Mine, in the silver district north of Yuma, wulfenite crystals form bright red chunky blades. Butterscotch-colored bladed crystals come from the Glove Mine, in the Santa Rita Mountains south of Tucson. These prized mineral specimens occur in a district famous for its lead-zinc-silver deposits.

Habit Bright yellow, wax yellow, yellow orange, bright orange, red orange or bright red; also gray, grayish white, rarely white or colorless, green, pale to dark blue, reddish brown, brown or black. Crystals commonly square and flat tabular but may be elongated or pyramidal; can be granular or massive. Subadamantine to greasy luster; transparent to opaque. Yellowish white streak.

Environment A secondary mineral found in the oxidized zone of deposits of lead- and molybdenum-containing minerals.

Notable Localities USA: Red Cloud and nearby mines, Silver district; Old Yuma Mine, near Tucson; Mammoth–St. Anthony Mine, Tiger; large crystals from Glove Mine, near Amado, Tyndall district; Hilltop Mine, Chiricahua Mountains; Defiance Mine, Gleeson — all in Arizona. Mexico: San Francisco Mine, Cerro Prieta, Magdalena, Sonora; Los Lamentos and Santa Eulalia, Chihuahua; Ojuela Mine, Mapimí, Durango. Europe: Bleiberg, Carinthia, Austria; Mežica (Mies) and Črna pri Prevaljah (Schwartzenbach), Slovenia. Africa: Tsumeb, Namibia. Asia: Sidjak, Uzbekistan. Australia: Christmas Mine, Chillagoe, Queensland.

Name Named after Franz Xavier Wulfen (1728–1805), an Austro-Hungarian Jesuit and mineralogist.

ABOVE: Wulfenite, Tsumeb, Namibia • 5 x 6 x 2 cm
RIGHT: Wulfenite, Defiance Mine, Gleeson, Arizona, USA • 12 x 14 x 12 cm

CHAPTER 9
Tectosilicates

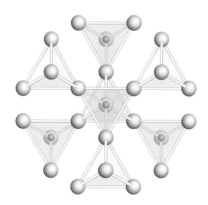

Tectosilicates form the largest mineral group, comprising nearly 75 percent of the crust of Earth. The basic motif of their structure is an SiO_4 tetrahedron, which is linked to other SiO_4 tetrahedra to form a network in three dimensions. The silicate tetrahedron has a pyramidal shape, with silicon (Si) in the center and four larger, negatively charged oxygen anions at the corners. Tectosilicates are also known as "framework silicates," and the chemical formula shows a ratio of two oxygen atoms for each silicon atom (SiO_2). The most familiar examples in this important family are quartz and the feldspar and zeolite groups. Quartz, the most common mineral in Earth's crust, is found in a wide range of varieties and shapes.

ABOVE: Relief-carved head (eastern Siberia, Russia), lazurite • 3.7 x 2.3 x 0.4 cm, 25.10 ct

RIGHT: Massive sodalite, Namibia • 20 x 18 x 14 cm

LEFT: Quartz (amethyst variety), Artigas, Uruguay • 7 x 6 x 1 cm

Quartz and Agate

Formula SiO$_2$

Crystal System hexagonal

Space Group $P3_121$

Hardness 7.0

Specific Gravity 2.66

Cleavage rarely observable

Fracture conchoidal

Tenacity brittle; tough when massive

Habit Colorless, white, rose pink to rose red, yellow to yellowish brown, green, blue, bluish violet or brown to black. Typically long prismatic crystals with steep pyramidal terminations, but may be short prismatic to nearly bipyramidal; fibrous for agate and chalcedony. Vitreous luster, but waxy to dull when massive; transparent to nearly opaque. White streak.

Environment The most common mineral found on Earth's surface and a significant component of many igneous, metamorphic and sedimentary rocks.

Notable Localities Quartz Canada: Thunder Bay area, Ontario. USA: Pala and Mesa Grande districts, California; Mt. Ida to Hot Springs, Ouachita Mountains, Arkansas; Ellenville, Middleville and Reel Mine, Iron Station, New York; Hiddenite, North Carolina. Latin America: Veracruz and Guerrero, Mexico; Rio Grande do Sul, Minas Gerais, Goiás, and Bahia, Brazil; around Artigas, Uruguay. Asia: Mursinka, Ural Mountains, Russia; Yamanashi and many other places in Japan. **Agate** Latin America: Chihuahua and Aguascalientes, Mexico; Minas Gerais, Brazil. Europe: Haut-Rhin, Alsace, France; Idar-Oberstein, Rhineland-Palatinate, Germany; Terlano Mine, Trentino–Alto Adige, Italy; Beroun (Beraun), Bohemia, Czech Republic.

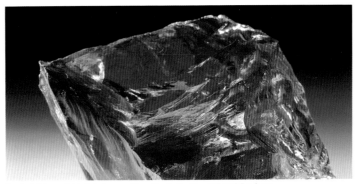

Quartz (citrine variety), Sete Lagoas, Minas Gerais, Brazil • 11.5 x 10.5 x 8 cm

ABOVE: Quartz (rock crystal variety), Madagascar • 17 x 14 x 7 cm
RIGHT: Quartz (agate variety), Brazil • 36 x 47 x 1 cm

Name Of obscure origin in the Middle Ages, the name *quartz* was first applied to gangue, or waste rock, in Saxony (now part of Germany). Agate, which is a form of microcrystalline quartz — chiefly chalcedony — was named by Theophrastus, a Greek philosopher and naturalist, who discovered the stone along the shoreline of the river Achates (now called Dirillo) in Sicily.

Agate is a common type of chalcedony, which is a compact, microcrystalline variety of quartz. Much of the sliced agate on the market today, particularly the brightly colored examples, has been dyed or stained to enhance its natural color.

Quartz, one of the most ubiquitous minerals on Earth's surface, formed in almost every geological environment and in a huge variety of shapes, sizes and colors. The most common color varieties of quartz are amethyst (purple), citrine (yellow), rose quartz (pink) and smoky quartz (brown to smoky gray to black).

Nepheline

Formula $(Na,K)AlSiO_4$

Crystal System hexagonal

Space Group $P6_3$

Hardness 5.5–6.0

Specific Gravity 2.66

Cleavage poor on $\{10\bar{1}0\}$ and $\{0001\}$

Fracture subconchoidal

Tenacity brittle

Habit Typically colorless, white, gray or yellow, but can be many colors. Stout six- or twelve-sided prisms, typically poorly formed; also granular, compact or massive. Vitreous to greasy luster; transparent to nearly opaque, from inclusions or alteration. White streak.

Environment Characteristic of alkalic rocks as nepheline syenites and gneisses and alkalic gabbros. Also occurs in sodium-rich hypabyssal rocks, tuffs and lavas and pegmatites and as a product of sodium metasomatism.

Notable Localities Canada: Bancroft district, Ontario; Mont-Saint-Hilaire, Quebec. USA: Iron Hill, Colorado; Granite Mountain, near Little Rock, Arkansas. Europe: Tunugdliarfik Fjord and Kangerdlugssuag Plateau, in the Ilímaussaq complex, Kitaa (West Greenland), Greenland; Lovozero Massif, Kola Peninsula, Russia; Monte Somma, Campania, Italy. Asia: Ilmen Mountains, southern Urals, Russia.

Name From the Greek word for "cloud," because it becomes cloudy when treated with strong acid.

Nepheline and schorlomite, Bou Agrao, High Atlas Mountains, Morocco • 5 x 3 x 3 cm

Leucite, Ariccia, Latium (Lazio), Italy • 25 x 24 x 21 cm

Leucite

Formula $KAlSi_2O_6$

Crystal System tetragonal

Space Group $I4_1/a$

Hardness 5.5–6.0

Specific Gravity 2.46

Cleavage very poor on $\{110\}$

Fracture conchoidal

Tenacity brittle

Habit White to gray. Commonly euhedral pseudo-cubic crystals, typically showing fine twin striae; also as disseminated grains, rarely granular, or massive. Vitreous luster; transparent to translucent. White streak.

Environment Occurs in potassium-rich mafic and ultramafic lavas and hypabyssal rocks.

Notable Localities USA: Bear Paw Mountains, Montana; Leucite Hills, Wyoming; Magnet Cove, Arkansas. Europe: Kitaa (West Greenland), Greenland; Lapanouse-de-Sévérac, Midi-Pyrénées, France; around the Laacher See, Eifel district, Germany; Monte Somma, Campania, Italy. Africa: Mt. Kilimanjaro, Tanzania. Asia: Borra, Andhra Pradesh, India.

Name From the Greek *leucos*, meaning "white," in allusion to its color.

Sodalite

Formula $Na_8Al_6Si_6O_{24}Cl_2$

Crystal System cubic

Space Group $P\bar{4}3n$

Hardness 5.5–6.0

Specific Gravity 2.31

Cleavage {110} poor

Fracture uneven to conchoidal

Tenacity brittle

Habit Colorless, white, yellow, green, various shades of blue or reddish. Crystals rare; typically massive. Vitreous to greasy luster; transparent to translucent. White streak.

Environment Found in nepheline syenites, phonolites, volcanic ejecta and metasomatized calcareous rocks.

Notable Localities Canada: Bancroft, Ontario; Mont-Saint-Hilaire, Quebec. USA: Bauxite Mines, Bauxite, and Magnet Cove, Arkansas; Cuttingsville, Vermont. Europe: Traprain Law, East Lothian, Scotland; Playa Blanca, Canary Islands, Spain. Africa: Western Bushveld complex, North West Province, South Africa.

Name Named for its sodium content.

Sodalite, Princess Quarry, Bancroft, Ontario, Canada • 22 x 20 x 7 cm

Haüyne, Niedermendig, Rhineland-Palatinate, Germany • 7 x 6 x 5 cm (entire sample)

Haüyne

Formula $(Na,Ca)_{4-8}Al_6Si_6(O,S)_{24}(SO_4,Cl)_{1-2}$

Crystal System cubic

Space Group $P\bar{4}3n$

Hardness 5.5–6.0

Specific Gravity 2.44–2.5

Cleavage {110} distinct

Fracture uneven to conchoidal

Tenacity brittle

Habit Bright blue to greenish blue, white or shades of black, gray, brown, green, yellow or red; may be patchy. Crystals dodecahedra or pseudo-octahedra; also rounded grains. Vitreous to greasy luster; transparent to translucent. Bluish white streak.

Environment Occurs in phonolites and related leucite- or nepheline-rich igneous rocks, and less commonly in nepheline-free extrusives.

Notable Localities Canada: Kimmirut (Lake Harbour), Baffin Island, Nunavut; Oka complex, Laurentides, Quebec. USA: Winnett, Montana; Edwards Mine, New York. Europe: Michels Quarry, Mendig, Rhineland-Palatinate, Mayen and elsewhere in the Eifel district, Germany; Lake Nemi, Latium, Italy. Asia: Niangniang Shan complex, Nanjing, Jiangsu, China. Pacific Ocean: Taiarupu, Tahiti.

Name Named in honor of Abbé René Just Haüy (1743–1822), a French crystallographer and mineralogist.

Plagioclase Series Feldspars

Formula $NaAlSi_3O_8$ to $CaAl_2Si_2O_8$

Crystal System triclinic

Space Group $C\overline{1}$

Hardness 6.0–6.5

Specific Gravity 2.6

Cleavage perfect on {001}; very good on {010}; imperfect on {110}

Fracture irregular/uneven, conchoidal

Tenacity brittle

Habit White to gray, bluish, green or red. Crystals common, can be tabular; also as aggregates, granular or massive. Vitreous luster, pearly on cleavages; transparent to translucent. White streak.

Labradorite, Ylämaa, Etelä-Suomen, Finland • 6 x 5 x 1 cm

ABOVE: Albite (cleavlandite variety), Rutherford Mine No. 2, Amelia, Virginia, USA • 18.5 x 15.5 x 11 cm

LEFT: Labradorite, Newfoundland and Labrador, Canada • 25 x 17 x 1 cm

The calcic middle-range member of the plagioclase feldspars is called labradorite. It was first described from the region around Nain, in Labrador, Canada, where it forms very large grains in the gabbros and anorthosites. It is most well-known for its blue and green play of colors, which is a result of light refracting within its lamellar intergrowths.

Environment A major constituent of granites and granite pegmatites, alkalic diorites and basalts; also found in hydrothermal and alpine veins. A product of potassium metasomatism, and also occurs in low-temperature and low-pressure metamorphic facies and some schists.

Notable Localities Albite Canada: Timmins, Ontario; Abitibi-Témiscamingue, Quebec; Stanley, New Brunswick. USA: Prince of Wales Island, Alaska; Pala and Mesa Grande districts, California. Latin America: Virgem da Lapa and Morro Velho, Minas Gerais, Brazil. Asia: Mursinka, Ural Mountains, and Miass, Ilmen Mountains (southern Urals), Russia. **Anorthite** Canada: Amitok Island, Labrador, Newfoundland and Labrador. USA: Great Sitkin Island, Aleutian Islands, Alaska; Grass Valley, California. Italy: Monte Somma and Mt. Vesuvius, Campania; Mt. Monzoni, Val di Fassa, Trentino–Alto Adige; Cyclopean Islands. Asia: Bogoslovsk and Barsowka, Ural Mountains, Russia.

Name *Albite* is from the Latin *albus*, meaning "white," for its characteristic color. *Anorthite* comes from the Greek for "not a right angle" or "oblique," in allusion to the oblique triclinic form of its crystals.

The plagioclase feldspars all contain a certain percentage of anorthite, indicated in parentheses in the following list. They form a series from albite, $NaAlSi_3O_8$ (0–10%), to anorthite, $CaAl_2Si_2O_8$ (90–100%). The minerals oligoclase (10–30%), andesine (30–50%), labradorite (50–70%) and bytownite (70–90%) make up the rest of the series.

Alkali Feldspars

Formula $(Na,K)(AlSi_3)O_8$

Crystal System monoclinic and triclinic

Space Group $C2/m$ and $C\bar{1}$

Hardness 6.0–6.5

Specific Gravity 2.5–2.6

Cleavage perfect on {001} and {010}

Fracture conchoidal to uneven

Tenacity brittle

Habit Colorless, white, gray, pale yellow, pink or green. Crystals commonly short, prismatic and tabular; also cleavable, granular or massive. Vitreous luster, but pearly on cleavages; transparent to translucent. White streak.

Environment The common feldspar of granites, granite pegmatites and syenites. Found in cavities in basalts, in high-grade metamorphic rocks and as a result of potassic hydrothermal alteration.

ABOVE: Microcline, Bedford, Ontario, Canada • 40 x 20 x 45 cm
RIGHT: Microcline and smoky quartz, Mt. Malosa, Zomba, Malawi • 7 x 6 x 4 cm

Notable Localities Orthoclase Canada: Rock Candy Mine, British Columbia. USA: Somerset, California; Granite Mountain complex, Sweet Home, Arkansas. Europe: Ticino (Tessin) and Wallis (Valais), Switzerland. Africa: Ampandrandava, Fianarantsoa and Itrongay, near Betroka, Madagascar. Asia: Tanokamiyama, Shiga, Japan. **Sanidine** Canada: Tanco Mine, Bernic Lake, Manitoba; Mont-Saint-Hilaire, Quebec. USA: Cottonwood Canyon, Peloncillo Mountains, Arizona. Europe: Mt. Dore, Auvergne, and Puy Gros du Laney, Puy-de-Dôme, France; Mt. Vesuvius and Monte Somma, Campania, and Monte Cimine, Lazio, Italy. Asia: Kanchin-do, Meisem-gun, Korea. **Anorthoclase** USA: Boron, California. Europe: Pantelleria and Ustica islands, Italy. Australia: Mt. Anakie and Mt. Franklin, Daylesford, Victoria. Antarctica: Mt. Erebus, Ross Island. **Microcline** USA: Pikes Peak area, Crystal Peak, and large crystals from Devil's Hole beryl mine, Colorado. Latin America: Fazenda do Bananal, Salinas, Urucum and Capelinha, Minas Gerais, Brazil. Europe: Mt. Greiner, Zillertal, Tyrol, Austria; St. Gotthard, Ticino, Switzerland.

Name *Orthoclase* comes from the Greek *orthos*, meaning "right," and *kalo*, meaning "I cleave," in allusion to the mineral's right angle of good cleavage. *Sanidine* is from the Greek word for "tablet" or "board," a reference to its common habit. *Anorthoclase* derives from the Greek for "oblique" and "fracture," descriptive of the mineral's cleavage. *Microcline* is from the Greek words for "little" and "inclined," for its small deviation from monoclinic symmetry.

Used in ceramics and as a mild abrasive, microcline is the most common feldspar mineral. Orthoclase is a major component of granite; its pink crystals give the rock its characteristic color.

Hyalophane, Busovača, Bosnia and Herzegovina • 13 x 13 x 7 cm. Hyalophane is an intermediate member of the alkali feldspars group.

Chabazite Group

Formula chabazite-(Ca) $Ca(Si_4Al_2)O_{12}\cdot 6H_2O$

Crystal System $P\bar{1}$

Space Group triclinic

Hardness 4.0–5.0

Specific Gravity 2.05

Cleavage $\{10\bar{1}1\}$ distinct

Fracture uneven

Tenacity brittle

Chabazite-(Ca), Wasson's Bluff, Cumberland County, Nova Scotia, Canada • 6 x 4.5 x 3.5 cm

Chabazite-(Ca), Cape d'Or, Bay of Fundy, Nova Scotia, Canada • 19.5 x 16 x 5 cm

The chabazite group is part of a larger group of minerals called zeolites. In zeolites large ions and molecules reside in and actually move around inside the overall crystal structure framework. They readily take up and release water and readily exchange sodium for calcium, and vice versa. This characteristic makes zeolites such as the minerals in the chabazite group useful as drying agents and water softeners.

Habit White, yellow, pink, red or colorless. Pseudo-rhombohedral crystals, nearly cubic in aspect; tabular, complex to rounded twinned forms; also anhedral, granular or massive. Vitreous luster; transparent to translucent. White streak.

Environment Occurs in volcanic rocks as basalts and in andesite; more rarely in limestones and schists or as hydrothermal deposits in cavities and joints in ore veins. Also found in bedded tuffs in lake deposits, altered from volcanic glass.

Notable Localities Canada: Chaudière-Appalaches, Québec; Bay of Fundy district, Nova Scotia. USA: Kalama area, Washington; Magnet Cove, Arkansas. Europe: Puy-de-Dôme, Auvergne, France; Colle del Lares, Trentino–Alto Adige, Italy. Asia: Irkutskaya Oblast, eastern Siberia, Russia; Hayata, Kyushu region, Japan.

Name From the Greek *chabazios*, an ancient name for a stone.

The chabazite group is actually made up of five minerals: chabazite-(Ca), containing calcium; chabazite-(K), with potassium; chabazite-(Mg), with manganese; chabazite-(Na), with sodium; and chabazite-(Sr), with strontium.

Lazurite

Formula $Na_3Ca(Si_3Al_3)O_{12}S$

Crystal System cubic; sometimes monoclinic or triclinic

Space Group $P\overline{4}3n$

Hardness 5.0–5.5

Specific Gravity 2.39–2.42

Cleavage {110} imperfect

Fracture uneven

Tenacity brittle

Habit Deep blue, azure, violet blue or greenish blue. Dodecahedral crystals or more rarely cubes; also granular, disseminated or massive. Vitreous luster; translucent to opaque. Light blue streak.

Environment A contact metamorphic mineral found in limestones.

Notable Localities Canada: north of Kimmirut (Lake Harbour), Baffin Island, Nunavut. USA: San Antonio Canyon, California; Little Rock, Arkansas. Latin America: Cerro Sapo, Cochabamba, Bolivia. Europe: Khibiny and Lovozero massifs, Kola Peninsula, Russia. Asia: Sar-e-Sang, Badakhshan, Afghanistan; Mogok, Myanmar (Burma).

Name From its resemblance in color to the mineral azurite, whose name comes from the Persian *lazhward*, meaning "blue."

Lazurite, Afghanistan • 10 x 5 x 5 cm

Lazurite is usually massive and forms the main component of lapis lazuli, a popular bright blue ornamental material that should be classified as a rock rather than a mineral. Most lapis lazuli also contains calcite (typically white) and pyrite (metallic yellow-gold), and usually some haüyne and sodalite (also blue) as well. Lapis has been used as a gemstone for millennia; the famous mask of Tutankhamen, for example, has lapis lazuli inlays. Powdered lapis was used for hundreds of years to make the pigment ultramarine but has now been replaced with a synthetic.

Lazurite, Sar-e-Sang district, Badakhshan, Afghanistan • 5 x 4 x 4.5 cm

Seal carved with coat of arms, lazurite (lapis lazuli) and gold, 7 x 2.5 x 2.5 cm.

Scapolite Group (Meionite and Marialite)

Formula **meionite** $(Ca,Na)_4(Si,Al)_{12}O_{24}(CO_3,SO_4,Cl)$

marialite $(Na,Ca)_4(Si,Al)_{12}O_{24}(Cl,CO_3,SO_4)$

Crystal System tetragonal

Space Group $I4/m$

Hardness 5.5–6.0

Specific Gravity 2.7

Cleavage {100} and {110} distinct

Fracture uneven to conchoidal

Tenacity brittle

Scapolite, Craigmont Mine, Raglan, Ontario, Canada • 26 x 20 x 7 cm

Scapolite was originally thought to be a single mineral, a calcium aluminosilicate, and the term is still used to describe its gemstone varieties. Now the group is defined as a series of closely related tetragonal aluminum silicates from calcium-bearing meionite to sodium-bearing marialite. Pure end members of this series do not form in nature. Several mineral names in this group, such as wernerite and mizonite, are no longer used.

Habit Bluish, brown, orange brown, colorless, violet, greenish or white. Crystals prismatic, typically with flat pyramidal terminations and striated; also granular or massive. Vitreous, resinous or pearly luster; transparent to opaque. White streak.

Environment Found in regional and contact metamorphic rocks, skarns, pegmatites, altered mafic igneous rocks and volcanic ejecta.

Notable Localities **Meionite** Canada: Gooderham, Ontario; Grenville, Quebec. USA: Bolton, Massachusetts; Rossie, New York; Cutcane Creek, Georgia. Europe: Pargas and Pusunsaari, Finland; Eifel district, Germany. Asia: Slyudyanka, near Lake Baikal, Siberia, Russia. **Marialite** Canada: Bancroft district, Ontario; Montérégie, Québec. USA: Hamburg and Franklin, New Jersey; Natural Bridge, Macomb and Olmsteadville, New York; French Creek, Pennsylvania. Europe: Extremadura, Spain; Pianura, Campania, Italy. Australia: Cygnet district, Tasmania.

Name Named in 1800 from the Greek *skapos*, meaning "rod," and *lithos*, meaning "stone."

The scapolite group is made up of two end members, meionite and marialite.

Golden scapolite, Tanzania • 3.2 x 2.6 x 2.2 cm, 104.40 ct

Stilbite Group

Formula **stilbite-(Ca)** $NaCa_4(Si_{27}Al_9)O_{72}·28H_2O$

stilbite-(Na) $Na_9(Si_{27}Al_9)O_{72}·28H_2O$

Crystal System monoclinic

Space Group $B2/m$

Hardness 3.5–4.0

Specific Gravity 2.23

Cleavage {010} perfect

Fracture uneven

Tenacity brittle

Habit White, yellowish, gray, pink, reddish, orange or light to dark brown. Crystals thin tabular, sheaf-like or in globular clusters. Vitreous luster, but pearly on cleavage; transparent to translucent. White streak.

Environment A low-temperature hydrothermal mineral found in amygdules and cavities in basalt.

Notable Localities Canada: Bay of Fundy, Nova Scotia. USA: Rocky Pass, Kuiu Island, Sitka, Alaska; Golden district, Colorado; Franklin mining district, New Jersey. Latin America: Guanajuato, Mexico. Europe: northwest Highland district, Scotland; Nowa Ruda Mine, Lower Silesia (Dolnośląskie), Poland. Africa: Palabora Mine, Limpopo, South Africa. Asia: Mumbai, Pune and Nasik districts, Maharashtra, India; Uzon Caldera, Kamchatka Peninsula, Russia.

Name From the Greek word for "luster," in reference to its pearly luster. The stilbite group is made up of two minerals, stilbite-(Ca) and stilbite-(Na).

Stilbite, Iceland • 12 x 8 x 9 cm

Analcime, Poudrette Quarry, Mont-Saint-Hilaire, Quebec, Canada • 10.5 x 10 x 4.5 cm

Analcime

Formula $Na(Si_2Al)O_6·H_2O$

Crystal System cubic

Space Group $Ia3d$

Hardness 5.0 5.5

Specific Gravity 2.27

Cleavage very poor on {100}

Fracture subconchoidal

Tenacity brittle

Habit White, colorless, gray, pink or greenish yellow. Crystals commonly trapezohedra; also granular, compact or massive, typically showing concentric structure. Vitreous luster; transparent to translucent. White streak.

Environment Occurs in the groundmass or vesicles of silica-poor intermediate and mafic igneous rocks, typically basalts and phonolites, originating from late-stage hydrothermal solutions or disseminated because of alteration. Also found in lakebeds, altered from pyroclastics or clays, or as a primary precipitate, and authigenic in sandstones and siltstones.

Notable Localities Canada: Tanco Mine, Bernic Lake, Manitoba; Poudrette Quarry, Mont-Saint-Hilaire, Québec; Cape d'Or, Bay of Fundy, Nova Scotia. Europe: Breidhdalsheidhi, Iceland; Bordoy Island, Faroe Islands, Denmark; around Glasgow, Dumbartonshire, Scotland. Asia: Kotchechovmo, Krasnoyarsk, Siberia, Russia.

Name From the Greek word for "weak," alluding to the weak electrostatic charge analcime develops when heated or rubbed.

CHAPTER 10
Phyllosilicates

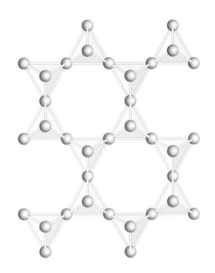

The phyllosilicates, also known as sheet silicates or disilicates, are an important group of minerals that includes the mica-group minerals, such as muscovite, chlorite and annite, and the clay minerals, such as kaolinite and vermiculite. They are made up of rings of tetrahedrons linked by shared oxygen atoms to other rings in a two-dimensional plane, which produces a sheet-like structure. The structure consists of six interconnected rings of SiO_4 tetrahedrons that extend outward in infinite sheets. Three out of the four oxygen atoms in each tetrahedron are shared with other tetrahedrons, leading to a basic unit of Si_2O_5 for single sheets or Si_4O_{10} for double sheets.

The typical crystal habit of phyllosilicates is flat, platy and book-like, and most of them display perfect basal cleavage — a result of the strong silicon-oxygen sheets forming their basic structure. These unique properties are particularly noticeable in the micas, which have been exploited for many industrial uses. Although members of the phyllosilicates group tend to be soft, they are remarkably resilient, often being the last to break down chemically during erosion and weathering processes. They can also withstand high pressures and temperatures, which is why they make up a large part of metamorphic rocks.

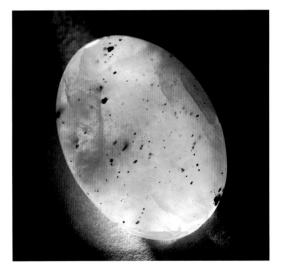

ABOVE: Antigorite (williamsite variety), Line Pit chromite mine, Cecil County, Maryland, USA • 41.5 x 31.2 x 8 mm, 82.80 ct

RIGHT: Clinochlore (kammererite variety), Kop Krom Mine, Kop Daglari, Erzerum, Turkey • 6 x 3 x 3 cm

LEFT: Chrysocolla, Inspiration Mine, Christmas, Arizona, USA • 7 x 9 x 6 cm

Serpentine Group
(Chrysotile and Antigorite)

Formula $Mg_3Si_2O_5(OH)_4$

Crystal System $A2/m$ and Cm

Space Group monoclinic

Hardness 2.5–4.0

Specific Gravity 2.5–2.6

Cleavage perfect on {001}; observed on {100} and {010}

Fracture conchoidal, splintery

Tenacity fibrous, flexible and elastic

Antigorite, East Broughton, Quebec, Canada • 19 x 46 x 3 cm

Chrysotile, Thetford Mines, Quebec, Canada • 9.5 x 9.5 x 7.5 cm

Among the serpentine group, the chrysotile minerals are more likely to form serpentine asbestos. Asbestos was heavily used in the mid-20th century for fire-retardant coatings, pipe insulation and fireproof drywall, roofing and flooring, but its use was discontinued when its fibers were found to pose a health hazard.

Habit White, gray, yellow to green or brown to black. Minute crystals, typically platy, rarely elongated; commonly bladed or fibrous. Silky, greasy or vitreous luster; translucent to opaque. White streak.

Environment Commonly replaces ultramafic rocks, pervasively or in crosscutting veinlets; also occurs as a replacement of siliceous dolostone along contacts with diabase sills.

Notable Localities Chrysotile Canada: Jericho kimberlite pipe, Contwoyto Lake, Northwest Territories; Prince George mining division, British Columbia; Bird River area, Manitoba. USA: Grand Canyon and Globe mining districts, Arizona. Europe: Lizard Peninsula, Cornwall, England; Zloty Stok, Dolnośląskie, Poland. Asia: Kop Krom Mine, eastern Anotolia, Turkey. **Antigorite** Canada: Timmins, Ontario; Asbestos, Quebec. USA: Texas; Pennsylvania; Brewster, Putnam County, New York; around Baltimore, Maryland; Buck Creek, North Carolina. Europe: Glen Urquhart, Highland district, Scotland; Val Antigorio, Piedmont, Italy. Asia: Hsiu-Yen Hsien, Liaoning, China.

Name Named in 1834 from the Greek *chrysos*, meaning "gold," and *tilos*, meaning "fiber."

The serpentine group describes a common group of minerals. *Serpentine* may refer to any of the 20 varieties belonging to this group; the main minerals are antigorite, chrysotile and lizardite.

Kaolinite

Formula $Al_2Si_2O_5(OH)_4$

Crystal System triclinic

Space Group $P1$

Hardness 2.0–2.5

Specific Gravity 2.6

Cleavage perfect on {001}

Fracture subconchoidal

Tenacity sectile

Habit White to cream and pale yellow; also often stained various hues, tans and browns being common. Rarely crystals, thin platy or stacked, to 2 mm. Pearly to dull earthy luster; translucent to opaque. White streak.

Environment A primary constituent of clay beds formed by decomposition of feldspar-bearing rocks.

Notable Localities Canada: Huberdeau, Quebec; near Walton, Nova Scotia. USA: Mesa Alta, New Mexico; near Murfreesboro and at Greenwood, Arkansas; near Webster, North Carolina; Dixie Clay Company mine and Lamar Pit, South Carolina; Macon, Georgia. Europe: near Dresden, Kemmlitz and Zettlitz, Saxony, and elsewhere in Germany.

Name Named for the ancient Chinese locality Kaoling (Gaoling), whose name means "high ridge."

Kaolinite pseudomorph after feldspar, Melbur china clay pit, Cornwall, England • 4 x 5 x 1.5 cm

Talc, Harford County, Maryland, USA • 24 x 18 x 1 cm

Talc

Formula $Mg_3Si_4O_{10}(OH)_2$

Crystal System triclinic

Space Group $P\bar{1}$

Hardness 1.0

Specific Gravity 2.8

Cleavage perfect on {001}

Fracture fibrous, micaceous

Tenacity sectile

Habit Colorless, white, pale green, bright emerald to dark green, brown or gray. Crystals platy; also fibrous, fine-grained compact or massive. Pearly, greasy, dull luster; transparent to translucent. White streak.

Environment A metamorphic mineral that results from metamorphism of magnesian minerals, such as serpentine, pyroxene, amphibole and olivine, in the presence of carbon dioxide and water.

Notable Localities Canada: Pickle Lake, Kenora District, and Timmins, Ontario; Francon Quarry, Montréal, and Val d'Or, Quebec. USA: Dexter Quarry, Lincoln, Rhode Island; Rochester, Vermont. Europe: Lizard Peninsula, Cornwall, England; Mt. Greiner, Zillertal, Tyrol, Austria; Pfitschtal, Trentino–Alto Adige, Italy.

Name From the Arabic *talq*, meaning "pure," probably alluding to the color of its powdered form.

Talc is used in many industries, including pharmaceuticals, cosmetics (talcum powder, baby powder to prevent diaper rash), ceramics (to prevent crazing), paper making (as a filler), plastics, rubber, paint and coatings.

Pyrophyllite, Tres Cerritos, Hornitos, California, USA • 20.5 x 12 x 7 cm

Pyrophyllite

Formula $Al_2Si_4O_{10}(OH)_2$

Crystal System monoclinic or triclinic

Space Group $C1$ or $C\bar{1}$

Hardness 1.0–2.0

Specific Gravity 2.7–2.9

Cleavage perfect on {001}

Fracture uneven or splintery

Tenacity flexible

Habit White, gray, pale blue, pale green, pale yellow or brownish green. Compact spherulitic aggregates of needle-like radiating crystals, fine-grained foliated laminae, granular or massive. Pearly to dull luster; translucent to opaque. White streak.

Environment Somewhat uncommon, found both in hydrothermal veins and in bedded deposits in schistose metamorphic rocks.

Notable Localities Canada: Iskut River, Liard mining division, British Columbia; Abitibi-Témiscamingue, Quebec; Cape Breton, Nova Scotia. USA: Champion Mine, White Mountains, California; Merrimac district, Nevada. Latin America: Ibitiara, Bahia, Brazil. Europe: St. Niklas, Zermatt, Valais, Switzerland; Monte Folgorito, Tuscany, Italy. Asia: Pyshminskoye deposit, Ural Mountains, Russia.

Name From the Greek words for "fire" and "leaf," for the way it exfoliates when heated.

Muscovite

Formula $KAl_2(Si_3Al)O_{10}(OH)_2$

Crystal System monoclinic

Space Group $C2/c$

Hardness 2.5

Specific Gravity 2.8

Cleavage perfect on {001}

Fracture uneven

Tenacity tough; laminae flexible and elastic

Habit Colorless, gray, brown, green, yellow or rose red. Crystals tabular to columnar with hexagonal or pseudo-hexagonal outline; also lamellar masses and fine-grained aggregates. Vitreous to pearly or silky luster; transparent to translucent. White streak.

Environment A common rock-forming mineral found in phyllites, schists and gneisses and in granites, granite pegmatites and aplites. Formed from other minerals under hydrothermal conditions.

Notable Localities Canada: Kimmirut (Lake Harbour), Baffin Island, Nunavut; Kenora District, Ontario. USA: Black Hills, in Pennington, Lawrence and Custer counties, South Dakota; Mt. Mica, near Paris, and elsewhere in Maine; Shelby, North Carolina. Latin America: Doce Valley and Antônio Dias, Minas Gerais, Brazil. Asia: Slyudyanka, near Lake Baikal, Siberia, and Mursinka, Ural Mountains, Russia; Nellore, Andhra Pradesh, India.

Name The name, first used in 1850, is derived from the term "Muscovy glass," because it was used for windows in Russia (Moscow, the Russian capital, was formerly called "Muscovy" in Western Europe).

Muscovite, Jose Pinto Mine, Jaguaraçu, Minas Gerais, Brazil • 12 x 19 x 6 cm

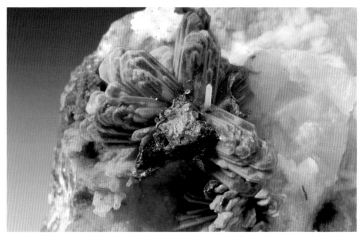

Chrysocolla, Dorothy Mine, Mungana, Queensland, Australia • 6.5 x 6 x 3.5 cm

Chrysocolla

Formula $(Cu,Al)_2H_2Si_2O_5(OH)_4 \cdot nH_2O$

Crystal System orthorhombic

Space Group not determined

Hardness 2.0–4.0

Specific Gravity 1.9–2.4

Cleavage none

Fracture conchoidal

Tenacity brittle to somewhat sectile

Habit Blue, blue green or green; brown to black when impure. Crystals very rare and rarely acicular, in radiating clusters; also fine fibrous, botryoidal or earthy; commonly cryptocrystalline, opaline or enamel-like. Vitreous, porcelaneous or earthy luster; translucent to opaque. Light green streak.

Environment Occurs in oxidized portions of many copper deposits, commonly associated with other secondary copper minerals.

Notable Localities Canada: Abitibi-Témiscamingue, Quebec. USA: Tintic district, Utah; Globe-Miami district and Christmas Mine, Banner district, Arizona; Santa Rita, New Mexico. Latin America: Cananea, Sonora, Mexico. Asia: Nizhni Tagil, Ural Mountains, Russia; Timna (King Solomon's) Mine, Israel. Australia: Chillagoe district, Queensland.

Name The name was first used by Theophrastus in 315 BCE and comes from the Greek *chrysos*, meaning "gold," and *kolla*, meaning "glue," in allusion to a material used to solder gold that may have been this mineral.

Annite ("Biotite")

Formula $KFe^{2+}_3(Si_3Al)O_{10}(OH)_2$

Crystal System monoclinic

Space Group $C2/m$

Hardness 2.5–3.0

Specific Gravity 3.3

Cleavage perfect on {001}

Fracture micaceous to uneven

Tenacity flexible

Habit Brown or black. Tabular to short prismatic crystals and cleavage fragments with pseudo-hexagonal outlines; commonly foliated masses. Adamantine luster; translucent to transparent. Brownish white streak.

Environment Forms large crystals in granites and granitic pegmatites.

Notable Localities Canada: Tanco Mine, Bernic Lake, Manitoba; Jeffrey Mine, Asbestos, Quebec. USA: Pegmatite Peak, Montana; Rockport, Massachusetts. Europe: Kitaa, Greenland; Iveland, Norway; Västmanland and Lappland, Sweden; Devon, England; Eifel Mountains, Rhineland-Palatinate, Germany; Thyon, Wallis (Valais), Switzerland. Africa: Mt. Malosa, Malawi. Australia: Broken Hill, New South Wales.

Name Named after Cape Ann, in Essex County, Massachusetts, where it is found.

"Biotite" is no longer a valid mineral name, but it is still commonly used, especially for dark micas.

Annite, Ontario, Canada • 53 x 44 x 7 cm

Vermiculite

Formula $Mg_{0.7}(Mg,Fe^{3+},Al)_6(Si,Al)_8O_{20}(OH)_4 \cdot 8H_2O$

Crystal System monoclinic

Space Group $C2/m$

Hardness 1.5–2.0

Specific Gravity 2.6

Cleavage perfect on {001}

Fracture uneven

Tenacity pliable

Habit Colorless, green, gray white or yellow brown. Tabular pseudo-hexagonal crystals or platy aggregates. Vitreous to dull luster; transparent to opaque. Greenish white streak.

Environment An alteration product of biotite-group minerals formed by weathering or hydrothermal action. Occurs at the contact between felsic and mafic or ultramafic rocks such as pyroxenites and dunites, in carbonatites and metamorphosed limestones, and as a clayey constituent of soils.

Notable Localities Canada: Verity property, Kamloops mining division, British Columbia. USA: Rutherford Quarry, near Tuxedo, North Carolina; Magnet Cove, Arkansas. Europe: Kovdor Massif, Kola Peninsula, Russia. Africa: Phalaborwa, Limpopo, South Africa. Asia: Potaninskoye deposit, southern Ural Mountains, Russia; Ajmer, Rajasthan, India. Australia: Mud Tank, Valley Bore, Northern Territory; Bulong, Western Australia.

Name From the Latin *vermiculare*, meaning "to breed worms," in allusion to its peculiar exfoliation on intense heating.

Vermiculite, Phalaborwa, Limpopo, South Africa • 14 x 14 x 3 cm

Phlogopite, Bedford, Ontario, Canada • 8 x 12 x 0.1 cm

Phlogopite

Formula $KMg_3(Si_3Al)O_{10}(OH)_2$

Crystal System monoclinic

Space Group $C2/m$

Hardness 2.0–3.0

Specific Gravity 2.8

Cleavage perfect on {001}

Fracture uneven

Tenacity tough; thin laminae flexible and elastic

Habit Brownish red, dark brown, yellowish brown, green or white. Crystals six-sided, thick tabular to prismatic, commonly tapered; also coarse-grained or platy. Pearly to submetallic luster; transparent to translucent. White streak.

Environment Found in contact and regional metamorphic limestones and dolomites and ultramafic rocks.

Notable Localities Canada: Jericho kimberlite pipe, Contwoyto Lake, Northwest Territories; Bancroft, Ontario; Témiscamingue, Quebec. USA: Franklin, New Jersey; Edwards and Pierrepont, New York. Europe: Campolungo, Ticino (Tessin), Switzerland; Trentino–Alto Adige and Malenco Valley, Lombardy, Italy. Africa: Saharakara and Ampandrandava, Madagascar. Asia: Madya Pradesh, India. New Zealand: Anxiety Point, Nancy Sound.

Name From the Greek *phlogopos*, meaning "resembling fire," in allusion to its red tint.

Palygorskite

Formula $(Mg,Al)_2Si_4O_{10}(OH)\cdot 4H_2O$

Crystal System monoclinic

Space Group $C2/m$

Hardness 2.0–2.5

Specific Gravity 2.1–2.2

Cleavage perfect on {110}

Fracture uneven

Tenacity tough

Habit White, grayish, yellowish or gray green. Crystals tiny laths; commonly fibrous, forming tangled mats termed "mountain leather"; also compact. Earthy to waxy luster; semitransparent. White streak.

Environment An alteration product of magnesium silicates in soils and sediments; in lacustrine marls, carbonate rocks and mafic igneous rocks; and in clay gouge associated with fault movement.

Notable Localities Canada: Golden mining division, British Columbia; Jeffrey Mine, Asbestos, Quebec. USA: New Melones Dam, California; Carlsbad, New Mexico; Blacksburg, Virginia. Europe: Warren Quarry, Enderby, Leicestershire, England. Africa: Tafraout, Morocco. Asia: Palygorskaya, Permskaya Oblast, Ural Mountains, Russia; Hyderabad deposit, Andhra Pradesh, India.

Name Named for its type locality, Palygorskaya, in the Perm district of the Ural Mountains in Russia.

Palygorskite, Metaline Falls, Pend Oreille County, Washington, USA • 26 x 22 x 12 cm

Saponite, Scotland • 8 x 10 x 4.5 cm

Saponite

Formula $(Ca,Na)_{0.3}(Mg,Fe^{2+})_3(Si,Al)_4O_{10}(OH)_2\cdot 4H_2O$

Crystal System monoclinic

Space Group not determined

Hardness 1.0–2.0

Specific Gravity 2.2–2.3

Cleavage perfect on {001}

Fracture uneven

Tenacity Plastic when hydrated, brittle when dry

Habit White, yellow, gray, blue, green, reddish or brown. Crystals minute, pseudo-hexagonal and tabular; bladed, fibrous, flaky or subparallel aggregates; also nodular, fine-grained or massive. Greasy luster; translucent. White streak.

Environment Hydrothermally deposited in mineralized veins and in vesicles in basalt and formed in fissures cutting calc-silicates, iron-rich skarns, amphibolites and serpentinites.

Notable Localities Canada: Thunder Bay District, Ontario; Poudrette Quarry, Mont-Saint-Hilaire, Quebec. USA: Carlsbad Caverns, New Mexico; near Milford, Utah. Europe: The Lizard, Cornwall, England; Frankenstein, Silesia, Poland. Africa: Krugersdorp, Guateng, South Africa.

Name From the Latin *sapo*, meaning "soap," which saponite resembles.

Prehnite

Formula $Ca_2Al(Si_3Al)O_{10}(OH)_2$

Crystal System orthorhombic

Space Group *P2cm*

Hardness 6.0–6.5

Specific Gravity 2.8–2.9

Cleavage good on {001}; poor on {110}

Fracture uneven

Tenacity brittle

Prehnite, Jeffrey Mine, Asbestos, Quebec, Canada • 5 x 8.3 x 4 cm

The rough natural state of prehnite hides its potential for beauty. The polishing process brings out a distinctive pearly luster, and its transparent nature gives this stone an almost luminous quality. Individual transparent, gem-quality crystals of prehnite are rare, and they are usually small.

Prehnite, Jeffrey Mine, Asbestos, Quebec, Canada • 8 x 6 x 5 cm

Habit Light to dark green, white, yellow, gray or pink. Tabular or prismatic to steep pyramidal crystals uncommon; aggregates fanlike, reniform, globular or stalactitic; also granular or compact. Vitreous luster; semitransparent to translucent. Colorless streak.

Environment A secondary or hydrothermal mineral in veins and cavities in mafic volcanic rocks; a typical product of low-grade metamorphism.

Notable Localities Canada: Bancroft district, Ontario; Thetford Mines, Quebec. Europe: Ilímaussaq complex, Narsaq, Kitaa, Greenland; Loanhead Quarry, Strathclyde (Ayrshire), Scotland; Jaén, Andalusia, Spain; Trentino–Alto Adige, Italy. Africa: Karoo dolerites, eastern Cape Province; South Africa. Asia: Khandivali Quarry, Mumbai district, Maharashtra, India.

Name Named for Hendrik von Prehn (1733–85), a Dutch colonel who discovered the mineral.

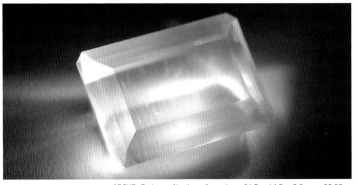

ABOVE: Prehnite, Northern Australia • 21.5 x 14.5 x 8.8 mm, 23.20 ct
RIGHT: Prehnite, Brandberg district, Erongo, Namibia • 10 x 13 x 9 cm

Carletonite

Formula $KNa_4Ca_4Si_8O_{18}(CO_3)_4(F,OH) \cdot H_2O$

Crystal System tetragonal

Space Group *P4/mbm*

Hardness 4.0–4.5

Specific Gravity 2.4

Cleavage perfect on {001}; good on {110}

Fracture conchoidal

Tenacity brittle

Habit Pink or pale to dark blue. Crystals prismatic or massive. Vitreous to pearly luster, and may become slightly waxy when exposed to air; transparent to translucent. White streak.

Environment Found in nepheline syenite in an intrusive alkalic gabbro-syenite complex.

Notable Localities Canada: Mont-Saint-Hilaire, Quebec.

Name Named after Carleton University, in Ottawa, Ontario, where it was first studied.

Carletonite, Poudrette Quarry, Mont-Saint-Hilaire, Quebec, Canada • 10 x 9 x 5.5 cm

Cavansite, Wagholi Quarry, Pune, Maharashtra, India • 15 x 8.5 x 10 cm

Cavansite

Formula $Ca(V^{4+}O)Si_4O_{10} \cdot 4H_2O$

Crystal System orthorhombic

Space Group *Pcmn*

Hardness 3.0–4.0

Specific Gravity 2.33

Cleavage distinct/good on {010}

Fracture none

Tenacity brittle

Habit Brilliant sky blue to greenish blue. Prismatic crystals or spherulitic rosettes. Vitreous luster; transparent. Bluish white streak.

Environment Found in basalts in association with zeolites and in tuffs.

Notable Localities USA: Owyhee Dam, Lake Owyhee State Park, and Chapman Quarry, Oregon. Asia: Wagholi, Pune, Maharashtra, India.

Name From the elements calcium, vanadium and silicon in its composition.

Apophyllite Group

Formula $(K,Na)Ca_4Si_8O_{20}(OH,F)\cdot 8H_2O$

Crystal System tetragonal

Space Group $P4/mnc$

Hardness 4.5–5.0

Specific Gravity 2.3–2.4

Cleavage perfect on {001}; imperfect on {110}

Fracture uneven

Tenacity brittle

Habit Colorless, white, pink, yellow or green. Crystals tabular to prismatic, commonly pseudo-cubic, with prism zone deeply striated; also granular. Vitreous to pearly luster; transparent to translucent. White streak.

Environment A product of low-grade regional and contact metamorphism and a late-stage hydrothermal mineral in some mineral deposits. Also a secondary mineral in amygdules or druses in basalts and in cavities in granite.

Notable Localities Apophyllite-(KF) USA: French Creek and Cornwall, Pennsylvania. Europe: Korsnäs, Finland; Sankt Andreasberg, Harz Mountains, Germany. Asia: Pune, Nasik and Mumbai districts, Maharashtra, India; Shaoguang, Guangdong, China. **Apophyllite-(KOH)** Africa: Kimberley and, in large crystals, near Kuruman, Cape Province, South Africa. Asia: Mumbai, Pune and Nasik districts, Maharashtra, India. **Apophyllite-(NaF)** Asia: Sampo Mine, west of Takahashi, Okayama, Japan.

Name From the Greek words for "away from" and "leaf," in allusion to its manner of exfoliating on heating.

Apophyllite-(KF), Momin Akhada, Maharashtra, India • 29 x 10.5 x 10.5 cm

Apophyllite-(KF), Mumbai, Maharashtra, India • 4 x 5 x 4 cm

Colorless and green apophyllite-group minerals from India are popular with collectors and are even faceted into gemstones. Apophyllite-group minerals are found in ancient lava and basalt flows. Cavities or other open spaces in the rock allow these blocky crystals to grow unimpeded. Apophyllite-group minerals are also found in voids in limestones, in the contact metamorphic zone that surrounds the intrusive rocks.

Clinochlore, Tilly Foster Mine, near Brewster, New York, USA • 12 x 10 x 7 cm

Clinochlore

Formula $Mg_6Si_4O_{10}(OH)_8$

Crystal System monoclinic

Space Group $C2/m$

Hardness 2.0–2.5

Specific Gravity 2.6–2.9

Cleavage perfect on {001}

Fracture uneven

Tenacity inelastic; lamellae flexible

Habit Grass green, olive green, yellowish, white or pink to rose red. Thin to thick pseudo-hexagonal crystals with tapering pyramidal faces; commonly foliated, fibrous, granular, earthy or massive. Pearly, greasy or dull luster; transparent to translucent. White streak.

Environment A hydrothermal alteration product of amphibole, pyroxene and biotite.

Notable Localities Canada: Sustut deposit, British Columbia; Cochrane and Algoma districts, Ontario; Rouyn-Noranda, Abitibi-Témiscamingue, Quebec. USA: Emery Mine, Massachusetts; Brinton's Quarry, Pennsylvania. Latin America: Petorca, Valparaíso region, Chile. Europe: Unst, Shetland Islands, Scotland; The Lizard, Cornwall, England; Rimpfischwänge, near Zermatt, Valais, Switzerland. Asia: Kop Krom Mine, eastern Anatolia, Turkey.

Name From its inclined optic axes and the Greek *chloros*, meaning "green," for its common color.

Petalite

Formula $LiAlSi_4O_{10}$

Crystal System monoclinic

Space Group $P2/a$

Hardness 6.5

Specific Gravity 2.4

Cleavage perfect on {001}; poor on {201}

Fracture imperfect conchoidal

Tenacity brittle

Habit Colorless, white or gray; rarely reddish or greenish. Crystals tabular or elongated and some faces may be striated; commonly foliated cleavable or massive. Vitreous luster, but pearly on some faces; transparent to translucent. Colorless streak.

Environment Found in granite pegmatites, locally constituting an ore of lithium.

Notable Localities Canada: Tanco pegmatite, Bernic Lake, Manitoba. USA: Queen and Hiriart mountains, Pala, California; Peru, Maine. Europe: Södermanland and Skellefteå, Västerbotten, Sweden. Asia: Mandalay, Myanmar (Burma). Australia: Utö, Londonderry Quarry, Coolgardie, Western Australia.

Name From the Greek word for "leaf," in allusion to its perfect basal cleavage.

Petalite, Maxixe pegmatite, Itinga, Minas Gerais, Brazil • 4 x 4 x 2 cm

Allophane, Magdalena, New Mexico, USA • 14 x 8 x 4 cm

Allophane

Formula $Al_2O_3(SiO_2)_{1.3-2.0} \cdot 2.5-3.0H_2O$

Crystal System amorphous

Space Group amorphous

Hardness 3.0

Specific Gravity 2.8

Cleavage none

Fracture conchoidal

Tenacity brittle

Habit White, pale blue to sky blue, green or brown. Hyaline crusts and masses, stalactites or flowstones. Vitreous to earthy or waxy luster; translucent. White streak.

Environment Found in hydrothermally altered igneous rocks, from the breakdown of feldspars, and in hydrothermal veins.

Notable Localities Canada: Montmagny, Chaudière-Appalaches, Quebec. USA: Red Mountain, Rand district, California; Globe-Miami and Ajo districts, Arizona; Hanover-Fierro district, New Mexico; Springfield and Bethel, Pennsylvania. Europe: Schneeberg district, Saxony, and Black Forest, Baden-Württemberg, Germany; Rosas Mine, Narcao, Sardinia, Italy. Asia: Bihoro Mine, Tokachi, Hokkaido, Japan. Australia: Rosebery district, Tasmania.

Name From the Greek words for "other" and "to appear," referring to its change of appearance under a blowpipe.

Sepiolite

Formula $Mg_4Si_6O_{15}(OH)_2 \cdot 6H_2O$

Crystal System orthorhombic

Space Group *Pncn*

Hardness 2.0

Specific Gravity 2.3

Cleavage not reported

Fracture conchoidal

Tenacity uneven

Habit White, light gray or light yellow. Compact nodular, earthy, clayey or massive; rarely fine fibrous. Dull luster; opaque. White streak.

Environment A sedimentary clay mineral also found in serpentine.

Notable Localities Canada: Cardiff uranium mine, Cardiff, Ontario. USA: Bisbee and Christmas Mine, Arizona. Latin America: Cerro de Mercado Mine, Durango, and Refugio Mine, Bonanza, Zacatecas, Mexico. Europe: Kongsberg, Buskerud, Norway; Cornwall, England; Bettolino, Baldissero Canavese, Piedmont, Italy. Africa: Bou Azzer district, Souss-Massa-Draâ region, Morocco. Asia: Sakhara Massif, Ural Mountains, Russia.

Name From the Greek *sepion*, meaning "cuttlefish bone," because of its low density and porous, bonelike appearance.

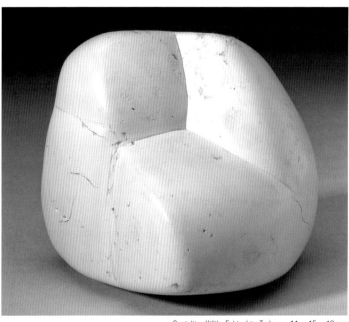

Sepiolite, Killik, Eskişehir, Turkey • 11 x 15 x 10 cm

CHAPTER 11

Single-Chain & Double-Chain Inosilicates

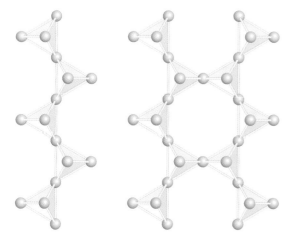

The inosilicates take their name from the Greek *inos*, meaning "chain." The silicate tetrahedrons in their structure point alternately to the left and right along a line formed by linked oxygen atoms. Then these chains are joined by other elements. The long chains common to these minerals account for the way their crystals often grow longer in one direction. A major group among the single-chain inosilicates is the pyroxenes. These are common rock-forming minerals, and one of them, jadeite, is an important gem material. The silicate part of the formula for pyroxene minerals is Si_2O_6, or a silicon-to-oxygen ratio of 1:3. In double-chain inosilicates, two single chains lie side by side so that the right-side tetrahedrons of the left chain are linked by an oxygen molecule to the left-side tetrahedrons of the right chain. The extra shared oxygen for every four silicon molecules reduces the ratio of silicon to oxygen to 4:11.

RIGHT: Maya pendant (Altun Ha, Belize, c. 650 CE), jade, 1.3 x 7 x 3 cm. Part of a royal raiment, this jade pendant comes from a tomb excavated by a ROM team in 1966. The human figure, arms crossed at the waist, is wearing a headdress that may represent the stylized face of a sun god.

RIGHT: Actinolite, Taiwan • 40 x 39 x 15 cm

LEFT: Orthoclase with aegirine, Mt. Malosa, Zomba, Malawi • 4.5 x 4 x 5 cm

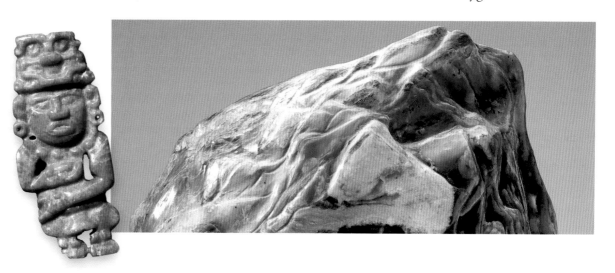

Pigeonite

Formula (Mg,Fe,Ca)SiO$_3$

Crystal System monoclinic

Space Group $P2_1/c$

Hardness 6.0

Specific Gravity 3.4

Cleavage {110} perfect

Fracture uneven to conchoidal

Tenacity brittle

Habit Brown or greenish brown to black. Prismatic crystals, granular or massive. Vitreous luster; semitransparent. Grayish white streak.

Environment Commonly occurs in rapidly cooled siliceous volcanic rocks. Inverted varieties with exsolved augite found in layered mafic intrusives; also in metamorphosed iron formations.

Notable Localities USA: Pigeon Point, Minnesota; Goose Creek Quarry, Leesburg, Virginia. Caribbean: Grande Rivière, Saint Lucia. Europe: Skaergaard intrusion, Qeqertarsuaq (Disko) Island, Kitaa, Greenland; Isle of Mull and Ardnamurchan, Lochaber, Scotland; Cogne, Italy. Africa: Eastern Bushveld complex, Limpopo, South Africa.

Name From its occurrence at Pigeon Point, Minnesota, in the United States.

Pigeonite, Richelieu Quarry, Mont-Saint-Bruno, Quebec, Canada • 7 x 5 x 4 cm

Enstatite, Kjerulfine Mine, Bamle, Telemark, Norway • 7 x 8 x 3 cm

Enstatite

Formula MgSiO$_3$

Crystal System orthorhombic

Space Group *Pbca*

Hardness 5.0–6.0

Specific Gravity 3.2

Cleavage {210} good

Fracture irregular/uneven

Tenacity brittle

Habit White, greenish white or gray, yellowish green, olive green or brown. Prismatic to lamellar, fibrous or massive. Vitreous to pearly luster on cleavages; translucent to opaque. Gray streak.

Environment Occurs in pyroxenites, peridotites and dunites, in ultramafic inclusions in alkalic olivine basalts and kimberlite, in mafic volcanics and rarely in felsic volcanics. Also found in granulite metamorphic facies, regionally metamorphosed rocks and metagabbros.

Notable Localities USA: Webster and Corundum Hill, North Carolina. Europe: Ødegården and Kjörrestad mines, Bamle, Norway; The Lizard, Cornwall, England; Kraubath, Styria, Austria. Asia: Embilipitiya, Sri Lanka.

Name From the Greek *enstates*, meaning "opponent," for its ability to retain strength under a blowpipe flame.

Aegirine

Formula $NaFe^{3+}Si_2O_6$

Crystal System monoclinic

Space Group $C2/c$

Hardness 6.0–6.5

Specific Gravity 3.5–3.6

Cleavage good on {110}

Fracture uneven

Tenacity brittle

Habit Dark green to greenish black, reddish brown or black. Prismatic crystals with blunt to steep terminations, striated lengthwise, that can be bent or twisted; also sprays of acicular crystals, fibrous or in radial concretions. Vitreous to slightly resinous luster; translucent to opaque. Yellowish gray streak.

Environment Common in alkalic igneous rocks, carbonatites and pegmatites. Also found in regionally metamorphosed schists, gneisses and iron formations, blueschist facies rocks and sodium metasomatism in granulites; an authigenic mineral in some shales and marls.

Notable Localities Canada: Mont-Saint-Hilaire, Quebec. USA: Yogo Peak intrusion, Montana; Magnet Cove, Arizona; north Cuyuna Range, Minnesota; Litchfield, Maine. Europe: Rundemyr, Eger and Kongsberg, Norway; Långban, Värmland, Sweden; S'Airde Beinn, Strathclyde, Scotland. Africa: Mbolwe Hill, Central, Zambia.

Name From Ægir, the Norse sea god, as the mineral was first described from Norway.

Aegirine, Mt. Malosa, Zomba, Malawi • 6 x 5 x 4 cm

Hedenbergite, Nordmark, Värmland, Sweden • 5.5 x 6 x 2 cm

Hedenbergite

Formula $CaFeSi_2O_6$

Crystal System monoclinic

Space Group $C2/c$

Hardness 5.5–6.5

Specific Gravity 3.56

Cleavage good on {110}

Fracture uneven to conchoidal

Tenacity brittle

Habit Black, dark green or green brown. Short prismatic crystals in columnar or acicular aggregates; also granular, lamellar or massive. Vitreous or dull luster; transparent to opaque. Whitish green streak.

Environment Occurs in metamorphosed iron formations, iron-manganese skarns, alkalic granites and xenoliths in kimberlite.

Notable Localities Canada: Gun Claim, Watson Lake mining district, Yukon; Marathon, Ontario. USA: Laxey Mine, South Mountain, Idaho; Iron Hill, Colorado; Marquette iron range, Michigan. Europe: Vesturhorn intrusion, southeast Iceland; Fürstenberg, Saxony, Germany; Prägraten, Tyrol, Austria. Asia: Skardu area, Pakistan; Tirodi, Madhya Pradesh, and Kacharwali, Nagpur district, Maharashtra, India; Dal'negorsk, Primorskiy Krai, Russia; Obira Mine, Bungo, Oita, Japan.

Name Named in honor of the Swedish chemist M.A. Ludwig Hedenberg, who first described the mineral.

Diopside

Formula CaMgSi$_2$O$_6$

Crystal System monoclinic

Space Group *C2/c*

Hardness 5.5–6.5

Specific Gravity 3.3

Cleavage distinct/good on {110}

Fracture uneven to conchoidal

Tenacity brittle

Habit Light to dark green, blue, brown, colorless, snow white or grey. Prismatic crystals with nearly square cross-sections; also granular, columnar or lamellar massive. Vitreous to dull luster; transparent to opaque. Whitish green streak.

Environment Typical of metamorphosed siliceous calcium- and magnesium-rich rocks of pyroxene-hornfels or epidote-amphibolite facies. Also found in some kimberlites, skarns and calcium- and magnesium-rich gneisses and schists; less common in alkalic olivine basalts and andesites.

Notable Localities Canada: Jericho kimberlite pipe, Contwoyto Lake, Northwest Territories; several localities in Bancroft district, Ontario; Jeffrey Mine, Asbestos, Quebec. USA: Garnet Ridge, Arizona; Murfreesboro, Arkansas. Latin America: Candelaria Mine, La Paz, Bolivia. Europe: Tyrol, Austria. Asia: Mogok, Myanmar (Burma).

Name From the Greek words for "double" and "appearance," apparently because there are two possible orientations of the prism zone.

ABOVE: Diopside, Birds Creek, Bancroft, Ontario, Canada • 10 x 16 x 7 cm
RIGHT: Diopside, Jeffery Mine, Asbestos, Quebec, Canada • 5 x 4.5 x 4 cm

Diopsides enriched with chrome tend to be found on top of or in close proximity to a kimberlite body. Kimberlite is a type of volcanic rock that forms deep within the mantle of Earth and is a host to diamonds. Diopsides are unusual among igneous rocks because they contain mineral species with chemical compositions not generally found in most other igneous rocks, making them particularly useful as indicators for kimberlites and, therefore, diamonds.

Trillium-cut diopside, Yakutia, eastern Siberia, Russia • 2.80 ct

Augite

Formula $(Ca,Mg,Fe)_2(Si,Al)_2O_6$

Crystal System monoclinic

Space Group $C2/c$

Hardness 5.5–6.0

Specific Gravity 3.2–3.6

Cleavage good on {110}

Fracture uneven to conchoidal

Tenacity brittle

Habit Black, brown, greenish or violet brown. Stubby prismatic crystals, square or octagonal in section; also acicular, skeletal or dendritic. Vitreous or resinous to dull luster; transparent to opaque. Greenish gray streak.

Environment Essential in mafic igneous rocks, basalt and gabbro; common in ultramafic rocks and occurs in some high-grade metamorphic rocks and metamorphosed iron formations.

Notable Localities Canada: Bancroft district, Ontario; Asbestos, Estrie and Mont-Saint-Hilaire, Quebec; Shambogamo Mine, Labrador City, Newfoundland and Labrador. USA: Twin Peaks, Utah; Elizabethtown, New York. Latin America: Potosí Department, Bolivia. Europe: Skaergaard complex, Greenland; Ersby, near Pargas, Finland; Mt. Vesuvius, Campania, Italy.

Name From the Greek *auge*, meaning "shine" or "luster," apparently because of the appearance of its cleavage surfaces.

Augite, Rondu, Baltistan, Pakistan • 3.5 x 2 x 2 cm

Jadeite, China • 11 x 8 x 7 cm

Jadeite

Formula $NaAlSi_2O_6$

Crystal System monoclinic

Space Group $C2/c$

Hardness 6.5

Specific Gravity 3.3

Cleavage good on {110}

Fracture splintery

Tenacity very tough when massive

Habit Greenish white, apple green, blue green or purplish blue. Sometimes prismatic but commonly massive; also fibrous, granular or compact. Subvitreous but pearly on cleavages; translucent. White streak.

Environment Occurs in high-pressure metamorphic rocks of glaucophane facies; also a component of eclogite.

Notable Localities USA: Cayucos and Paso Robles, California. Asia: Myanmar (Burma); Kunlun Mountains, Xinjiang (Uyghur Autonomous Region), and Lianyungang Prefecture, Jiangsu, China; Kotaki, Niigata, and elsewhere in Japan.

Name From the Spanish *piedra de yjada*, meaning "stone of the side," because it was believed to have a curative effect in kidney ailments.

Jadeite is only one of several varieties of jade.

Spodumene

Formula LiAlSi$_2$O$_6$

Crystal System monoclinic

Space Group *C2/c*

Hardness 6.5–7.0

Specific Gravity 3.2

Cleavage good on {110}

Fracture uneven to subconchoidal

Tenacity brittle

Habit Colorless, greenish or grayish white, yellowish green, emerald green, yellow, pink or violet; may be bicolor. Crystals prismatic, typically flattened and striated; also commonly massive. Vitreous but pearly on cleavage; transparent to translucent. White streak.

Environment A common constituent of lithium-rich granite pegmatites and also occurs in aplites and gneisses.

Notable Localities Canada: Tanco Mine, Bernic Lake, Manitoba. USA: Harding Mine, Dixon, New Mexico; Etta Mine, near Keystone, and elsewhere in the Black Hills, South Dakota. Latin America: Resplendor, Minas Gerais, Brazil. Europe: Varuträsk pegmatite, Sweden. Africa: Bikita, Zimbabwe.

Name From the Greek for "ash-colored," in allusion to its color.

Spodumene (kunzite variety), Itambacuri, Minas Gerais, Brazil • 18 x 13.5 x 6 cm

Kunzite, the pink gem variety of spodumene, was named after New York jeweler and gemstone specialist George Frederick Kunz (1856–1932). Kunz was the first person to describe the stone, in 1902. The appeal of kunzite lies in its clarity and fine, delicate pink nuances, which often display a hint of violet, depending on the angle from which you view the stone.

Spodumene, Nuristan, Afghanistan • 18 x 21 x 10 cm

Oval mixed-cut spodumene (kunzite variety), Minas Gerais, Brazil • 5.6 x 4.2 x 2.8 cm, 463.60 ct

Rhodonite

Formula $Mn^{2+}SiO_3$

Crystal System triclinic

Space Group $C\bar{1}$

Hardness 5.5–6.5

Specific Gravity 3.5–3.7

Cleavage perfect on {110} and {1$\bar{1}$0}; good on {001}

Fracture irregular/uneven

Tenacity brittle

Rhodonite is primarily opaque and sometimes streaked with black veins of manganese oxide. The bright pink-to-red color of this mineral can be quite attractive when it is cut cabochon-style for jewelry, and it is also used as a carving material. Very rarely transparent rhodonite is found, and it can be faceted into a gemstone.

Habit Pink to rose red. Rounded crystals, masses or grains, often coated or veined black with manganese oxides. Vitreous, somewhat pearly on cleavages; transparent to translucent. White streak.

Environment Found in manganese deposits formed by sedimentary or hydrothermal contact or regional metamorphic processes.

Notable Localities USA: Franklin and Sterling Hill, New Jersey. Latin America: Morro da Mina, Conselheiro Lafaiete, Minas Gerais, Brazil. Europe: Värmland, Sweden. Africa: Kombat Mine, Namibia. Asia: Yekaterinburg (Sverdlovsk), Ural Mountains, Russia; Tirodi, Madhya Pradesh, India.

Name From the Greek *rhodon*, meaning "rose," because of its characteristic pink color.

Rhodonite has been used as a manganese ore in India, but it is more often mined as a gem or ornamental stone.

BELOW: Rhodonite, Broken Hill, New South Wales, Australia • 14.3 x 10.6 x 7.4 mm, 10.90 ct

OPPOSITE: Rhodonite, Madagascar • 30 x 22 x 0.5 cm

Astrophyllite, Poudrette Quarry, Mont-Saint-Hilaire, Quebec, Canada • 7 x 6 x 5 cm

Astrophyllite

Formula $K_2NaFe^{2+}_7Ti_2(Si_4O_{12})_2O_2(OH)_4F$

Crystal System triclinic

Space Group $A\overline{1}$

Hardness 3.0–4.0

Specific Gravity 3.3–3.4

Cleavage perfect on {001}; poor on {100}

Fracture none

Tenacity brittle

Habit Bronze yellow, golden yellow or brown to reddish brown. Blades up to 15 cm long and in stellate aggregates; also foliated or massive. Greasy, pearly submetallic luster; opaque to translucent in thin leaves. Yellowish brown streak.

Environment Found in nepheline syenites and alkali granites.

Notable Localities Canada: Mont-Saint-Hilaire, Quebec. Europe: Låven, near Brevik, Langesundsfjorden, Norway; Mt. Yukspor and Mt. Eveslogchorr, Khibiny Massif, Kola Peninsula, Russia; Pontevedra, Spain. Africa: Los Islands, Guinea; Mt. Charib, Egypt; Pilanesberg, North West Province, South Africa.

Name From the Greek *astron*, meaning "star," and *phyllon*, meaning "leaf," referring to its starburst-like sprays and micaceous cleavage.

Wollastonite-1A

Formula $CaSiO_3$

Crystal System triclinic

Space Group $P\overline{1}$

Hardness 4.5–5.0

Specific Gravity 2.8–2.9

Cleavage perfect on{001}; good on $\{\overline{1}02\}$

Fracture irregular/uneven

Tenacity brittle

Habit White, gray white, light green, pinkish, brown, red or yellow. Tabular short or long prismatic crystals; also commonly fibrous, compact or massive. Vitreous or pearly luster; transparent to translucent. White streak.

Environment Occurs in thermally metamorphosed siliceous carbonates, igneous rocks and skarn deposits.

Notable Localities Canada: Lac de Gras, Northwest Territories; Ice River complex, Ottertail Range, British Columbia; Bancroft district, Ontario; Black Lake, Thetford Mines and Oka carbonatite complex, Quebec. USA: Jacumba district, Imperial County, California. Europe: Kangerlussuaq Fjord, Tunu, Greenland; Alnö, Sweden; Isle of Mull, Scotland; Mounts Somma, Vesuvius and Peloritani, Sicily, Italy; Santorini volcano, Greece; Dognecea, Banat, Romania.

Name Named after William Hyde Wollaston (1766–1828), the English chemist and mineralogist who discovered palladium in 1804 and rhodium in 1809.

Wollastonite is used extensively in the ceramics industry. The insulators in most spark plugs are made from wollastonite, and the fibrous material is used as a replacement for asbestos insulation and in the manufacture of floor and wall tiles.

Wollastonite, Gouverneur Talc Company No. 4 Quarry, Diana, New York, USA • 10 x 6.5 x 3 cm

Pectolite, Black Lake, Quebec, Canada • 4 x 11 x 4.5 cm

Pectolite

Formula $NaCa_2Si_3O_8(OH)$

Crystal System triclinic

Space Group $P\bar{1}$

Hardness 4.5–5.0

Specific Gravity 2.7–2.9

Cleavage perfect on {100} and {001}

Fracture uneven

Tenacity brittle

Habit Colorless, white, pale pink, greenish or pale blue. Crystals may be tabular but also commonly acicular, radiating fibrous, spheroidal or columnar; also fine-grained or massive. Silky, subvitreous luster; translucent to opaque. White streak.

Environment A primary mineral in nepheline syenites. Also found as a hydrothermal mineral in cavities in basalts and diabases and in serpentinites and peridotites.

Notable Localities Canada: Jeffrey Mine, Asbestos, and Mont-Saint-Hilaire, Quebec. USA: Magnet Cove and Granite Mountain, near Little Rock, Arkansas; Paterson and Bergen Hill, New Jersey. Europe: Lovozero and Khibiny massifs, Kola Peninsula, Russia. Africa: Bou Agrao, High Atlas Mountains, Morocco; Pilanesberg, North West Province, South Africa. Asia: Ahmadnagar, Maharashtra, India.

Name From the Greek *pektos*, meaning "congealed" or "well put together," in allusion to its resistance to pulverization.

Some specimens of pectolite are triboluminescent: they give off light when friction is applied.

Sérandite

Formula $NaMn^{2+}_2Si_3O_8(OH)$

Crystal System triclinic

Space Group $P\bar{1}$

Hardness 5.0–5.5

Specific Gravity 3.2–3.4

Cleavage perfect on {001} and {100}

Fracture uneven

Tenacity brittle

Habit Pale pink, rose red, salmon red, deep orange, brown or colorless. Prismatic to acicular, bladed, blocky or tabular crystals; also radiating crystal aggregates or massive. Vitreous or greasy luster; transparent to translucent. White streak.

Environment Occurs in sodalite zenoliths and pegmatites, phonolite and contact metamorphic rocks.

Notable Localities Canada: Mont-Saint-Hilaire, Quebec. Europe: Mt. Karnasurt, Lovozero Massif, Kola Peninsula, Russia. Asia: Tumannoe deposit, Bol'shoi Santar Island, Sea of Okhotsk, Russia; Tanohata Mine, Iwate, Japan.

Name Named after J.M. Sérand, a mineral collector from West Africa who assisted in obtaining the first samples.

Sérandite, Poudrette Quarry, Mont-Saint-Hilaire, Quebec, Canada • 12.5 x 11.5 x 4 cm

Hornblende Group

Formula ferrohornblende $Ca_2(Fe^{2+}_4Al)(Si_7Al)O_{22}(OH)_2$

magnesiohornblende $Ca_2[Mg_4(Al,Fe^{3+})]Si_7AlO_{22}(OH)_2$

Crystal System monoclinic

Space Group $C2/m$

Hardness 5.0–6.0

Specific Gravity 3.1–3.3

Cleavage perfect on {110}, intersecting at 56° and 124°

Fracture uneven

Tenacity brittle

Habit Green, dark green to brownish green to black. Prismatic crystals, but more commonly bladed and unterminated. Vitreous to pearly luster; semitransparent. White streak.

Environment Occurs widely in metamorphic rocks, especially in amphibolites, hornblende schists, gneisses and mafic igneous rocks.

Notable Localities Ferrohornblende Canada: Bancroft, Pakenham and Eganville, Ontario. USA: Franklin and Sterling Hill, Ogdensburg, New Jersey; Edwards, Pierrepont and Gouverneur, New York. Europe: Kragerö, Arendal and around Langesundsfjord, Norway; Pargas, Finland; Bílina and Schima, Czech Republic. **Magnesiohornblende** USA: Sierra Nevada batholiths, California. Europe: Mounts Vesuvius and Somma, Campania, Italy.

Name From Old German words meaning "horn" and "blind" or "to deceive," alluding to the fact that it occurs in ore deposits but does not yield any metal.

Chemical analysis is necessary to distinguish between hornblendes. The two end members of this group are ferrohornblende, which contains iron, and magnesiohornblende, which contains magnesium.

Magnesiohornblende, Renfrew County, Ontario, Canada • 8 x 5 x 3

Pargasite, Aliabad, Hunza Valley, Gilgit, Pakistan • 3 x 4 x 2 cm

Pargasite

Formula $NaCa_2(Mg_4Al)(Si_6Al_2)O_{22}(OH)_2$

Crystal System monoclinic

Space Group $C2/m$

Hardness 5.0–6.0

Specific Gravity 3.07–3.5

Cleavage perfect on {110}

Fracture subconchoidal to splintery

Tenacity brittle

Habit Light brown, brown or greenish brown to dark green and black. Stout prismatic crystals or granular. Vitreous luster; transparent to translucent. White streak.

Environment Found in skarns metamorphosed from siliceous limestones, schists and amphibolites; also forms in andesitic volcanic and altered ultramafic rocks.

Notable Localities Canada: southern Baffin Island, Nunavut; Kirkland Lake area, Ontario. USA: Jensen Quarry, California; Stillwater complex, Montana; San Carlos, Arizona; Burlington, Pennsylvania. Latin America: Tinaquillo, Venezuela. Europe: Långban, Värmland, Sweden; Pargas Valley, Finland; Sau Alpe, Carinthia, Austria.

Name From its occurrence in the Pargas Valley, Finland.

Tremolite

Formula $Ca_2Mg_5Si_8O_{22}(OH)_2$

Crystal System monoclinic

Space Group $C2/m$

Hardness 5.0–6.0

Specific Gravity 2.9–3.4

Cleavage perfect on {110}, intersecting at 56° and 124°

Fracture splintery

Tenacity brittle

Habit White, gray or lavender to pink. Elongated, stout prismatic or flattened bladed crystals; also fibrous, granular or columnar aggregates. Vitreous luster; transparent to translucent. White streak.

Environment Formed by contact metamorphism of calcium-magnesium siliceous sediments. Occurs in greenschist facies metamorphic rocks derived from ultramafic or magnesium carbonate rocks.

Notable Localities Canada: Wilberforce, Ontario; Mont-Saint-Hilaire, Quebec. USA: Pierrepont, Gouverneur, Edwards and Macomb, New York; Franklin, New Jersey; Lee, Massachusetts. Latin America: Brumado Mine, Bahia, Brazil. Europe: St. Marcel, Piedmont, Italy. Africa: Lelatema, Tanzania. Asia: Kozano, Badakhshan, Afghanistan.

Name From its occurrence in the Tremola Valley (Val Tremola), Central St. Gotthard Massif, Switzerland.

Tremolite, Kuran wa Munjan, Badakhshan, Afghanistan • 8 x 4 x 2 cm

Tremolite, Haliburton, Ontario, Canada • 36 x 19 x 16 cm

Tremolite is an important mineral to petrologists because at high temperatures it is unstable and will convert to diopside ($CaMgSi_2O_6$). When tremolite but no diopside is found, this indicates that the rock has not endured extremely high temperatures. Without trace amounts of iron in its crystal structure, tremolite has a typical creamy white color, but with just a small amount of iron it becomes green. Increased iron content raises the specific gravity and index of refraction and darkens the green color.

Actinolite (Nephrite)

Formula $Ca_2(Mg,Fe^{2+})_5Si_8O_{22}(OH)_2$

Crystal System monoclinic

Space Group $C2/m$

Hardness 5.0–6.0 (6.5 for nephrite)

Specific Gravity 3.03–3.24

Cleavage good on {110}

Fracture uneven

Tenacity brittle; tough in fibrous aggregates

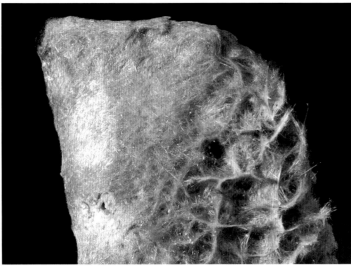

ABOVE: Actinolite (byssolite variety), Centreville Quarry, Centreville, Virginia, USA. This variety of actinolite is made up of free-growing, often matted, hair-like fibers. • 14 x 20 x 6 cm

RIGHT: Massive nephrite jade, New Zealand • 29 x 18 x 0.5 cm

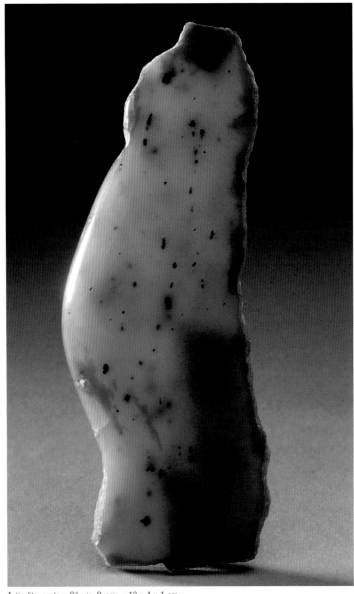

Actinolite, eastern Siberia, Russia • 13 x 4 x 1 cm

Habit Usually green, but can range from white to gray to black. In euhedral crystals, short to long prismatic, but more commonly bladed crystals or in aggregates, as radiating groups; compact, tough aggregates of short, tightly interlocking fibers with subparallel alignment. Vitreous to silky luster; transparent to translucent. White streak.

Environment Produced by low-grade regional or contact metamorphism of magnesium carbonate or mafic or ultramafic rocks; also occurs in glaucophane-bearing blueschists.

Notable Localities Canada: Fraser River, British Columbia. USA: around Jade Mountain, near Kobuk River, Alaska; Lander, Wyoming. Europe: Mt. Greiner, Zillertal, and Untersulzbachtal, Austria. Asia: Kunlun Mountains, Xinjiang (Uyghur Autonomous Region), China. New Zealand: around Mt. Cook, South Island.

Name From the Greek for "ray," in allusion to the mineral's common radiating fibrous habit. *Nephrite* comes from the Latin for kidney, in reference to its alleged beneficial effect in kidney ailments.

Nephrite is a form of actinolite and one of the two mineral species called jade. Nephrite can be found in a translucent white to very light yellow form known in China as mutton-fat jade. It also occurs as an opaque white to very light brown or gray known as chicken-bone jade, as well as a variety of greens. Nephrite is used as an ornamental stone for beads, carvings and jewelry.

Hastingsite, Obira Mine, Ono-gun, Oita, Kyushu, Japan • 6 x 7 x 2 cm

Hastingite

Formula $NaCa_2(Fe^{2+}_4Fe^{3+})(Si_6Al_2)O_{22}(OH)_2$

Crystal System monoclinic

Space Group $C2/m$

Hardness 5.0–6.0

Specific Gravity 3.35–3.5

Cleavage perfect on {110}

Fracture subconchoidal to splintery

Tenacity brittle

Habit Black, dark green, green brown or yellow. Prismatic crystals. Vitreous luster; semitransparent. Greenish gray streak.

Environment Occurs in nepheline syenite and granite and in schists, gneisses and amphibolites.

Notable Localities Canada: near Crescent Lake, Cassiar Mountains, Yukon; Bancroft and elsewhere in Hastings County, Ontario. USA: Iron Hill, Colorado; Franklin, New Jersey; Cornwall, New York. Europe: Tysfjord, Norway; Almunge, Sweden. Asia: Goubensky Massif, southern Ural Mountains, Russia; Obira Mine, Ogato, Kyushu, Japan.

Name From its occurrence in Hastings County, Ontario.

The Royal Ontario Museum houses the "type" material for hastingite, which is the reference specimen for this mineral.

Riebeckite

Formula $Na_2(Fe^{2+}_3Fe^{3+}_2)Si_8O_{22}(OH)_2$

Crystal System monoclinic

Space Group $C2/m$

Hardness 6.0

Specific Gravity 3.3–3.4

Cleavage perfect on {110}, intersecting at 56° and 124°

Fracture conchoidal to uneven

Tenacity brittle

Habit Black to dark blue. Prismatic crystals; commonly fibrous, asbestiform, earthy or massive. Dull to vitreous luster; semitransparent. Greenish brown streak.

Environment Occurs in alkalic granites and syenites, more rarely in felsic volcanics and granite pegmatites, and in some schists. Found in iron formations as asbestiform "crocidolite."

Notable Localities Canada: Mont-Saint-Hilaire, Quebec; Red Wine complex, Labrador, Newfoundland and Labrador. USA: Washington Pass, Washington State; St. Peter's Dome, near Pikes Peak, Colorado; Quincy, Massachusetts. Latin America: around Chapare, Cochabamba, Bolivia. Europe: Cornwall, England. Asia: Socotra Island, Aden, Yemen.

Name Named in honor of Emil Riebeck (1853–85), a German explorer.

Riebeckite inclusions in quartz, Mt. Malosa, Zomba, Malawi • 9 x 8 x 6 cm

Gedrite, Bamle, Telemark, Norway • 8 x 6 x 5 cm

Gedrite

Formula $Mg_2(Mg_3Al_2)(Si_6Al_2)O_{22}(OH)_2$

Crystal System orthorhombic

Space Group *Pnma*

Hardness 5.5–6.0

Specific Gravity 3.15–3.57

Cleavage perfect on {210}

Fracture subconchoidal to uneven

Tenacity brittle

Habit White, gray, brown or green. Bladed and prismatic crystals or fibrous. Vitreous luster; transparent to translucent. Gray white streak.

Environment Widespread in medium- to high-grade metamorphic rocks; also occurs in metasomatized contact metamorphic rocks.

Notable Localities Canada: Geco Mine, Manitouwadge, Ontario; Île-du-Grand-Calumet (Calumet Island), Quebec. USA: Haddam, Connecticut. Europe: Strathy and Glen Urquhart, Highland district, Scotland; Héas, Gèdre, France. Asia: Wakamatsu Mine, Tottori, and Iratsuyama, Ehime, Japan.

Name From its occurrence in the Gèdre area of France, which is in the Pyrenees Mountains, very close to Spain.

Neptunite

Formula $KNa_2LiFe^{2+}_2Ti_2Si_8O_{24}$

Crystal System monoclinic

Space Group *Cc*

Hardness 5.0–6.0

Specific Gravity 3.19–3.23

Cleavage perfect on {110}

Fracture conchoidal

Tenacity brittle

Habit Black. Prismatic crystals, typically with square cross-sections, and may be curved or twisted. Vitreous luster; nearly opaque. Brown streak.

Environment Occurs in natrolite veins cutting a glaucophane schist inclusion in a serpentinite body.

Notable Localities Canada: Mont-Saint-Hilaire, Quebec; Seal Lake, Labrador, Newfoundland and Labrador.

Name Named for Neptune, the sea god of Roman mythology, because of the close association of its type occurrence with aegirine, the name of which derives from Ægir, the Scandinavian sea god.

Neptunite, San Benito County, California, USA • 9 x 4 x 9 cm

CHAPTER 12

Cyclosilicates

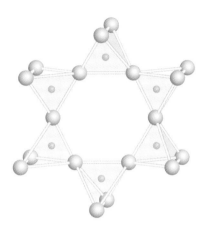

Cyclosilicates form chains like those in the inosilicates, except that the ends of the chains are linked to form rings. The rings can be made of the minimum three tetrahedrons to form triangular rings, such as in benitoite (Si_3O_9), while four tetrahedrons can form a roughly square shape, as in axinite (Si_4O_{12}). Six tetrahedrons form hexagonal shapes, which are found in beryl, cordierite and the members of the tourmaline group (Si_6O_{18}). There are even eight-member rings (Si_8O_{24}) and yet more complicated ring structures. Several gemstone minerals are represented in this group, which is generally notable for its hardness, luster and durability.

ABOVE: Beryl (morganite variety), Barra da Salinas, Minas Gerais, Brazil • 77 x 58 x 52 cm, 1,625.00 ct

RIGHT: Dioptase, Tsumeb, Namibia • 8 x 5 x 3 cm

LEFT: Tourmaline-group minerals, Mt. Tsilaizina, Antananarivo, Madagascar • 11 x 11 x 0.5 cm

Dioptase

Formula $CuSiO_3 \cdot H_2O$

Crystal System hexagonal

Space Group $R\bar{3}$

Hardness 5.0

Specific Gravity 3.3

Cleavage perfect on $\{10\bar{1}1\}$

Fracture conchoidal to uneven

Tenacity brittle

Habit Emerald green or blue green. Commonly prismatic to rhombohedral crystals; also as indistinct crystalline aggregates or massive. Vitreous luster; transparent to translucent. Green streak.

Environment Occurs as a secondary mineral in oxidized zones of copper deposits.

Notable Localities USA: Harquahala Mine, California; Bisbee, Arizona. Latin America: Chiviquin, Córdoba, Argentina. Europe: Piedmont, Italy. Africa: Tsumeb, Guchab and Omaue deposit, Kaokoveld, Namibia. Asia: Altyn-Tyube, Karaganda Oblast, Kazakhstan.

Name From the Greek words for "through" and "to see," in allusion to the high visibility of its internal cleavage planes.

Dioptase, Tsumeb Mine, Tsumeb, Namibia • 4.5 x 6 x 5 cm

Sugilite, Wessels Mine, Hotazel, Northern Cape, South Africa • 24 x 12 x 2 cm

Sugilite

Formula $KNa_2Fe^{3+}{}_2(Li_3Si_{12})O_{30}$

Crystal System hexagonal

Space Group $P6/mcc$

Hardness 5.5–6.5

Specific Gravity 2.74

Cleavage $\{0001\}$ poor

Fracture subconchoidal

Tenacity none

Habit Light brownish yellow to bright magenta. Crystals, shaped like slender prisms, rare; commonly in interlocking aggregates of subhedral grains, compact to massive. Vitreous luster; transparent to translucent. White streak.

Environment Found in strata-bound metamorphosed manganese deposits and peralkaline igneous rocks.

Notable Localities Canada: Mont-Saint-Hilaire, Quebec. Africa: Wessels and N'Chwaning mines, near Kuruman, Cape Province, South Africa. Asia: Iwagi islet, Ehime, Japan.

Name Named for Professor Ken-ichi Sugi (1901–48), the Japanese petrologist who discovered the mineral.

Cordierite

Formula $Mg_2Al_4Si_5O_{18}$

Crystal System orthorhombic

Space Group *Cccm*

Hardness 7.0–7.5

Specific Gravity 2.5

Cleavage fair on {100}; poor on {001} and {010}

Fracture subconchoidal

Tenacity brittle

Habit Blue, smoky blue, bluish violet, greenish, yellowish brown or gray. Crystals short prismatic; typically granular to compact or massive. Vitreous luster; transparent to translucent. White streak.

Environment Occurs in thermally metamorphosed argillaceous sediments and high-grade regionally metamorphosed schists, gneisses and granulites. Also found in mafic igneous rocks and granites and as a detrital mineral.

Notable Localities Canada: Thompson, Manitoba. USA: Richmond, New Hampshire; Haddam, Connecticut. Europe: Orijärvi and Leppävirta, Finland. Africa: Treasure Casket Claims, Fungure Reserve, Zimbabwe. Asia: Tiruchchirappalli and Coimbatore, Tamil Nadu, India; gem gravels in Sri Lanka. Australia: Harts Range, Northern Territory.

Name Named in honor of Pierre Louis A. Cordier (1777–1861), the French mining engineer and geologist who first studied the species.

Cordierite, India • 12 x 11 x 0.3 cm

Round-cut cordierite (iolite variety) (source unknown) • 2.5 x 2.5 x 8 cm, 5.90 ct

Iolite is the gem-quality variety of the mineral cordierite. Pleochroism is very pronounced in iolite, producing three different colors in the same stone: violet blue, yellow gray and light blue. The major sources of gem-grade iolite are Sri Lanka, India, Madagascar and Myanmar (Burma); it is sometimes used as a less expensive alternative to sapphire.

Tourmaline Group
(Schorl and Elbaite)

Formula schorl $NaFe^{2+}_3Al_6(BO_3)_3Si_6O_{18}(OH)_4$

elbaite $Na(Al_{1.5}Li_{1.5})Al_6(BO_3)_3Si_6O_{18}(OH)_4$

Crystal System hexagonal

Space Group $R3m$

Hardness 7.0

Specific Gravity 3.24

Cleavage very poor on $\{11\bar{2}0\}$ and $\{10\bar{1}1\}$

Fracture uneven to conchoidal

Tenacity brittle

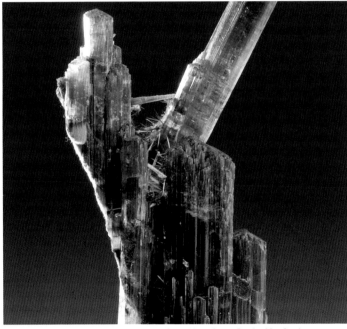

ABOVE: Tourmaline, Cruzeiro Mine, São José da Safira, Minas Gerais, Brazil • 22 x 6 x 4 cm

BELOW: Bicolor tourmaline gemstone (source unknown) • 2.1 x 2.9 x 1 cm, 63.00 ct

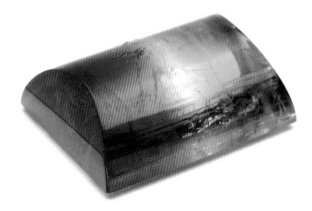

ABOVE: Schorl, Erongo Mountains, Namibia • 7 x 8 x 6 cm
RIGHT: Elbaite, Minas Gerais, Brazil • 14 x 8.5 x 12 cm

Habit Black, brownish black or bluish black (schorl); green, blue, red, orange, yellow or colorless (elbaite); zoning common, parallel to trigonal outline (both). Crystals prismatic to acicular, with prominent trigonal prism and pyramid, commonly hemimorphic; also radial, fibrous or massive. Vitreous to resinous luster; transparent to translucent to nearly opaque. White streak.

Environment Both types found in granites and granite pegmatites, high-temperature hydrothermal veins and some metamorphic rocks; also as detrital sediments.

Notable Localities Schorl USA: Little Three Mine, Ramona, California. Latin America: Santa Cruz, Sonora, Mexico. Europe: Sonnenberg, Harz Mountains, Germany. Asia: Nuristan district, Laghman, Afghanistan; around Alabashka and Mursinka, Ural Mountains, Russia. **Elbaite** USA: Pala and Mesa Grande districts, California. Latin America: Araçuaí-Itinga-Salinas and Itatiaia district, Governador Valaderes, Minas Gerais, Brazil. Europe: around San Piero, Campo, Elba, Italy.

Name *Schorl* comes from the Old German *Schürl*, which perhaps means "impurities." Elbaite is named from its occurrence on the island of Elba, Italy.

The tourmaline group includes many minerals of different chemistries and therefore different colors. The black version, schorl, is the most common, accounting for more than 95 percent. The remaining 5 percent represents the more attractive, gem-quality stones.

Beryl

Formula $Be_3Al_2Si_6O_{18}$

Crystal System hexagonal

Space Group *P6/mcc*

Hardness 7.5–8.0

Specific Gravity 2.7

Cleavage imperfect on {0001}

Fracture conchoidal to uneven

Tenacity brittle

Red beryl, Wah Wah Mountains, Beaver County, Utah, USA • 4 x 4 x 3 cm

ABOVE: Beryl (emerald variety), Coscuez Mine, Muzo, Boyacá, Colombia • 3.5 x 3.5 x 3 cm

LEFT: Art Deco ring (Colombia), beryl (emerald variety) in tiered platinum and diamond setting, 20.00 ct.

Habit Colorless, white, pale blue to sky blue, bluish green through green to greenish yellow or yellow, rose to peach, or deep pink to raspberry red; may be zoned. Crystals prismatic to tabular and may be complexly terminated by pyramids, as well as radial, trapiche or columnar; also granular to compact. Vitreous, resinous luster; transparent to translucent. White streak.

Environment Commonly occurs in pegmatites. Red beryl is found in topaz rhyolites.

Notable Localities Canada: Bernic Lake, Manitoba. USA: Pala and Rincon districts, California; Sawtooth Mountains, Idaho; Wah Wah Mountains, Utah; Mt. Antero, Colorado; Hiddenite, North Carolina. Latin America: Muzo and Chivor districts, Boyacá, Colombia. Europe: Volhynia, Ukraine. Africa: Rafin-Gabas Hills, near Jos, Nigeria; Muiâne pegmatite, Alto Ligonha, Mozambique; Ampandramaika-Malakialina pegmatite field, Madagascar. Asia: Khenj, Panjshir Valley, Afghanistan; Skardu and Hunza districts, Pakistan; Yekaterinburg (Sverdlovsk), Ural Mountains, and Nerchinsk, Chitinskaya Oblast, eastern Siberia, Russia.

Name Possibly from the Greek *beryllos*, which in antiquity referred to a number of blue-green stones.

Beryl is the mineral name, but its associated gem names are based on color. They include, among others, emerald (green), goshenite (clear or white), aquamarine (blue), heliodor (yellow) and morganite (pink).

Eudialyte

Formula $Na_{15}Ca_6Fe_3Zr_3Si(Si_{25}O_{73})(O,OH,H_2O)_3(Cl,OH)_2$

Crystal System hexagonal

Space Group $R\bar{3}c$

Hardness 5.0–6.0

Specific Gravity 2.74–3.1

Cleavage perfect to indistinct on {0001}; imperfect on {11$\bar{2}$0}

Fracture uneven

Tenacity brittle

Habit Brown, yellow brown, yellow, pink, rose red or cherry red. Crystals short rhombohedral to long prismatic; more commonly irregular masses and vein fillings. Vitreous to dull luster; translucent. White streak.

Environment Occurs in nepheline syenites, alkalic granites and associated pegmatites. May be a major constituent of both magmatic and late-stage pneumatolytic origin.

Notable Localities Canada: Shefield Lake complex, Kipawa River, Villedieu, Mont-Saint-Hilaire and near Saint-Amable, Quebec; Seal Lake and Red Wine complex, Labrador, Newfoundland and Labrador. USA: Pajarito Mountain, New Mexico; Magnet Cove, Arkansas. Europe: Kangerdlugssuaq Plateau, Ilímaussaq intrusion, Narssârssuk, Greenland.

Name From the Greek words for "easily" and "dissolved," alluding to its ready dissolution in acids.

Eudialyte, Kipawa complex, Les Lacs-du-Témiscamingue, Quebec, Canada • 13 x 9 x 6 cm

Benitoite, San Benito County, California, USA • 9 x 8 x 4.5 cm

Benitoite

Formula $BaTiSi_3O_9$

Crystal System hexagonal

Space Group $P\bar{6}2c$

Hardness 6.0–6.5

Specific Gravity 3.68

Cleavage poor on {10$\bar{1}$1}

Fracture conchoidal

Tenacity brittle

Habit Sapphire blue, white to colorless or pink; commonly bicolor. Flat prismatic crystals, tabular, triangular or hexagonal in outline. Vitreous luster; transparent to translucent. White streak.

Environment Occurs in compact granular natrolite veins cutting glaucophane schist interlayered with serpentine.

Notable Localities USA: Dallas Gem Mine, San Benito County, California; Diamond Jo Quarry, Magnet Cove, Arkansas. Asia: Ohmi, Niigata, Japan. Australia: Broken Hill, New South Wales.

Name From the type locality, San Benito County, California.

Catapleiite

Formula $Na_2ZrSi_3O_9 \cdot 2H_2O$

Crystal System monoclinic

Space Group *I2/c*

Hardness 5.5–6.0

Specific Gravity 2.65–2.9

Cleavage {100} perfect; {101} and {102} imperfect

Fracture conchoidal

Tenacity brittle

Catapleiite, Mont-Saint-Hilaire, Quebec, Canada • 8 x 7.5 x 1 cm

Catapleiite is a rare zirconium mineral that forms magnificent rosette clusters in specimens from Mont-Saint-Hilaire, Quebec, in Canada. Catapleiite is just one of the minerals that can form in those rarely encountered rocks that are low in silica and have high concentrations of alkali metals — truly unique chemical environments.

Catapleiite, Mont-Saint-Hilaire, Quebec, Canada • 10 x 6 x 5 cm

Habit Colorless, light gray, beige to tan, light yellow, orange or light blue. Crystals pseudo-hexagonal, thin tabular; rosettes of crystal plates. Weakly vitreous or dull luster; transparent to translucent to opaque. White streak.

Environment Occurs in syenites and nepheline syenites and in pegmatites, typically the result of metasomatic alteration of eudialyte.

Notable Localities Canada: Ice River Valley, south of Field, British Columbia; Mont-Saint-Hilaire, Miron Quarry, Montreal, and near Saint-Amable, Quebec. Europe: Ilímaussaq intrusion, Narssârssuk, and Kangerlussuaq Fjord, Greenland; Norra Kärr complex, near Gränna, Sweden; Khibiny and Lovozero massifs, Kola Peninsula, Russia.

Name From the Greek *kata* and *pleios*, meaning "with many," for its association with many other rare minerals.

ABOVE: Catapleiite, Mont-Saint-Hilaire, Quebec, Canada • 1.1 x 0.7 x 0.5 cm, 2.50 ct

RIGHT Catapleiite, Poudrette Quarry, Mont-Saint-Hilaire, Quebec, Canada • 9 x 7 x 4.5 cm

CHAPTER 13

Sorosilicates

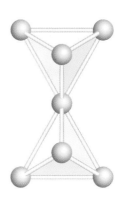

Sorosilicates have two silicate tetrahedrons linked by one oxygen ion, which means the basic chemical unit is the anion group Si_2O_7. Most of the minerals in the sorosilicate group are rare, but epidote is widespread in many metamorphic environments. Epidote — its formula is $Ca_2Al_2FeO[SiO_4][Si_2O_7](OH)$ — has single and paired SiO_4 tetrahedra; it provides an example of a silicate with two types of SiO_4 tetrahedral arrangements in the same structure. Another, more common sorosilicate mineral is hemimorphite: $Zn_4(Si_2O_7)(OH)_2 \cdot H_2O$. Hemimorphite is a secondary mineral (meaning that it is an alteration product) found in the oxidized portions of zinc ore deposits.

ABOVE: Suolunite, Black Lake, Quebec, Canada • 4 x 5 x 2 cm

RIGHT: Epidote, Brazil • 7 x 7.5 x 4 cm

LEFT: Vesuvianite, Asbestos, Quebec, Canada • 4.5 x 4 x 4.5 cm

Danburite, Charcas, San Luis Potosí, Mexico • 7 x 7 x 7 cm

Danburite

Formula $CaB_2Si_2O_7O$

Crystal System orthorhombic

Space Group *Pnam*

Hardness 7.0–7.5

Specific Gravity 3.0

Cleavage no distinct cleavage

Fracture subconchoidal to uneven

Tenacity brittle

Habit Colorless, white, amber, yellow, pink or yellow brown. Granular to glassy and prismatic; can easily be confused with topaz. Vitreous luster; transparent to translucent. White streak.

Environment Occurs in moderate- to low-temperature conditions as a contact metamorphic mineral.

Notable Localities USA: Danbury, Connecticut; Russell, New York. Europe: Kragerø district, Norway; Graubünden and Uri, Switzerland; Presov, Slovakia.

Name From its type locality, Danbury, Connecticut.

Axinite-(Fe)

Formula $Ca_2FeAl_2[BSi_4O_{15}](OH)$

Crystal System triclinic

Space Group $P\overline{1}$

Hardness 6.5–7.0

Specific Gravity 3.2–3.3

Cleavage {100} good; {001}, {110} and {011} poor

Fracture uneven to conchoidal

Tenacity brittle

Habit Usually gray to bluish gray, brown, honey brown or violet; less commonly green. Thin, wedge-shaped "ax-head" crystals common, frequently arranged in rosettes; also massive or granular. Vitreous luster; transparent to translucent. White streak.

Environment Most commonly found in high-grade metamorphic zones, hydrothermal metasomatism of granite or aplite, and igneous contacts with sedimentary rocks.

Notable Localities Canada: Timmins, Ontario. USA: Franklin and Bridgeville, New Jersey; King Mountain, North Carolina. Latin America: San Sebastian Mine, San Luis Potosí, Mexico; several localities in Brazil. Europe: Devon, England; Bourg d'Oisans and La Balme d'Auris, France; Uri, Switzerland; Premia, Italy. Asia: several localities in Japan. Australia: New South Wales.

Name From the ax-head shape of the crystals and its iron content.

Axinite-(Fe), Saranpaul, Khanty-Mansi, western Siberia, Russia • 6 x 5 x 3 cm

Ilvaite, Dal'negorsk, Primorskiy Krai, Russia • 3 x 2 x 2 cm

Ilvaite

Formula $CaFe_3O[Si_2O_7](OH)$

Crystal System orthorhombic

Space Group *Pnam*

Hardness 5.5–6.0

Specific Gravity 4.0

Cleavage {010} and {001} distinct; {100} indistinct

Fracture uneven

Tenacity brittle

Habit Iron black or dark grayish black. Crystals short to long prismatic, commonly striated vertically; also coarsely crystalline, massive or granular. Submetallic luster; opaque, but translucent in thin fragments. Brownish black streak.

Environment Occurs in contact metasomatic iron, zinc and copper ores, as well as in sodalite syenites and associated with zeolites.

Notable Localities USA: Laxey Mine, Idaho; Balmat, New York. Europe: Ilímaussaq complex, Greenland; Thyrill, Iceland; Fossum, Norway; Elba, Italy. Africa: Constantine, Algeria. Asia: Dal'negorsk, Russia; a few localities in Japan.

Name Named for the location of its discovery — Elba, Italy — which was called Ilva in Latin.

Clinozoisite

Formula $Ca_2(Al,Fe^{3+})Al_2(SiO_4)(Si_2O_7)(O)(OH)$

Crystal System monoclinic

Space Group $P2_1/m$

Hardness 6.5

Specific Gravity 3.2–3.4

Cleavage {001} and {100} perfect

Fracture uneven

Tenacity brittle

Habit Colorless, pale yellow, pink, red, gray or green. Prismatic crystals elongated in one direction, often striated; may be granular, massive or fibrous. Vitreous luster; transparent to translucent. Grayish white streak.

Environment Occurs in regional metamorphic rocks, particularly in greenschist and epidote-amphibolite facies, pegmatites and veins. Also found in acid igneous rocks contaminated with calc-silicate material.

Notable Localities Canada: Timmins, Ontario. USA: Allenspark, near Boulder, Colorado; Eden Mills, Vermont. Mexico: Pinos Altos, Gavilanes and Arroyo Puerto Nuevo, Baja California; Alamos, Sonora. Europe: Switzerland; Austria; Italy. Africa: Madagascar.

Name From the crystal system, which is a monoclinic dimorph of zoisite.

Clinozoisite, Fenomeno Mine, Rosa de Castillo, Baja California Norte, Mexico • 3.5 x 1 x 0.5 cm

Hemimorphite

Formula $Zn_4[Si_2O_7](OH)_2 \cdot H_2O$

Crystal System orthorhombic

Space Group *Imm*2

Hardness 4.5–5.0

Specific Gravity 3.4–3.5

Cleavage {110} perfect; {101} good; {001} poor

Fracture uneven

Tenacity brittle

Hemimorphite, Tri-State Mining District, Joplin, Missouri, USA • 12 x 16 x 11 cm

Hemimorphite tends to have two main forms. One is very glassy, clear or white thin-bladed crystals, often well-formed and showing many faces. The other form is a blue to blue-green botryoidal crust that resembles smithsonite or prehnite.

ABOVE: Hemimorphite, Ojuela Mine, Mapimí, Durango, Mexico • 6 x 6 x 4 cm
RIGHT: Hemimorphite, Durango, Mexico • 8 x 6 x 6 cm

Habit Usually colorless or white; less commonly pale yellow, light green, sky blue or brown. Isolated or radiating groups of distinctly hemimorphic crystals, prismatic and flattened to a greater or lesser degree parallel to {010}; also botryoidal, massive, granular or fibrous or form incrustations. Vitreous luster; transparent to translucent. White streak.

Environment A widespread phase in the oxidation zone of zinc deposits.

Notable Localities USA: Sterling Hill, New Jersey; with zinc ores, Tri-State Mining District, especially Granby, Missouri; several other U.S. localities. Latin America: El Potosí and San Antonio mines, Santa Eulalia, and other localities, Mexico. Europe: Roughten Gill and Alston Moor, Cumberland, England; Aachen area, Belgium and Germany; Almeria and Santander provinces, Spain. Africa: northwest of Setif, Algeria; Tsumeb, Namibia. Australia: Broken Hill, New South Wales.

Name From the Greek *hemi*, meaning "half," and *morphie*, meaning "form," a reference to its crystal form.

Vesuvianite

Formula $Ca_{10}(Mg,Fe)_2Al_4(SiO_4)_5(Si_2O_7)_2(OH)_4$

Crystal System tetragonal

Space Group *P4/nnc*

Hardness 6.5

Specific Gravity 3.3–3.45

Cleavage poor

Fracture subconchoidal to uneven

Tenacity brittle

Habit Green or chartreuse, but may be white, yellow, pink, yellow brown, greenish yellow, brown, red, black, purple or blue. Commonly short pyramidal to long prismatic crystals, but can be in many forms, even on one sample; columnar, granular and massive also common. Vitreous to resinous luster; transparent to translucent. White streak.

Environment A rock-forming or accessory mineral in skarns, rodingites and altered alkali syenites; frequently associated with grossular, wollastonite, diopside and calcite.

Notable Localities Canada: Black Lake, Quebec. USA: San Benito, California; Sanford, Maine; Olmsteadville, New York; Franklin, New Jersey. Europe: Eger, Norway; Mt. Vesuvius, Italy. Asia: Muslim Bagh, Pakistan; Yakutia, Russia.

Name From the locality where it was discovered, Mount Vesuvius, in Italy.

Vesuvianite, Jeffrey Mine, Asbestos, Quebec, Canada • 2.5 x 2.5 x 2.5 cm

Zoisite, Arusha, Tanzania • 1.5 x 2.5 x 1 cm

Zoisite

Formula $Ca_2Al_3(SiO_4)(Si_2O_7)O(OH)$

Crystal System orthorhombic

Space Group *Pnma*

Hardness 6.0–7.0

Specific Gravity 3.15–3.3

Cleavage {100} perfect; {010} difficult

Fracture conchoidal to uneven

Tenacity brittle

Habit Yellowish green, green, brown, blue (tanzanite); colorless, purple, gray or pink (thulite). Crystals prismatic, vertically striated. Vitreous luster, sometimes pearly on cleavage; transparent to translucent. White streak.

Environment Occurs in regional and contact metamorphic rocks; also in quartz veins, pegmatites and some eclogites.

Notable Localities Europe: Gefrees, Germany; Vipiteno and Passiria, Italy. **Thulite** Canada: Remigny, Quebec. USA: Pilar, New Mexico. Europe: Sauland and Lexviken, Norway. Asia: Ural Mountains, Russia. **Tanzanite** Africa: Merelani Hills, Tanzania. Asia: Baltistan, Pakistan.

Name Named for Siegmund Zois, Baron von Edelstein (1747–1819), an Austrian natural scientist.

Piemontite

Formula (Ca,Mn)(Ca,Sr,REE)(Mn,Fe)(Al,Mn)Al(SiO$_4$)(Si$_2$O$_7$)(OH,F)(O)

Crystal System monoclinic

Space Group $P2_1/m$

Hardness 6.0–6.5

Specific Gravity 3.4–3.6

Cleavage {001} perfect

Fracture uneven

Tenacity brittle

Habit Reddish brown, black or red. Crystals prismatic and elongate on b. Vitreous luster; translucent to nearly opaque. Red streak.

Environment Occurs in regional metamorphosed rocks of greenschist and amphibolite facies, in metasomatized manganese deposits and in low-temperature hydrothermal veins in altered rhyolites, andesite and diorites.

Notable Localities USA: Tucson Mountains, Arizona; Pine Mountain, Pennsylvania. Europe: Piedmont, Italy. Africa: Wessels Mine, near Kuruman, Cape Province, South Africa. Asia: Kajlidongri Mine, Jhabua district, Madhya Pradesh, India.

Name From the locality where it was discovered, Piedmont, Italy, which is Piemonte in Italian.

Piemontite, Saint-Marcel, Valle d'Aosta, Italy • 7.5 x 5.5 x 3 cm

Allanite-(Ce), Ontario, Canada • 10 x 6 x 6 cm

Allanite-(Ce)

Formula (Ce,Y,Ca)$_2$(Fe^{2+},Fe^{3+})Al$_2$(SiO$_4$)(Si$_2$O$_7$)(O)(OH)

Crystal System monoclinic

Space Group $P2_1/m$

Hardness 5.0–6.5

Specific Gravity 3.4–4.2

Cleavage {001} imperfect; {100} and {110} poor

Fracture conchoidal to uneven

Tenacity brittle

Habit Light brown to black. Crystals tabular to long prismatic; can be granular as well; often metamict. Resinous to submetallic luster; translucent to opaque. Weakly radioactive. Grayish brown streak.

Environment A common accessory mineral in many igneous rocks, especially felsic and metamorphosed igneous rocks. Also occurs in pegmatites, skarns and tactites.

Notable Localities Canada: Murchison, Ontario. Europe: Avigeit, eastern Greenland; Vaarala, Finland; Ytterby, Riddarhyttan and Finbo, Sweden; Isle of Skye, Scotland; Luzenac, France. Africa: Sama, Madagascar. Asia: Ural and Vishnevye mountains, Russia.

Name Named for Thomas Allan (1777–1833), the Scottish mineralogist who first observed the mineral.

Axinite-(Fe)

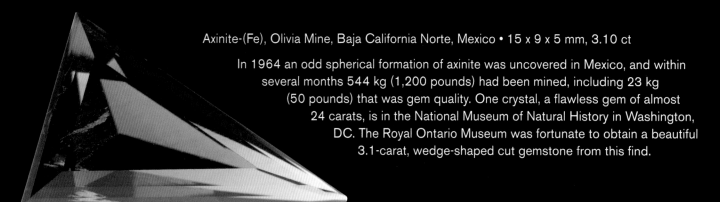

Axinite-(Fe), Olivia Mine, Baja California Norte, Mexico • 15 x 9 x 5 mm, 3.10 ct

In 1964 an odd spherical formation of axinite was uncovered in Mexico, and within several months 544 kg (1,200 pounds) had been mined, including 23 kg (50 pounds) that was gem quality. One crystal, a flawless gem of almost 24 carats, is in the National Museum of Natural History in Washington, DC. The Royal Ontario Museum was fortunate to obtain a beautiful 3.1-carat, wedge-shaped cut gemstone from this find.

Vesuvianite

Vesuvianite, known as idocrase to the gem world, typically forms short to long transparent prismatic crystals in various colors, of which green, yellow and brown are the most common. The Jeffrey Mine in Quebec, Canada, which was the largest open-pit asbestos mine in the world, is a prolific source of fine gem and mineral specimens. The mine is well-known for producing beautiful transparent pink and green vesuvianite crystals.

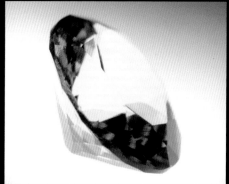

ABOVE: Mixed brilliant-cut vesuvianite, Jeffrey Mine, Asbestos, Quebec, Canada • 0.6 x 0.5 x 0.3 cm, 0.70 ct

LEFT: Vesuvianite, Asbestos, Quebec, Canada • 2.5 x 2.5 x 2.5 cm

Tanzanite (Zoisite)

Brooch/pendant, Birks (Canada), tanzanite, diamonds and yellow gold, 3.6 x 2.7 x 1.5 cm, 48.00 ct. This versatile piece of jewelry contains a large oval tanzanite of 30.00 carats accompanied by 26 diamonds totaling 2.00 carats. It can be used in several different ways to suit the wearer's needs. The back of the brooch has a clip called a "bead enhancer," which allows the piece to be worn as a single pendant on a chain or attached to a strand of pearls to "enhance" them.

Epidote

Formula $Ca_2(Fe^{3+},Al)_3(SiO_4)(Si_2O_7)(O,OH)_2$

Crystal System monoclinic

Space Group $P2_1/m$

Hardness 6.5

Specific Gravity 3.3–3.5

Cleavage {001} perfect; {100} good

Fracture conchoidal, uneven or splintery

Tenacity brittle

Habit Light to dark pistachio green. Crystals short to long prismatic, often striated, but also thick tabular or acicular; commonly massive, coarse to fine granular, or fibrous. Pearly or resinous luster; transparent to nearly opaque. Grayish white streak.

Environment Very common in regional and contact metamorphic rocks and as a product of hydrothermal alteration of plagioclase.

Notable Localities Canada: Hemlo, Ontario. USA: Haddam, Connecticut. Europe: Arendal, Norway; Outokumpu area, Finland; Cornwall, England; Zermatt, Switzerland; Knappenwand, Untersulzbachtal River, Salzburg, and Zillertal, Austria; Piedmont, Italy. Africa: Namibia. Asia: Ural Mountains, Russia; Gilgit, Tormiq and Dusso, northwestern Pakistan; Tawmaw, Myanmar (Burma).

Name From the Greek *epidosis,* meaning "increase," because the base of the prism has one side longer than the other.

Epidote, Sulzbach, Tyrol, Austria • 3.5 x 7.5 x 4.5 cm

Perhaps the most famous source of world-class epidote specimens is Knappenwand, in the Hohe Tauern Mountains of Salzburg, Austria. Epidotes from this locality tend to be a dark olive green, with deep striations and sharp terminations. This fairly dense but fragile mineral has distinct cleavage; it is rarely cut into gemstones.

BELOW: Epidote, Copper Mountain, Prince of Wales Island, Alaska, USA • 12.5 x 25 x 12 cm

LEFT: Epidote, Knappenwand, Untersulzbachtal, Salzburg, Austria • 6 x 8 x 2 cm

Prismatine, Gatineau River, Hincks Bridge, Quebec, Canada • 12 x 11 x 5 cm

Kornerupine and Prismatine

Formula **kornerupine** $(Mg,Fe^{2+})_4Al_6(Si,Al,B)_5O_{21}(OH)$

prismatine $(Mg,Al,Fe)_6Al_4(Si,Al)_4(B,Si,Al)(O,OH,F)_{22}$

Crystal System orthorhombic

Space Group *Cmcm*

Hardness 6.5–7.0

Specific Gravity 3.3–3.5

Cleavage {110} distinct prismatic; {001} poor

Fracture none

Tenacity brittle

Habit Typically dark to sea green but also colorless, white, blue, pink, greenish yellow or black. Crystals rod-like to fibrous, with long prisms. White streak.

Environment Occurs in silicon-poor, magnesium- and aluminum-rich gneisses, often associated with cordierite, sapphirine, corundum and sillimanite.

Notable Localities Less than 60 localities known. Canada: Opinicon Lake, Ontario; Lac-Sainte-Marie, Quebec. Europe: Fiskenaesset region, Greenland; Kola Peninsula, Russia; Saxony, Germany.

Name Kornerupine was named in honor of the Danish geologist Andreas Nikolaus Kornerup (1857–83).

Leucophanite

Formula $NaCaBeSi_2O_6F$

Crystal System orthorhombic or triclinic

Space Group $P2_12_12_1$ or $P\bar{1}$

Hardness 3.0–4.0

Specific Gravity 3.0

Cleavage {001} perfect; {100} and {010} distinct

Fracture none

Tenacity brittle

Habit Colorless, pale yellow or light green. Short prismatic to tabular crystals. Vitreous luster; transparent to translucent. White streak.

Environment Found in nepheline-syenite pegmatites.

Notable Localities Canada: Mont-Saint-Hilaire, Quebec. Europe: Narssârssuk, Greenland; Langesundsfjord, Norway; Kola Peninsula, Russia.

Name From the Greek for "white" and "to appear," for its usual color.

Leucophanite, Poudrette Quarry, Mont-Saint-Hilaire, Quebec, Canada • 1.5 x 2 x 1.5 cm

Lawsonite, Reed Station, Tiburon Peninsula, Marin County, California, USA • 9 x 6 x 4 cm

Lawsonite

Formula $CaAl_2Si_2O_7(OH)_2 \cdot (H_2O)$

Crystal System orthorhombic

Space Group *Ccmm*

Hardness 6.0

Specific Gravity 3.0

Cleavage {100} and {010} perfect; {101} imperfect

Fracture none

Tenacity brittle

Habit Colorless, white, gray, pale blue or pink. Crystals commonly prismatic, tabular to 5 cm.; also granular or massive. Vitreous to greasy luster; translucent. White streak.

Environment Characteristic of low-temperature metamorphism, commonly occurring in glaucophane schists with chlorite, epidote and pumpelyite.

Notable Localities USA: numerous localities in California, including near Reed Station and elsewhere on the Tiburon Peninsula, Marin County. Latin America: Santa Clara, Cuba. Europe: Anglesey, Wales; Alpine regions; Calabria, Italy; Corsica; Crete. Asia: Tavsanli region, Turkey. New Zealand: Nelson.

Name Named in honor of a Scottish-American geologist at the University of California, Andrew Cowper Lawson (1861–1952).

Suolunite

Formula $Ca_2Si_2O_5(OH)_2 \cdot H_2O$

Crystal System orthorhombic

Space Group *Fdd*2

Hardness 3.5

Specific Gravity 2.6–2.7

Cleavage none

Fracture none

Tenacity brittle

Habit Colorless, white, yellow, green, blue or purple. Occurs as concretionary aggregates or fine-grained granular masses; small bladed crystals rare. Vitreous to resinous luster; transparent to translucent. White streak.

Environment Forms in ultrabasic serpentinized rocks.

Notable Localities Canada: Jeffrey Mine, Asbestos, Quebec. Asia: Muscat, Oman; Suolun, Mongolia, China.

Name From the locality where it was first discovered, Suolun, Mongolia.

Suolunite, Lake Asbestos Mine, Thetford Mines, Quebec, Canada • 13 x 16.5 x 11 cm

CHAPTER 14
Nesosilicates

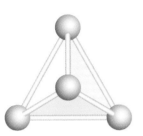

Nesosilicates (sometimes called orthosilicates) include all the silicates in which the SiO_4 tetrahedron is not bonded to other tetrahedrons connected by other kinds of atoms. The silicate part of the chemical formula is usually written SiO_4. The structure of nesosilicates produces stronger bonds and more closely packed ions, and therefore they a have higher density, index of refraction and hardness than chemically similar silicates in other subclasses. These properties mean that there are several gem minerals in this group, such as topaz, tsavorite and members of the garnet group. Minerals in the garnet group all have the same crystal structure, but with different kinds of elements that can replace one another. This replacement allows chemical variations among some of the species.

Andalusite is a common regional metamorphic mineral that forms under low pressure and moderate to high temperatures. The minerals kyanite and sillimanite are polymorphs of andalusite, meaning that they all have the same mineral formula (Al_2SiO_5) but different structures. Each forms under different temperature/pressure regimes, so they are rarely found together in the same rock. Because of this, the three minerals are a useful tool to help identify the pressure and temperature under which rocks were formed.

ABOVE: Spessartine garnet (source unknown) • 0.8 x 1.0 x 0.5 cm, 3.30 ct

RIGHT: Andalusite (chiastolite variety), Lancaster, Massachusetts, USA • 37.5 x 16 x 3 cm

LEFT: Grossular, Asbestos, Quebec, Canada • 7 x 8.5 x 0.5 cm

Olivine Group
(Forsterite and Fayalite)

Formula $(Mg,Fe)_2SiO_4$

Crystal System orthorhombic

Space Group *Pbmn*

Hardness 6.5–7.0

Specific Gravity 3.2–4.3

Cleavage forsterite {100} and {010} indistinct to good; {001} poor to fair **fayalite** {010} moderate; {100} weak

Fracture conchoidal

Tenacity brittle

Habit Pale yellow to olive green, greenish yellow, yellow brown or brown to black; color intensifies with increasing iron content. Subhedral to euhedral crystals, typically thick with striations, with wedge-shaped terminations; commonly granular or compact massive. Vitreous to resinous luster on fractures, gradating to dull or submetallic; transparent to translucent. White streak.

Environment Occurs in ultramafic volcanic and plutonic rocks; less common in felsic plutonic rocks.

Notable Localities USA: San Carlos, Arizona. Europe: Rhineland-Palatinate, Germany; Mt. Vesuvius and Monte Somma, Italy. Asia: Ural Mountains, Russia.

Name Forsterite was named after Adolarius Jacob Forster (1739–1806), a noted English mineral collector. Fayalite was named for the locality where it was first discovered, Fayal (or Faial) Island in the Azores.

Olivine is a major component of Earth's upper mantle and is also found in pallasites and other meteorites.

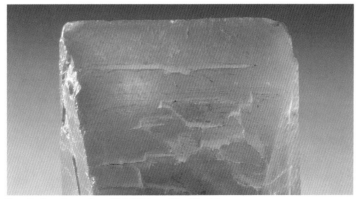

Forsterite, Suppatt, near Dasu, Gilgit, Pakistan • 3.5 x 2.5 x 1.5 cm

Monticellite, Magnet Cove, Arkansas, USA • 10 x 8.5 x 4 cm

Monticellite

Formula $MgSiO_4$

Crystal System orthorhombic

Space Group *Pbnm*

Hardness 5.5

Specific Gravity 3.0–3.3

Cleavage {010} poor

Fracture conchoidal

Tenacity brittle

Habit Colorless to white to gray, greenish gray, greenish yellow or amber. Short, rounded prismatic crystals. Vitreous luster, or slightly resinous when massive; transparent to translucent. White streak.

Environment Forms in skarns and marbles during high-temperature metasomatism or metamorphism; associated with apatite, calcite, diopside, dolomite, forsterite and similar minerals.

Notable Localities Canada: Elwin Bay diatreme, Northwest Territories; Mineral Mountain and Copper Butte, British Columbia; Bancroft, Ontario; Oka, Quebec. USA: Magnet Cove, Arizona; Cascade slide, New York. Europe: Inverness, Scotland; County Louth, Ireland; Mt. Vesuvius, Campania, Italy. Asia: Siberia, Russia; Kushiro, Hokkaido, Japan. Australia: Hobart, Tasmania.

Name Named for Teodoro Monticelli (1759–1845), an Italian mineralogist.

Pyrope

Formula $Mg_3Al_2(SiO_4)_3$

Crystal System isometric

Space Group *Ia3d*

Hardness 7.0–7.5

Specific Gravity 3.6

Cleavage none

Fracture conchoidal

Tenacity brittle

Habit Dark red, violet red, red, rose red or reddish orange. Subhedral to euhedral crystals showing dodecahedral or trapezohedral forms; also granular or massive. Vitreous luster; transparent to translucent. White streak.

Environment A high-pressure mineral that occurs in magmatic ultrabasic rocks, kimberlites and peridotites. Also found in alluvial deposits and as a detrital mineral in sedimentary rocks.

Notable Localities Canada: Gauthier, Ontario. USA: Larimer County, Colorado. Europe: Bavaria, Germany; Bohemia, Czech Republic. Africa: Tanzania; Zimbabwe. Asia: India; Ratnapura, Sri Lanka.

Name From the Greek for "fire" and "to appear," because of its red color.

Pyrope in eclogite, Dutoitspan Mine, near Kimberley, South Africa • 18 x 10 x 5 cm

Spessartine, Equador, Rio Grande do Norte, Brazil • 8 x 8 x 8 cm

Spessartine

Formula $Mn_3Al_2(SiO_4)_3$

Crystal System isometric

Space Group *Ia3d*

Hardness 7.0–7.25

Specific Gravity 3.9–4.2

Cleavage none

Fracture uneven to conchoidal

Tenacity brittle

Habit Pale yellow to deep red and sometimes brown to black. Commonly euhedral crystals, dodecahedra or trapezohedra or in combination with other cubic forms; also fine or coarse granular, compact or massive. Vitreous luster; transparent to translucent. White streak.

Environment Found in manganese-rich metamorphic rocks and igneous rocks; most commonly occurs in pegmatites, aplites and granites.

Notable Localities Canada: Quebec. USA: Ramona, California; Rutherford Mine, Virginia. Europe: Trondheim, Norway; Spessart, Bavaria, Germany. Asia: Ratnapura, Sri Lanka; Xinjiang (Uyghur Autonomous Region), China. Australia: Broken Hill, New South Wales.

Name From the locality where it was first found, near Spessart, Germany.

Almandine, Mtoko, Mashonaland, Zimbabwe • 5 x 5 x 5 cm

Almandine

Formula $Fe_3Al_2(SiO_4)_3$

Crystal System isometric; sometimes tetragonal

Space Group $Ia3d$ ($I4_1/acd$)

Hardness 7.0–7.5

Specific Gravity 3.8–4.3

Cleavage none

Fracture subconchoidal

Tenacity brittle

Habit Deep red, brownish red or red violet; rarely black. Typically well-formed dodecahedra or trapezohedra; also in rounded grains or massive. Vitreous to resinous luster; transparent to translucent. White streak.

Environment The most common garnet, found in contact and regional metamorphic rocks. Occurs in both granites and eclogites and sedimentary rocks, as a detrital mineral and rarely as inclusions in diamonds.

Notable Localities Canada: Baffin Island, Nunavut. USA: North Creek and Gore Mountain, New York. Latin America: Minas Gerais, Bahia and Rio de Janeiro, Brazil. Europe: Cumbria, England; Saar-Pfalz and Bavaria, Germany. Asia: Alabanda, Turkey; Rajputana, northern India.

Name From the ancient city of Alabanda (now Araphisar), Turkey, where garnets were cut and polished for hundreds of years.

Grossular

Formula $Ca_3Al_2(SiO_4)_3$

Crystal System isometric

Space Group $Ia3d$

Hardness 6.5–7.0

Specific Gravity 3.5

Cleavage none

Fracture uneven to conchoidal

Tenacity brittle

Habit Colorless, white, pink, orange, red, honey-colored, green, emerald green (gem quality, called tsavorlite in Europe and tsavorite in North America), reddish brown (hessonite) or brown; rarely black. Commonly in dodecahedra or trapezohedra with striated faces; also granular, compact or massive. Vitreous luster; transparent to opaque. Brownish white streak.

Environment Ordinarily found in both regional and thermal calcium-rich metamorphic rocks; also occurs in association with serpentine and rodingites.

Notable Localities Canada: Near Bancroft, Ontario; Jeffrey Mine, Asbestos, and Orford nickel mine, Quebec. USA: Snohomish, Washington; Lowell, Vermont. Latin America: Zacatecas, Mexico. Europe: Auerbach, Germany; Elba and Monte Somma, Italy. Africa (tsavorite): near Voi, Taita Hills, Kenya; Merelani Hills, Tanzania. Asia: Sri Lanka (hessonite); Yakutia, Russia.

Name From the Latin botanical name for gooseberry (*Ribes grossularia*), because of its greenish color.

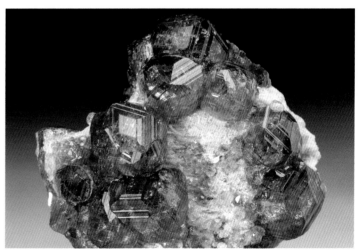

Grossular, Asbestos, Quebec, Canada • 7 x 8 x 3 cm

Zircon, Mt. Malosa, Zomba, Malawi • 2 x 2 x 2 cm

Zircon

Formula $ZrSiO_4$

Crystal System tetragonal

Space Group $I4_1/amd$

Hardness 7.5

Specific Gravity 4.6–4.7

Cleavage imperfect

Fracture uneven to conchoidal

Tenacity brittle

Habit Reddish brown, yellow, green, blue, gray or colorless. Prismatic to dipyramidal crystals. Vitreous to adamantine luster, but greasy when metamict; transparent to opaque. White streak.

Environment An accessory mineral in igneous and metamorphic rocks. Large crystals found in mafic pegmatites and carbonatites; also occurs in sedimentary rocks and alluvial heavy-mineral sands.

Notable Localities Canada: Macdonald Mine, Eganville, Ontario; Mont-Saint-Hilaire, Quebec. USA: Washington Pass area, Washington; Litchfield, Maine. Europe: northern Norway. Asia: Matura and Saffragam districts, Sri Lanka (alluvial gem gravels); Chiang Mai district, Thailand.

Name From the Arabic *zarqun*, which is thought to derive from the Persian *zar*, for "gold," and *gun*, meaning "color."

Zircon has been mined from the gem gravels of Sri Lanka for more than 2,000 years. It was used as a gemstone in Greece and Italy as far back as the sixth century CE.

Topaz

Formula $Al_2SiO_4(F,OH)_2$

Crystal System orthorhombic

Space Group *Pbnm*

Hardness 8.0

Specific Gravity 3.4–3.5

Cleavage perfect basal

Fracture subconchoidal to uneven

Tenacity brittle

Habit Mostly colorless, shades of blue, or straw to wine yellow, but can also be pink, green or red; rarely other colors. Well-formed crystals common, typically morphologically complex, long to short prismatic, with prism faces commonly vertically striated; also columnar, compact or massive. Vitreous luster; transparent to opaque with inclusions. White streak.

Environment Occurs in veins and cavities in granites and granitic pegmatites and in fluorine-rich vapors in rhyolites and greisens; also found in alluvial deposits.

Notable Localities USA: Pikes Peak region, Colorado; Llano Uplift, Texas. Latin America: Ouro Preto area, Minas Gerais, and São Domingos Mine, Mugui, Espirito Santo, Brazil. Europe: Volyn region, Ukraine. Asia: Alabaschka-Mursinka region, Ural Mountains, Russia; Katland, Mardan, Pakistan.

Name From the Greek *topazion*, meaning "to seek," or possibly from *tapaz*, the Sanskrit word meaning "fire."

The Greek *topazion* may allude to the Egyptian island of Zabargad (or St. Johns) in the Red Sea. This island was known for olivine (also called peridot or chrysolite), which has been referred to since antiquity as topaz. Most blue topaz on the market is actually irradiated, heat-treated colorless topaz.

Topaz, Dasu, Gilgit, Northern Areas, Pakistan • 9 x 7 x 6 cm

Pyrope

Round brilliant-cut dark red pyrope, Kenya • 1.6 x 1.6 x 0.9 cm, 17.10 ct

Titanite

Zircon

Titanite, Baja California, Mexico • 1.1 x 0.7 x 0.7 cm, 5.60 ct

Teardrop-cut blue zircon (source unknown) •
2.2 x 1.9 x 1.2 cm, 61.70 ct

Topaz

Imperial topaz crystal, Brazil • 1.5 x 4.5 x 1 cm

Rectangular mixed-cut imperial topaz crystal • 3.3 x 2.7 x 1.8 cm, 159.10 ct

Square step-cut unheated blue topaz, Brazil • 9 x 6.3 x 5 cm, 3,000.00 ct

Colorless topaz crystal, Klein Spitzkopje, Swakopmund, Erongo, Namibia • 3.5 x 3.5 x 3 cm

Andalusite

Formula Al_2OSiO_4

Crystal System orthorhombic

Space Group *Pnnm*

Hardness 7.5

Specific Gravity 3.1–3.2

Cleavage {110} good to perfect; {100} poor

Fracture uneven to subconchoidal

Tenacity brittle

Andalusite, Sri Lanka • 1.5 x 1.3 x 1 cm, 11.70 ct

Andalusite is a strongly pleochroic gemstone, meaning that it displays different colors depending on the direction from which it is viewed — in this case, shades of yellow, olive and reddish brown. Depending on the cut, each stone has two colors that differ in intensity or blend into a mosaic; cutters try to orient the gem to get the most pleasing mix.

Andalusite (chiastolite variety), Tanjianshan Mine, Qinghai, China • 6 x 3 x 3 cm

Habit Pale to deep pink or reddish brown, white, gray, violet, yellow, green or blue. Euhedral crystals or columnar aggregates with nearly square cross-sections, commonly elongated; also fibrous, compact or massive. Vitreous luster; transparent to opaque. White streak.

Environment Characteristic of low-grade metamorphism of pelitic sediments (clastic rocks with a grain size of less than 0.06 mm), primarily in contact zones, but also in regional metamorphism. Occurs less commonly in granites and pegmatites.

Notable Localities USA: Champion Mine, Mono County, California. Europe: near Var, Provence, France; Andalusia, Spain; Steinbach, Bavaria, and Darmstadt, Germany. Asia: Ratnapura district, Sri Lanka. Australia: Bimbowrie, South Australia.

Name From the province of Andalusia in Spain.

Sillimanite

Formula Al_2OSiO_4

Crystal System orthorhombic

Space group *Pnma*

Hardness 7.0

Specific Gravity 3.2

Cleavage {010} perfect

Fracture uneven

Tenacity splintery

Habit Colorless or white to gray; also brown, yellow, yellow green, gray green, blue green or blue. Crystals prismatic and may be acicular, with square cross-sections, rounded and striated, poorly terminated; also as fibrous mats, rarely radiating. Vitreous to subadamantine luster; transparent to translucent. White streak.

Environment Characteristic of high-temperature regional and thermal metamorphism of pelitic rocks; occurs in amphibolite to granulite facies.

Notable Localities Canada: Romaine, Quebec. USA: Yorktown, New York. Latin America: Minas Gerais, Brazil. Europe: Pontgibaud, France; Vltava, Sušice, Czech Republic. Asia: Sri Lanka; Mogok district, Myanmar (Burma).

Name Named for Benjamin Silliman (1779–1864), an American chemist and geologist at Yale University.

Sillimanite (pseudomorph after andalusite), Lüsenser Tal, Sellraintal, Tyrol, Austria • 9 x 5.5 x 7 cm

Kyanite, Bahia, Brazil • 11 x 11 x 12 cm

Kyanite

Formula Al_2OSiO_4

Crystal System triclinic

Space Group $P\bar{1}$

Hardness 4.5–6.5

Specific Gravity 3.6

Cleavage {100} perfect; {010} good; {001} parting

Fracture none

Tenacity splintery

Habit Blue, green, colorless, gray or, most recently discovered, orange. Commonly bladed, elongated in one direction and flattened in another. Vitreous luster; translucent to transparent. White streak.

Environment Typically occurs in regional metamorphic or pelitic rocks; can be found as a detrital mineral.

Notable Localities USA: Hanover, Jaffrey and Lyme, New Hampshire. Latin America: Minas Gerais, Brazil. Europe: Zillertal, Austria. Africa: Karai, Zimbabwe; Arusha region, Tanzania (orange).

Name From the Greek *kuanos*, meaning "dark blue," for its most common color.

Titanite, Bear Lake, Tory Hill, Monmouth, Ontario, Canada • 22 x 18 x 7 cm

Titanite

Formula $CaTiSiO_5$

Crystal System monoclinic

Space Group $P2_1/a$ or $A2/a$

Hardness 5.0–5.5

Specific Gravity 3.5–3.6

Cleavage imperfect

Fracture conchoidal

Tenacity brittle

Habit Black, brown, gray, colorless, green, yellow or red. Can be wedge-shaped and also as prismatic crystals; sometimes metamict. Vitreous to greasy luster; transparent to opaque. Reddish white streak.

Environment A common accessory mineral in igneous and metamorphic rocks; less common in volcanic rocks.

Notable Localities Canada: Litchfield, Quebec. USA: Franklin, New Jersey. Latin America: Pino Solo, El Rodeo and La Huerta, Baja California, Mexico; gem-quality material from Minas Gerais, Brazil. Europe: Nordmark, Värmland, Sweden; Maronne, France; Eifel, Germany. Africa: Maevatanana, Madagascar. Asia: gem-quality material from Sri Lanka.

Name From the titanium in its composition.

Staurolite

Formula $Fe^{2+}Al_9Si_4O_{23}(OH)$

Crystal System monoclinic

Space Group $C2/m$

Hardness 7.0–7.5

Specific Gravity 3.7–3.8

Cleavage {010} fair

Fracture subconchoidal

Tenacity brittle

Habit Reddish to blackish brown or yellowish brown; rarely blue. Short to long prismatic crystals, commonly cruciform twins, or "fairy crosses." Subvitreous to resinous luster; transparent to opaque. Gray streak.

Environment Characteristic of intermediate-grade metamorphism of aluminum-rich rocks, with staurolite-almandine-kyanite being a common assemblage. Also forms at lower metamorphic grades with chloritoid or in schists, emery deposits or metamorphosed ultrabasic rocks.

Notable Localities USA: Rio Arriba, Taos County and Truchas Mountains, New Mexico; Pearl Hill, Fitchburg, Massachusetts. Latin America: Minas Gerais, Brazil. Europe: Keivy, Kola Peninsula, Russia; numerous localities in Great Britain; Brittany, France; Mt. Campione, Switzerland. Australia: Broken Hill, New South Wales.

Name From the Greek *stauros*, meaning "cross," in allusion to the common cruciform twins crystal formation.

The cruciform twins are sometime used as ornaments and amulets. Staurolite is an index mineral for interpreting metamorphic grades, since it forms only in a narrow range of pressures and temperatures.

Staurolite, Windham, Maine, USA • 3.5 x 3.5 x 2.5 cm

Willemite

Formula Zn_2SiO_4

Crystal System hexagonal

Space Group $R\bar{3}$

Hardness 5.0–5.5

Specific Gravity 4.0–4.2

Cleavage $\{11\bar{2}0\}$ good to poor; $\{0001\}$ poor

Fracture conchoidal to uneven

Tenacity brittle

Willemite, Tsumeb, Namibia • 4 x 8 x 6 cm

Habit Colorless to white, gray, red brown, dark brown, honey yellow, apple green or blue. Crystals prismatic; coarse to fine granular, disseminated and in fibrous aggregates, botryoidal or massive. Vitreous to resinous luster; translucent to transparent. White streak.

Environment Found in oxidized zones of zinc deposits and in metamorphosed environments such as metamorphosed limestones.

Notable Localities Canada: Mont-Saint-Hilaire, Quebec. USA: Sterling Hill and Franklin, New Jersey. Europe: Ilímaussaq, Greenland; Långban, Värmland, Sweden; Altenberg, Belgium; Attica, Greece.

Name Named in honor of Willem I (1772–1843), king of the Netherlands from 1813 to 1840.

Willemite is a somewhat rare zinc mineral that is found in great abundance at Franklin, New Jersey, the USA's "fluorescent mineral capital of the world." Nearly all willemite specimens fluoresce bright yellow green in shortwave ultraviolet light. The mineral is usually associated with calcite, which fluoresces reddish orange, making these samples very striking when viewed under UV lighting.

Willemite, Tsumeb, Namibia • 6 x 8 x 2 cm

Phenakite

Formula Be_2SiO_4

Crystal System hexagonal

Space Group $R\bar{3}$

Hardness 7.5–8.0

Specific Gravity 2.9–3.0

Cleavage $\{11\bar{2}0\}$ distinct; $\{10\bar{1}1\}$ imperfect

Fracture conchoidal

Tenacity brittle

Habit Colorless, white, yellow or pale red. Crystals rhombohedral, tabular to prismatic, less commonly acicular and granular. Vitreous luster; transparent to translucent. White streak.

Environment Found in granitic pegmatites and schists and as a product of beryl alteration.

Notable Localities USA: Mt. Antero, Colorado; Lord Hill, Maine. Latin America: Marambaia, Minas Gerais, Brazil. Europe: Framont, Vosges, France. Africa: Swakopmund, Namibia; Anjanabonoina, Madagascar. Asia: Takovaya, Sverdlovsk, Ural Mountains, Russia.

Name From the Greek for "deceiver," because it is often mistaken for quartz.

Phenakite, Minas Gerais, Brazil • 3.5 x 6 x 3.5 cm

Euclase, Last Hope Mine, Karoi, Mashonaland West, Zimbabwe • 5.5 x 5 x 4 cm

Euclase

Formula $BeAlSiO_4OH$

Crystal System monoclinic

Space Group $P2_1/a$

Hardness 7.5

Specific Gravity 3.1

Cleavage $\{010\}$ perfect

Fracture conchoidal

Tenacity brittle

Habit Colorless, white, pale green to deep yellowish green, greenish blue or pale blue to deep blue. Prismatic crystals and striated, with terminations complex, less commonly flattened. Vitreous luster, somewhat pearly on cleavage faces; transparent to translucent. White streak.

Environment A product of decomposition of beryl in pegmatites; also occurs in low-temperature alpine veins.

Notable Localities USA: Boomer Mine, Colorado. Latin America: Gachalá Mine, Las Cruces, near Chivor, Colombia; Minas Gerais, Brazil. Africa: Miami district, Zimbabwe. Asia: Orenburg district, southern Ural Mountains, Russia.

Name From the Greek *eu klasis*, meaning "good fracture," in allusion to its perfect cleavage.

Gadolinite-(Y)

Formula $FeBe_2Y_2Si_2O_{10}$

Crystal System monoclinic

Space Group $P2_1/a$

Hardness 6.5–7.0

Specific Gravity 4.0–4.7

Cleavage no or very poor cleavage on {100}

Fracture conchoidal to splintery

Tenacity brittle

Habit Pale green, green or blue green when unaltered and nonmetamict; black or red brown when partly altered and metamict. Generally found in compact masses, but when crystals form, they are prismatic; often metamict or partly so. Vitreous to greasy luster; opaque, but nearly transparent in thin fragments. Greenish gray streak.

Environment Occurs most often in alkalic granitic pegmatites or granites.

Notable Localities Canada: Loughborough Township, Ontario. USA: Baringer Hill and Rhode Ranch pegmatites, Texas. Europe: Ytterby, Sweden; Iveland, Norway; Kimito, Finland; Kola Peninsula, Russia; Baveno, Italy. Asia: several localities in Japan.

Name Named for J. Gadolin (1760–1852), a Finnish chemist, who first separated out yttrium in 1794.

Gadolinite, Mt. Malosa, Zomba, Malawi • 3 x 2 x 1 cm

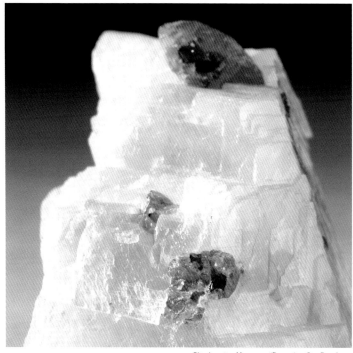

Clinohumite, Myanmar (Burma) • 6 x 5 x 4 cm

Clinohumite

Formula $(Mg,Fe)_9(SiO_4)_4(F,OH)_2$

Crystal System monoclinic

Space Group $P2_1/b$

Hardness 6.0

Specific Gravity 3.2–3.4

Cleavage {001} poor

Fracture uneven to subconchoidal

Tenacity brittle

Habit Yellow, brown, white, orange or reddish orange. Crystals complex, highly modified; massive. Vitreous luster; transparent to translucent. White streak.

Environment Occurs in kimberlite, carbonatites, peridotites, metadunites and serpentinites in orogenic belts such as the Alps and the Apennines.

Notable Localities Canada: Cargill Lake, Ontario. USA: Twin Lakes, California; Tilly Foster iron mine, Brewster, New York. Latin America: Jacupiranga Mine, São Paulo, Brazil. Europe: Mounts Somma and Vesuvius, Italy; Piedmont, Italy. Asia: Kuche-Lal, Pamir Mountains, Tajikistan.

Name Named for its crystal system — monoclinic — and its position in the humite group.

Glossary

Acicular the fragile, needle-like habit of some mineral crystals.

Adamantine very bright luster, typically found in transparent minerals.

Allochromatism a range of colors in minerals caused by the presence of foreign elements.

Arborescent the treelike habit of some mineral crystals, with branches spreading in one or more directions.

Conchoidal a type of fracture resulting in smoothly curved concentric rings around the stress point, generating a shell-like appearance. Quartz is an example of a mineral with conchoidal fracture.

Cleavage a plane of structural weakness at the atomic level, along which a mineral is likely to split smoothly.

Crystal habit the favored growth pattern of the crystals of a mineral, both individually and in aggregate.

Drusy a type of habit in which the surface of the mineral is covered with a fine dusting of tiny crystals.

Facies a distinctive body of rock that forms under certain conditions, reflecting a particular process or environment with specified characteristics.

Fracture the non-directional characteristic mark left when a mineral chips or breaks.

Gangue commercially worthless rock surrounding or closely mixed with an economically important mineral in an ore deposit.

Granite a common type of intrusive felsic igneous rock with a medium- to coarse-grained texture, comprising quartz, plagioclase feldspar and alkali feldspar.

Hackly a fractured surface with multiple small, sharp, jagged irregularities.

Hydrothermal pertains to the circulation of hot aqueous fluids or gases within Earth's crust.

Idiochromatic refers to a mineral color derived directly from the presence of one or more elements.

Iridescence a rainbow of colors caused by the interference of light in thin films of different refractive indices and varying thicknesses.

Luster the overall sheen of a mineral, caused by the quantity and quality of light reflected from its exterior surfaces.

Malleable describes a mineral that can easily be hammered into thin sheets.

Metallic a mineral luster that is opaque and very reflective because of a high absorptive index.

Non-metallic a type of luster that causes a mineral to look not at all like a metal.

Opalescence an opal-like play of light in which reflections off the mineral produce flashes of different colors.

Pegmatite a coarse-grained igneous rock with interlocking grains of about 2.5 cm or larger.

Pelitic describes sedimentary rock composed of fine fragments such as clay or mud.

Rhyolite an extrusive igneous rock of felsic composition, typically comprised of quartz, alkali feldspar and plagioclase. It can have a variety of textures and ranges from fine- to coarse-grained, depending on its cooling rate.

Sectile describes a mineral that can easily be cut with a knife.

Space group in crystallography, describes the symmetry of the crystal; can be one of 230 types.

Streak the color of the powder left after a mineral has been rubbed across unglazed porcelain.

Striation shallow parallel grooves or lines along flat crystal faces.

Subconchoidal a type of mineral fracture that falls somewhere between conchoidal and even; the broken surface is smooth, with irregularly rounded corners.

Submetallic a luster that has the look of a metal dulled by weathering or corrosion, typically on opaque minerals.

Tenacity a mineral's resistance to breaking, bending or otherwise being deformed.

Tri-State Mining District a historic mining district in southwest Missouri, southeast Kansas and northeast Oklahoma. It is one of the major lead and zinc mining areas in the world and has produced a variety of exemplary mineral specimens.

Additional Reading

Books

Anthony. J.W., et al. *Handbook of Mineralogy.* 5 vols. Tucson, AZ: Mineral Data Publishing, 1997–2003.

Blackburn, W.H., and W.H. Dennen. *Encyclopedia of Mineral Names.* Ottawa: Canadian Mineralogist, 1997.

Bloss, Donald F. *Crystallography and Crystal Chemistry.* Chantilly, VA: Mineralogical Society of America, 1994.

Bonewitz, Ronald L. *Rock and Gem: A Definitive Guide to Rocks, Minerals, Gems and Fossils.* New York: DK Publishing, 2008.

Deer, W.A., R.A. Howie and J. Zussman. *An Introduction to the Rock-Forming Minerals,* 2nd ed. London: Prentice Hall, 1996.

de Fourestier, J. *Glossary of Mineral Synonyms.* Ottawa: Canadian Mineralogist, 1998.

Gaines, Richard V., et al. *Dana's New Mineralogy,* 8th ed. New York: John Wiley and Sons, 1997.

Klein, Cornelius, and Barbara Dutrow. *Manual of Mineralogy,* 23rd ed. New York: John Wiley and Sons, 2008.

Mandarino, Joseph, and M.E. Back. *Fleischer's Glossary of Mineral Species.* Tucson, AZ: Mineralogical Record, 2007.

Mineral Society of America. "Reviews in Mineralogy" series. A new volume is published about once a year, often based on a short course at their annual meeting. Each volume typically deals with a specific group of minerals or some mineral-related topic.

Putnis, A. *An Introduction to Mineral Sciences.* New York: Cambridge University Press, 1992.

Journals

Peer-reviewed publications in mineralogy are published in several journals in a variety of languages. The most widely circulated English journals are *American Mineralogist*, published by the Mineralogical Society of America, *Canadian Mineralogist*, published by the Mineralogical Association of Canada, and *Mineralogical Magazine*, published by the Mineralogical Society of Great Britain. *Elements* is a bimonthly magazine that explores themes of broad and current interest in the mineral sciences; it is published cooperatively by several mineral associations.

Websites

The RRUFF website (rruff.info) has photos, spectral data and diffraction data on thousands of minerals, available to search. The official International Mineralogical Association (IMA) database can be found at rruff.info/ima. Founded in 1958, the IMA is the world's largest organization promoting mineralogy. The Nomenclature and Classification subcommittee of the IMA Commission on New Minerals reviews and approves new minerals when they are discovered.

Mindat.org is the largest mineral database and mineralogy reference website on the Internet. This site contains worldwide data on minerals, mineral collecting, mineral localities and other information.

Acknowledgments

I would like to sincerely thank my fellow curator and the technicians and students of the Mineralogy and Geology section of the Royal Ontario Museum, namely Malcolm Back, Veronica Di Cecco, Katherine Dunnell, Brendt Hyde, Emily Kwan, Ian Nicklin, Michelle Thompson, Heidi Tomes, Bob Ramik, Katrina van Drongelen and Vincent Vertolli, for assisting with images, proofreading and general discussions about the content of this book. I would also like to thank Mark Engstrom and Julian Siggers for their assistance.

Much of the material in the introduction has been adapted from text prepared by the Earth Sciences Gallery Team for the Teck Suite of Galleries: Earth's Treasures, at the Royal Ontario Museum.

The hard work of Brian Boyle and Miguel Hortiguela is evident: they are responsible for the beautiful photography. Thanks also to Wanda Dobrowlanski and Carole Iritz for putting up with my multiple requests for images, and to Glen Ellis and Nicola Woods for their assistance as well.

This book would not have been possible but for the wonderful organization and editing skills of Gillian Watts, and of Kathleen Fraser in the early stages. As well, many thanks are due to Joseph Gisini of PageWave Graphics for his keen designer's eye in the layout of the book. I would also like to thank Michael Worek at Firefly for his encouragement and support.

Index